CAMBRIDGE STUDIES IN MEDIEVAL LITERATURE 48

Gestures and Looks in Medieval Narrative

In medieval society, gestures and speaking looks played an even more important part in public and private exchanges than they do today. Gestures meant more than words, for example, in ceremonies of homage and fealty. In this, the first general study of its kind in English, John Burrow examines the role of non-verbal communication in a wide range of narrative texts, including Chaucer's *Troilus and Criseyde*, the anonymous *Sir Gawain and the Green Knight*, Malory's *Morte Darthur*, the romances of Chrétien de Troyes, the Prose *Lancelot*, Boccaccio's *Il Filostrato*, and Dante's *Commedia*. Burrow argues that since non-verbal signs are in general less subject to change than words, many of the behaviours recorded in these texts, such as pointing and amorous gazing, are familiar in themselves, yet may prove easy to misread, either because they are no longer common, like bowing, or because their use has changed, like winking.

JOHN BURROW is Emeritus Professor and Research Fellow in the Department of English at Bristol University. He has published widely on Middle English literature. His books include *Medieval Writers and Their Work* (1982).

CAMBRIDGE STUDIES IN MEDIEVAL LITERATURE

General editor
Alastair Minnis, *University of York*

Editorial board
Patrick Boyde, *University of Cambridge*
John Burrow, *University of Bristol*
Rita Copeland, *University of Pennsylvania*
Alan Deyermond, *University of London*
Peter Dronke, *University of Cambridge*
Simon Gaunt, *King's College, London*
Nigel Palmer, *University of Oxford*
Winthrop Wetherbee, *Cornell University*

This series of critical books seeks to cover the whole area of literature written in the major medieval languages – the main European vernaculars, and medieval Latin and Greek – during the period c. 1100–1500. Its chief aim is to publish and stimulate fresh scholarship and criticism on medieval literature, special emphasis being placed on understanding major works of poetry, prose, and drama in relation to the contemporary culture and learning which fostered them.

Recent titles in the series
Margaret Clunies Ross *Old Icelandic Literature and Society*
Donald Maddox *Fictions of Identity in Medieval France*
Rita Copeland *Pedagogy, Intellectuals and Dissent in the Later Middle Ages: Lollardy and Ideas of Learning*
Kantik Ghosh *The Wycliffite Heresy: Authority and Interpretation of Texts*
Mary C. Erler *Women, Reading, and Piety in Late Medieval England*
D.H. Green *The Beginnings of Medieval Romance: Fact and Fiction, 1150–1220*

A complete list of titles in the series can be found at the end of the volume.

Gestures and Looks in Medieval Narrative

J. A. BURROW

CAMBRIDGE UNIVERSITY PRESS
Cambridge, New York, Melbourne, Madrid, Cape Town, Singapore, São Paulo

Cambridge University Press
The Edinburgh Building, Cambridge CB2 8RU, UK

Published in the United States of America by Cambridge University Press, New York

www.cambridge.org
Information on this title: www.cambridge.org/9780521815642

© J. A. Burrow 2002

This publication is in copyright. Subject to statutory exception
and to the provisions of relevant collective licensing agreements,
no reproduction of any part may take place without the written
permission of Cambridge University Press.

First published 2002
This digitally printed version 2008

A catalogue record for this publication is available from the British Library

ISBN 978-0-521-81564-2 hardback
ISBN 978-0-521-05066-1 paperback

For Diana

Such shapes, such gesture, and such sound expressing
(Although they want the use of tonge) a kinde
Of excellent dumbe discourse.
The Tempest

Contents

Acknowledgements	*page* x
List of abbreviations	xi
1 Introduction	1
2 Gestures	11
3 Looks	69
4 Two Middle English narratives	114
5 Dante's *Commedia*	156
6 Afterword	180
Bibliography	186
Index of names and titles	196
Index of signs	199

Acknowledgements

I am grateful to colleagues who have given me advice and information: Richard Gregory, Nick Havely, Christian Kay, Richard Lewis, Bella Millett, Jonathan Nicholls, John Parkin, Rhiannon Purdie, Ad Putter, Frank Shaw, Myra Stokes, Matthew Strickland, and Barry Windeatt.

I have also enjoyed and benefited from discussions at the Oxford Dante Society, the St Andrews Medieval Society, the Second International Langland Conference, and the Bristol Centre for Medieval Studies. The Bristol University Library and its Interlibrary Loans department have done much to facilitate my work.

Abbreviations

DOST	*Dictionary of the Older Scottish Tongue*
EETS	Early English Text Society (E.S. Extra Series, S.S. Supplementary Series)
MED	*Middle English Dictionary*
NVC	non-verbal communication
OED	*Oxford English Dictionary*
STS	Scottish Text Society

I

Introduction

Much attention has been paid in recent decades, by social psychologists and others, to non-verbal communication – those forms of bodily behaviour, supplementing or replacing speech, by which people convey their thoughts and feelings to each other. Modern experts have studied, often in minute detail, such things as facial expression, gaze, gesture, and posture.[1] When medieval commentators touched on these matters, as they sometimes did, they were most often concerned with gestures, and in particular with what was proper or improper in such bodily movements – the disciplines of decent gesture.[2] There was also at that time, however, a scholastic tradition which considered non-verbal messages as part of a general theory of signs, *signa* – for semiology, though the term is modern, was not the creation of Peirce or Saussure, as their successors sometimes claim. A main authority for such discussions 'de signis' was a section of the *De Doctrina Christiana* of St Augustine; and since Augustine's understanding of the matter lies quite close to that adopted in this book, it seems appropriate to start with what he has to say.

At the beginning of Book Two of the *De Doctrina*, Augustine turns from 'things' (*res*, the subject of Book One) to 'signs' (*signa*).[3] After offering a general definition, he goes on to draw a distinction: 'Some signs are natural [*naturalia*], others given [*data*]'. Natural signs 'are those which,

---

[1] For a comprehensive survey, see Michael Argyle, *Bodily Communication*, 2nd edn (London, 1988).
[2] See especially J.-C. Schmitt, *La raison des gestes dans l'occident médiéval* (Paris, 1990). An influential treatment of such decorum, the *De Institutione Novitiorum* of Hugh of St Victor, will be considered later.
[3] I quote text and translation from R. P. H. Green, ed. and transl., *De Doctrina Christiana* (Oxford, 1995), II 1–7.

without a wish or any urge to signify [*sine voluntate atque ullo appetitu significandi*], cause something else beside themselves to be known from them'. He cites examples: smoke as a sign of fire, footprints as signs of a passing animal, and facial expressions where they are involuntary signs of emotion. Of these last, he observes that 'the expression of an angry or depressed person signifies an emotional state even if there is no such wish on the part of the person who is angry or depressed'. By contrast, 'given' signs are so called because the signer intentionally gives, or transmits, them in order to communicate something: 'Given signs are those which living things give to each other, in order to show, to the best of their ability, the emotions of their minds, or anything they have felt or learnt'. Here Augustine raises in passing the question of whether animals can be credited with that *voluntas significandi* upon which his prime distinction turns: do cocks or doves intend to signify when they crow or coo?[4]

Leaving that question aside, Augustine passes on to treat signs 'given' by human beings. He classifies them according to the sense at which they are directed: some to the eyes, most to the ears, and a few to the other senses. Words form by far the most important type of audible signs (he also mentions the music of trumpet, flute, and lyre); but especially relevant here are his observations on signs directed to the eyes:

> When we nod, we give a sign just to the eyes of the person whom we want, by means of that sign, to make aware of our wishes. Certain movements of the hands signify a great deal. Actors, by the movement of all their limbs, give certain signs to the cognoscenti and, as it were, converse with the spectators' eyes; and it is through the eyes that flags and standards convey the wishes of military commanders. All these things are, to coin a phrase, visible words [*verba visibilia*].[5]

---

[4] See U. Eco, R. Lambertini, C. Marmo, and A. Tabarroni, 'On Animal Language in the Medieval Classification of Signs', in U. Eco and C. Marmo, eds., *On the Medieval Theory of Signs* (Amsterdam, 1989), pp. 3–41. This essay is helpful on medieval semiotic systems generally.

[5] *De Doctrina*, II 5: 'Nam cum innuimus non damus signum nisi oculis eius quem volumus per hoc signum voluntatis nostrae participem facere. Et quidem motus manuum pleraque significant, et histriones omnium membrorum motibus dant signa quaedam scientibus et cum oculis eorum quasi fabulantur, et vexilla draconesque militares per oculos insinuant voluntatem ducum. Et sunt haec omnia quasi quaedam verba visibilia.' In an earlier work, *De Magistro*, Augustine had already distinguished signs according to the receiving sense,

Introduction

This passage was commonly referred to by medieval writers. In it one sees some prime instances of 'non-verbal communication' – movements of the head and hands especially – firmly embedded as *verba visibilia*, along with military flags, in a strong general theory of signs.

The texts studied in this book deal mostly in visible signs such as gestures and looks, and it is with these that I shall be chiefly concerned, for only a few involve (non-verbal) sound: laughs, an occasional meaning cough, and a diabolical fart. More important is Augustine's other distinction between 'natural' and 'given' signs, for I shall be occupied here only with the latter. The criterion is the presence of a *voluntas significandi*. A version of this criterion has been adopted by some – but by no means all – modern experts on non-verbal communication. Thus one of the best of them, Adam Kendon, has defined gesture as 'any distinct bodily action that is regarded as part of the process of deliberate utterance or expression'. 'The action,' he adds, 'has to be seen as having a communicative function and it has to be seen as being something that the individual could have avoided doing.'[6] Similarly, a writer on communication theory argues that a distinction must be drawn between non-verbal behaviour '*calculated* to inform the observer' on the one hand and 'the passive manifestation of a symptom' on the other. 'Blushing,' he remarks later, 'is a *symptom*, not a *message*.'[7]

Some modern observers object to the criterion of intentionality on the grounds that, since intentions are themselves not open to inspection, they can only be inferred, and that uncertainly.[8] But this objection hardly has any force for a student not of behaviours but of texts. Unlike real people, persons in texts have no inaccessible insides, nor can they harbour intentions beyond what their author states or implies. So one

---

specifying words for hearing and gestures (*gestus*) for sight: Chapter 4, Para. 8, in *Patrologia Latina*, Vol. XXXII.

[6] A. Kendon, 'Geography of Gesture', *Semiotica*, 37 (1981), 129–63 (pp. 134–5). For similar remarks see also Kendon's essay 'The Study of Gesture: Some Observations on its History', *Recherches Sémiotiques / Semiotic Enquiry*, 2 (1982), 45–62 (pp. 45–6); and his statement on p. 49 of D. McNeill, ed., *Language and Gesture* (Cambridge, 2000). Like most of his colleagues, Kendon appears to be unaware of Augustine and of the medieval semiological tradition.

[7] D. M. MacKay, 'Formal Analysis of Communication Processes', in R. A. Hinde, ed., *Non-Verbal Communication* (Cambridge, 1972), pp. 3–25 (pp. 5, 19, with the author's italics). This collection has a number of valuable essays.

[8] See the criticisms of MacKay's essay on pp. 86–8 of Hinde's volume.

can apply the Augustinian test with some confidence, even to the less straightforward cases. Social behaviours such as pointing a finger or winking an eye are nothing if not acts of communication; and the same can almost be said of smiles and frowns. I further include actions of a more formal and even ceremonious kind – frequently encountered in the texts – for these also carry messages: hand-clasping, kissing, and bowing, for example.[9] At the other end of the scale, I exclude from discussion such bodily 'symptoms' as blushing and weeping (even though, as we shall see, a cynical Scottish poet asserts that women can deliberately weep for effect). There remain – in between, as it were – those actions which may or may not be intended to carry a message. As Augustine noted, facial expressions (*vultus*) sometimes express anger or sorrow 'even if there is no such wish on the part of the person who is angry or depressed'; yet, as this indeed implies, expressions of anger and the like are also commonly directed as signals at others, and it is as such that I shall be concerned with them here.[10] Simply to look at another person – glancing, gazing, or staring – can also be full of meaning. Some looks are just looks, intended only to acquire information; but others are 'speaking' looks, intended to convey it.[11] Even coughs, normally just physical symptoms, may be produced as deliberate signals, to attract attention or convey a warning.

Having introduced the principle governing my choice of examples, I shall now explain the choice of texts from which the examples are taken. First, let me briefly locate the present study in relation to some of the scholarly work that has already been done.[12] Non-verbal communication in the medieval West is, needless to say, a vast and varied

---

[9] For an account of the role of gestures in human communication, see A. Kendon, 'Do Gestures Communicate? A Review', *Research on Language and Social Interaction*, 27 (1994), 175–200.

[10] On facial signalling by animals, see Argyle, *Bodily Communication*, Chapter 3.

[11] See ibid., Chapter 10, 'Gaze'.

[12] I confine myself here to book-length studies. The most recent bibliographies of books and articles in the field may be found on pp. 411–20 of Schmitt, *Raison des gestes*, and on pp. 219–21 in M. Mostert, ed., *New Approaches to Medieval Communication* (Turnhout, 1999). There is a more selective bibliography in J. Bremmer and H. Roodenburg, eds., *A Cultural History of Gesture: From Antiquity to the Present Day* (Oxford, 1991, paperback, 1993), pp. 255–7.

Introduction

subject, and only some few patches of it have so far been investigated. One approach taken by scholars has been to focus on the evidence provided by a single author or artist. Thus, R. G. Benson selected Chaucer's writings for his study of 'medieval body language', and the art historian M. Barasch devoted an excellent book to the 'language of gesture' in the paintings of Giotto.[13] An alternative method is to concentrate on a single type of action, as Barasch does in his other book, on gestures of depair, or P. Ménard does in a remarkable survey of Old French smiles and laughter.[14] Or a study may confine itself to some particular genre of writing, as in D. Peil's comparative investigation into some Arthurian romances in medieval French and German.[15] So far as medieval English is concerned, the only really substantial study to date is W. Habicht's monograph on body language in Old and Middle English poetry, a book to which the present study owes a debt.[16]

My own interest in the subject was prompted first by the non-verbal signs in Middle English poems, notably *Sir Gawain and the Green Knight* and Chaucer's *Troilus and Criseyde*. It seemed to me that readers, myself included, were inclined to underestimate the weight and force of many of these signs. Nor could their meanings always be taken for granted, as we are also inclined to do – as if fourteenth-century kisses, for example, had just the same range of meanings as modern ones. So, having modern readers of literature chiefly in mind, I set out to observe the workings of non-verbal communication in some of the narrative texts that they were most likely to encounter, extending my range to include some medieval French classics and also, more rashly, Dante's *Commedia*. So the bulk of the examples considered here will be drawn from the following core texts:

---

[13] M. Barasch, *Giotto and the Language of Gesture* (Cambridge, 1987); R. G. Benson, *Medieval Body Language: A Study of the Use of Gesture in Chaucer's Poetry*, Anglistica 21 (Copenhagen, 1980). Benson's disappointing book takes 'body language' in a very broad sense.
[14] M. Barasch, *Gestures of Despair in Medieval and Early Renaissance Art* (New York, 1976); P. Ménard, *Le rire et le sourire dans le roman courtois au moyen âge (1150–1250)* (Geneva, 1969). The book of essays edited by C. Davidson, *Gesture in Medieval Drama and Art* (Kalamazoo, 2001), appeared too late for me to use it here.
[15] D. Peil, *Die Gebärde bei Chrétien, Hartmann und Wolfram: Erec–Iwein–Parzival* (Munich, 1975).
[16] W. Habicht, *Die Gebärde in englischen Dichtungen des Mittelalters* (Munich, 1959).

English: Chaucer's *Troilus*, Langland's *Piers Plowman*, Gower's *Confessio Amantis*, *Sir Gawain and the Green Knight*, Malory's *Morte Darthur*.
French: the romances of Chrétien de Troyes, the Prose *Lancelot*, Froissart's *Chronicles*.
Italian: Dante's *Commedia*.

These texts are particularly rich in non-verbal signs; but I have taken many other examples from a variety of other writings in these languages (listed in the Bibliography) and also, on occasion, from citations in dictionaries.

In life, non-verbal signs form a frequent, sometimes a continuous, accompaniment to speech; but in texts, not least in medieval texts, they are recorded only sporadically. Hence they can readily be neglected by readers. It is the general purpose of this study simply to help remedy that neglect, by drawing attention to occasions when such acts as gestures or looks play a significant part in the medieval writer's representation of exchanges and relationships between characters. A secondary aim is to encourage the realisation that non-verbal signs, like words, need to be understood historically. One must be prepared to find that they too may have undergone change over time. Some of the more formal gestures, such as bowing and kneeling, are now largely obsolete in the West; so we are inclined to underestimate their significance and force, and also fail to appreciate the subtleties that may attend their performance: in medieval Europe, as in modern Japan, an underperformed bow does not pass unnoticed. Other actions, more familiar in themselves, lie open to misreading because the conventions governing their use have changed. They are the non-verbal equivalents of those misleadingly familiar words sometimes referred to as false friends. It should cause no surprise, after all, to find that certain of these signs – headshakes and winks, for example – had somewhat different meanings then from what we are accustomed to today.

I would have welcomed some theoretical guidance on this general question of diachronic change in non-verbal signs, but that has proved hard to find, either from cultural historians or from modern observers. As already noticed, scholars have produced studies of gestures and looks in the Middle Ages, as in other periods. Yet the history of individual

Introduction

gestures over time remains largely unexplored. An excellent essay by H. Roodenburg on the history of the handshake in early modern times shows what can be done; but even here, the patchiness of the evidence allows only an imperfect account of what was evidently a complex set of developments.[17] Again, the book entitled *Gestures: Their Origins and Distribution* by Desmond Morris and others, while throwing new light on the current geographical distribution of their twenty selected gestures, arrives at very few secure conclusions about the origins or development of these. As the authors are themselves aware, this is an area where the non-verbal equivalent of folk etymology flourishes, and where errors are blindly repeated.[18] Social scientists, in fact, rarely touch on such matters. Yet they do address themselves to a question which has a real bearing, indirectly, on the problem of diachronic change. How like language itself is non-verbal communication? On this question, which chiefly arises for social scientists when comparing NVC in different modern cultures, there appear to be two broad schools of thought.[19]

One of these schools of thought may be traced back to a remarkable book published by Charles Darwin in 1872, *The Expression of the Emotions in Man and Animals*.[20] Being concerned with the derivation of the human species from lower animals, Darwin was particularly interested in those gestures and expressions which might be shown to be 'innate or universal' rather than 'conventional or artificial' (p. 50). Although Quintilian had long before described hand-gestures as 'a language common to all men',[21] Darwin was rightly suspicious of such

---

[17] H. Roodenburg, 'The "Hand of Friendship": Shaking Hands and Other Gestures in the Dutch Republic', in Bremmer and Roodenburg, eds., *A Cultural History of Gesture*, pp. 152–89.

[18] D. Morris, P. Collett, P. March, and M. O'Shaughnessy, *Gestures: Their Origins and Distribution* (London, 1979). See for example their discussion of the supposed origins of the thumb-up gesture in the Roman amphitheatre, pp. 186–7.

[19] The literature on contemporary NVC is very extensive. For a fairly recent bibliography, see Argyle, *Bodily Communication*, pp. 310–47.

[20] I quote from the photographic reprint in paperback (Chicago, 1965). Darwin's conclusions find general support in P. Ekman, ed., *Darwin and Facial Expression: A Century of Research in Review* (New York, 1973).

[21] *Institutio Oratoria*, ed. and transl. H. E. Butler, Vol. IV (New York, 1922), XI iii 87. See D. Knox, 'Ideas on Gesture and Universal Languages, *c.* 1550–1650', in J. Henry and S. Hutton, eds., *New Perspectives on Renaissance Thought* (London, 1990), pp. 101–36.

ill-founded assertions; and he set out to study the matter scientifically, both by his own observations and by questionnaires sent out to correspondents in several parts of the world. He stated his main conclusion as follows: 'I have endeavoured to show in considerable detail that all the chief expressions exhibited by man are the same throughout the world' (p. 359). The modern ethologist Eibl-Eibesfeldt arrives at similar results, in particular by employing the camera to produce 'cross-cultural documentation of human expressive behaviour'.[22] Much like Darwin, he finds 'similarities in expressive movements between cultures', in 'such basic expressions as smiling, laughing, crying and the facial expressions of anger' (p. 299). Like Darwin, too, he proposes evolutionary origins for a number of these basic expressions, tracing them also in sub-human primates. Neither writer, of course, claims that all facial expressions – still less, all gestures – can be so explained; but both place their emphasis on phylogenetic factors and on the significance of cross-cultural similarities.

Other observers are inclined to see NVC as functioning much more like the distinctively human institution of language, its items being generally determined not by evolutionary or other natural factors, but by the diverse cultures of humanity. The social anthropologist Edmund Leach presents a particularly challenging statement of this position.[23] He asserts that 'cross-species ethological comparisons between men and animals are nearly always thoroughly misleading' (p. 331); and he is equally sceptical about attempts to establish 'any consistent relationship between non-verbal signal and response when such signals are observed in differing cultural environments' (p. 329). Such signals are, he says, 'related to one another as a total system after the fashion of a language' (p. 318); so comparisons between individual items abstracted from their different systems must be misleading. Similar structuralist

---

[22] I. Eibl-Eibesfeldt, 'Similarities and Differences between Cultures in Expressive Movements', in Hinde, ed., *Non-Verbal Communication*, pp. 297–312. See also, for similar conclusions, P. Ekman, 'Cross-Cultural Studies of Facial Expression', in Ekman, ed., *Darwin and Facial Expression*, pp. 169–222; also Chapter XIX in P. Ekman, W. V. Friesen, and P. Ellsworth, *Emotion in the Human Face* (New York, 1972).

[23] E. Leach, 'The Influence of Cultural Context on Non-Verbal Communication in Man', in Hinde, *Non-Verbal Communication*, pp. 315–44. The general editor comments on the disagreements between Leach and Eibl-Eibesfeldt on pp. 344–6.

Introduction

arguments are put forward by Ray Birdwhistell, under the influence of what he calls 'anthropological linguistics'.[24] In an interesting essay entitled 'There are Smiles...', Birdwhistell describes how he came to abandon a Darwinian belief in the smile as a single, natural form of expression, and learned to perceive its differing physical forms and, especially, its varying significations and uses, from one culture to another. He states his general conclusion as follows: 'Insofar as I have been able to determine, just as there are no universal words...which carry the same meaning the world over, there are no body motions, facial expressions, or gestures which provoke *identical* responses the world over.'[25]

The issues discussed here have an evident bearing upon the present study, for it is itself cross-cultural, albeit across time rather than space in the main. Insofar as NVC signals can safely be regarded as products of long-term evolutionary processes, one may expect them to change rather little, if at all, over a mere few centuries. Insofar as they are 'language-like', on the other hand, they may be expected to vary over much shorter periods of time both in form and in meaning, as words so evidently do. The matter is, I believe, still controversial; yet I find that many of the experts agree, from their different standpoints, in allowing more variability to gestures than to facial expressions. Thus Michael Argyle, in his survey of modern work, reports extensive evidence for Darwin's theory that 'facial expression evolved for communication purposes' out of what were originally non-communicative acts among primates. But of gesture he writes: 'There are extensive cultural variations in the use of gesture, showing that it is the non-verbal signal that is most affected by socialization and by cultural history.'[26] Distinctions such as these, however, can suggest no more than general probabilities, so far as concerns the history of any given signal. 'Language-like' gestures

[24] R. L. Birdwhistell, *Kinesics and Context: Essays on Body-Motion Communication* (London, 1971). He observes that 'kinesic structure is parallel to language structure' (p. 80, 'kinesics' being his term for NVC). On the structuralist approach, see A. Kendon, 'The Organization of Behavior in Face-to-Face Interaction', in K. R. Scherer and P. Ekman, eds., *Handbook of Methods in Nonverbal Behavior Research* (Cambridge, 1982), pp. 440–505.
[25] *Kinesics and Context*, p. 34 (author's italics).
[26] *Bodily Communication*, pp. 75, 191.

Gestures and looks in medieval narrative

can show considerable persistence over time;[27] and conversely, 'natural' facial expressions are very far from immune to cultural pressures.[28]

Of the following chapters, the two first concern, respectively, gestures and 'looks' – taking advantage of the ambiguity of the latter term to treat both facial expressions and glances or speaking looks. The following chapters offer more detailed discussions of individual works which have proved particularly rich in representations of non-verbal signs: Chaucer's *Troilus* and the anonymous *Sir Gawain and the Green Knight* in Chapter 4, and Dante's *Commedia* in Chapter 5. I conclude with an Afterword.

---

[27] Kendon observes the persistence of many gestural forms: 'In this they appear to show a contrast with linguistic forms. Their stability is probably connected to the fact that enacted gestures are not part of a gestural system, and also that, unlike linguistic forms, they are not segmental in structure, but unitary... In some cases it is possible to observe changes in the meanings of the gesture, but the form itself does not alter': A. Kendon, 'Did Gesture Have the Happiness to Escape the Curse at the Confusion of Babel?', in A. Wolfgang, ed., *Nonverbal Behavior: Perspectives, Applications, Intercultural Insights* (Lewiston, N.Y., 1984), pp. 75–114. See also Kendon, 'Geography of Gesture', p. 151.

[28] Ekman's essay 'Cross-Cultural Studies', while arguing powerfully that, as Darwin maintained, 'there are some facial expressions of emotion that are universally characteristic of the human species', allows that they may be prompted by different 'elicitors' in different cultures, and also that they may be affected by culturally varying 'display rules' (pp. 219, 220).

2

Gestures

Jean-Claude Schmitt has written eloquently about the significance of gesture in medieval societies, citing Jacques Le Goff's characterisation of that period as 'une civilisation du geste'. No doubt Le Goff had chiefly in mind those formal public gestures which most interest historians – physical actions which had legally binding consequences, in ceremonies of homage, oath-swearing, and the like.[1] Beginning with these, the first section of the present chapter goes on to consider gestures of a generally less consequential kind, in particular bowing and kneeling as signs of submission, deference, or petition; and it concludes with the polite everyday rituals of greeting and farewell. The second section treats those gestures which more directly signify interpersonal feelings and attitudes such as grief, anger, and affection. It is here, somewhat uneasily, that kissing belongs. The third and last section concerns what many modern writers on NVC call 'emblems'. These small behaviours are more language-like than other items in the gestural repertoire, for they have direct verbal equivalents. Here I discuss beckoning, pointing, headnodding, and headshaking.

Gestures played an essential part in the solemn ceremonies of homage and fealty, in which men bound themselves together as lord and vassal 'by mouth and by hand'.[2] To become another's man (homage), it was necessary, as well as declaring one's willingness in words, to place one's

---

[1] *Raison des gestes*, pp. 14–18, citing (p. 14) J. Le Goff, *La civilisation de l'occident médiéval* (Paris, 1964), p. 440. M. T. Clanchy observes that 'dependence on symbolic gestures and the spoken word persisted in law and literature, and throughout medieval culture, despite the growth of literacy', *From Memory to Written Record*, 2nd edn (Oxford, 1993), p. 278.

[2] For full description and analysis of the ceremonial, see J. Le Goff, 'Le rituel symbolique de la vassalité', in his book *Pour un autre moyen âge* (Paris, 1977), pp. 349–420. Also

Gestures and looks in medieval narrative

two hands joined between the hands of the lord, usually on bended knee. The vassal then engaged his faith (fealty) by swearing an oath, with one hand on some sacred text or relic, and the mutual *fidelitas* was sealed by a kiss, mouth-to-mouth. Froissart, in his *Chronicles*, gives a partial account of these ceremonies when he describes how English lords renewed their allegiance to King Richard II on the occasion of his reaching his majority in 1388:

> Aprez la messe, en cause d'hommaige, les oncles du roy baisierent le roys comme ses tenaulz et fievez et luy firent et jurerent foy et hommaige à tenir à perpetuelité. Aprez, les contes et les barons luy jurerent ... et baisoient par foy et hommaige, leurs mains jointes, ainsi comme il appartient, le roy en la bouche.
>
> ['After mass, the king's uncles by way of homage kissed him as fief-holders and made and swore fealty and homage in perpetuity. After that, the counts and lords swore to him ... and kissed the king on the mouth by way of fealty and homage, with their hands joined, as is right'.][3]

The most distinctive gesture in these ceremonies was the *immixtio manuum*. By placing his hands palm-to-palm between the palms of his lord, the vassal both symbolically and in reality ceased to be his own man. So the romances sometimes single out this particular act. In the Prose *Lancelot*, Pharien recalls how he and others have 'done fealty and homage with joined hands' to their lord;[4] and in the *Chevalier de la Charrete* of Chrétien de Troyes, Meleagant protests to his father at the idea that he should submit in this way to his enemy Lancelot:

> Et dit: 'Joinz piez et jointes mains,
> Volez espoir que je devaigne
> Ses hom et de lui terre taigne?'

M. Bloch, *Feudal Society*, transl. L. A. Manyon (London, 1961), pp. 145–6 and Plates II, III, and IV.

[3] *Chroniques de J. Froissart*, ed. S. Luce *et al.*, 15 vols., in progress (Paris, 1869–): Vol. XIV, ed. A. Mirot (Paris, 1966), p. 81 (Book III, Section 200).

[4] 'Feauté faite et homage a jointes mains', *Lancelot do Lac: The Non-Cyclic Old French Prose Romance*, ed. E. Kennedy, 2 vols. (Oxford, 1980), 86.7–8. All citations, by page and line number, are from this edition.

Gestures

['And he says: "I suppose you want me to become his man, with joined feet and joined hands, and to hold my land from him?"'.][5]

Another passage in Froissart's *Chronicles* shows how seriously such 'mixing of hands' was taken. In 1329, the young Edward III of England travelled to Amiens to do homage, as Duke of Guienne, to King Philip VI of France; but, according to Froissart, he omitted the joining of hands: 'Et me samble que li rois Edouwars d'Engleterre fist adonc hommage, de bouce et de parolle tant seulement, sans les mains mettre entre les mains dou roy de France' ['And, as I believe, King Edward of England did homage by mouth and word only, without placing his hands between the hands of the king of France'].[6] Froissart may have been misinformed (other sources report that hands were in fact joined), but his account illustrates the high importance attached to such symbolic acts. Gestures as well as words may be performative. Edward, according to the chronicler, was ready to swear an oath ('parolle') and exchange the kiss ('bouce'); but, by withholding his hands, he reserved his position on a matter of extreme delicacy in Anglo-French relations.[7]

Rather less grand were the rituals by which individuals swore an oath or plighted their troth to another; but these actions also had a legalistic force and imposed binding obligations of a kind easily underestimated by readers today. In its simplest form, the ritual required no more than the holding up of hands. Thus, towards the beginning of Chaucer's *Canterbury Tales*, the Host invites the pilgrims to submit to his authority with the words 'Hold up youre hondes, withouten moore speche.'[8]

---

[5] *Le Chevalier de la Charrete*, ed. M. Roques (Paris, 1978), ll. 3224–6. 'Joinz piez' suggests kneeling on both knees: see below, p. 19.

[6] *Chroniques*, Vol. 1, ed. S. Luce (Paris, 1869), p. 95 (Book 1, Section 45). Modern historians report that Edward did in fact perform the crucial *immixtio manuum*: E. Perroy, *The Hundred Years War*, transl. D. C. Douglas (London, 1951), p. 82.

[7] 'Et n'en volt adonc li dis rois d'Engleterre, par le conseil qu'il eut, dou dit hommage proceder plus avant' ['And the said King of England did not wish, on advice, to proceed any further in the said homage', ibid.]. Ten years later, Edward sent a letter to Philip promising that he 'tenra ses mains entre les mains dou roy de France', but he never did so (ibid., p. 98).

[8] *Canterbury Tales* I 783. All Chaucer quotations are from *The Riverside Chaucer*, 3rd edn, ed. L. D. Benson (Boston, 1987). On gestures of trothplight, see R. F. Green, *A Crisis of Truth: Literature and Law in Ricardian England* (Philadelphia, Pa., 1999), pp. 57–9; Peil, *Die Gebärde bei Chrétien, Hartmann und Wolfram*, pp. 195–8; and Habicht, *Gebärde*, pp. 122–3.

It is not a vote that he is asking for. By holding up their hands, a gesture accompanied by oath-swearing and the common drinking of wine, the pilgrims bind themselves to submission for the duration of the pilgrimage – an obligation later acknowledged, significantly, by the Man of Law himself (II 35–45). Elsewhere in the *Canterbury Tales*, the Pardoner's three rioters plight their troths as sworn brothers in the same way: 'Lat ech of us holde up his hand til oother, / And ech of us bicomen otheres brother.'[9] But where faith is engaged between two individuals, the hands must be touched or clasped – the right hands, and without glove or gauntlet.[10] Certain expressions in Middle English suggest that this action was understood as effecting a hand-transfer of something from one party to the other, or from each to each. The transfer is one of 'troth'. One may recall what 'plight' means, in the expression 'plight one's troth'. The *OED* explains: 'To put (something) in danger or risk of forfeiture; to give in pledge; to pledge or engage (one's troth, faith, oath, promise, etc.)' (*Plight* v.¹, sense 2). Hence, to plight one's troth, or 'give one's word', is to leave it in pawn with another, as it were, 'in danger or risk of forfeiture' unless one later redeems it by fulfilling the terms of the oath or promise. Troth may be understood here as one's reputation for integrity, to be maintained or forfeited; but medieval English treats it as rather more thingy than that. As one scholar says of the early folklaw of Western Europe: 'One's word is no mere abstraction; it takes on some of the qualities of a piece of property to be defended against the world.'[11]

Such a conception of troth evidently lies behind expressions such as that used in Chaucer's Friar's Tale: 'Everych in oother es hand his trouthe leith, / For to be sworne bretheren til they deye' (III 1404–5). By

---

[9] *Canterbury Tales* VI 697–8. In the romance *Amis and Amiloun*, the two heroes 'held up her hond' in swearing brotherhood: ed. M. Leach, EETS, 203 (1937), l. 156 (with other examples in the editor's note). Knights pledge agreement by raising their hands: 'Har gloves up þey held / In forward as Y teld', *Lybeaus Desconus*, ed. M. Mills, EETS, 261 (1969), Cotton Ms, ll. 814–15.

[10] 'Your bond / That ye have sworn with your ryght hond', Chaucer, *House of Fame*, ll. 321–2; 'de ma main destre / Vos plevirai', Chrétien de Troyes, *Yvain*, ed. T. B. W. Reid (Manchester, 1942), ll. 5750–1; 'me fianciez de vostre main nue', Prose *Lancelot* 523.11. Many examples from classical and biblical antiquity are given by John Bulwer in his *Chirologia* (1644): ed. J. W. Cleary (Carbondale and Edwardsville, 1974), pp. 77–88. Bulwer observes that '*faith* consists wholly in the right hand and the left hath no obligatory force or virtue in it' (p. 83).

[11] Green, *A Crisis of Truth*, p. 47.

Gestures

a handclasp, each of the parties places his troth in the hand of the other. Similarly in the Wife of Bath's Tale, when the old woman asks the young knight to promise to do her will, she says 'Plight me thy trouthe heere in myn hand'; and the knight responds with 'Have heer my trouthe.'[12] At the same moment in John Gower's version of the same story, the old woman is more specific:

> 'er thou be sped,
> Thou schalt me leve such a wedd,
> That I wol have thi trowthe in honde
> That thou schalt be myn housebonde'.

After first refusing, Florent agrees:

> 'Have hier myn hond, I schal thee wedde.'
> And thus his trowthe he leith to wedde.[13]

Both parties here refer to the knight's troth as a 'wedd', that is, 'a pledge, something deposited as security for a payment or the fulfilment of an obligation' (*OED Wed* sb.). To leave one's troth thus, as a 'wed' in the hand of another, brings out clearly the inner logic of such plighting by handclasp. A common shorthand expression for this act was 'handfast', a word most often applied to marriage vows, as in Malory: 'And anone he made them honde-faste and wedded them.'[14] Even under quite unlikely circumstances handfasting was thought necessary to effect a formal agreement, as a curious episode in Froissart shows. Soldiers holding with the English party in the Auvergne have scaled the outer walls of one of the Dauphin's castles, and the French captain of the castle, Geraudon, has taken refuge in the great tower. The attackers' leader, Aimerigos, parleys with Geraudon, asking for the keys to the outer gate and promising that they will then go peacefully away. When Geraudon understandably expresses some scepticism, Aimerigos offers to swear an oath, whereupon Geraudon ill-advisedly puts his hand out through a little window in the tower door 'pour faire jurer sa foi'. Once Aimerigos has got hold of the

---

[12] *Canterbury Tales* III 1009, 1013. In the Franklin's Tale, Aurelius reminds Dorigen that 'in myn hand youre trouthe plighten ye / To love me best', v 1328–9.

[13] *Confessio Amantis* I 1557–60, 1587–8, ed. G. C. Macaulay, *John Gower's English Works*, 2 vols., EETS, E.S. 81, 82 (1900, 1901).

[14] *The Works of Sir Thomas Malory*, ed. E. Vinaver, 3 vols (Oxford, 1947), 642.27–8. Citations are by page and line number. See *MED hond-festen* v. and *OED Handfast* v.

hand, he threatens to nail it to the door with his dagger unless Geraudon yields up the keys of castle and tower alike. This he does, 'with his other hand'.[15]

Other gestures serve to associate an oath with some sacred object. These acts declare the increased 'risk of forfeiture' for the swearer, if he fails to redeem a pledge made, not only to a human being, but also to God and his saints. In the Prose *Lancelot*, knights hold their right hands out towards some neighbouring church or chapel and swear by 'les sainz de cele eglise'.[16] Where the saints were physically on the spot, as relics, a potent gesture was to swear on a reliquary. Schmitt reproduces a scene from the Bayeux tapestry showing Harold touching two reliquaries as he swears his oath to William.[17] In Chrétien's *Perceval*, Gawain swears a solemn oath on 'un molt prescieus saintuaire', and the same phrase is used when Laudine swears her oath in *Yvain*.[18] The latter scene is quite elaborate. Her attendant lady, Lunete, brings out the reliquary, and Laudine kneels before it, raises her right hand, and swears 'einsi m'ait Des et li sainz' ('as God and the saints may aid me'; ll. 6630–58). The English version of Chrétien's poem, *Ywain and Gawain*, elaborates further – surprisingly, since it generally abbreviates such ceremonial details. Alundyne first promises to plight her troth; but Lunet insists on a formal oath: 'I most nedes have of ȝow an ath, / So þat I mai be sertayn'.[19] Accordingly she brings out relics, a chalice, and a mass-book, and Alundyne kneels before them, places her hand on the book, and, after swearing, kisses it. The act of touching or kissing a sacred book accompanies oaths quite commonly in English texts. To swear such a

---

[15] *Chroniques*, Vol. XI, ed. G. Raynaud (Paris, 1899), pp. 142–3 (Book II, Section 394). On 'acts of hand-giving which stood for an end of hostility, an act of friendship, a pledge of faith or a sign of surrender' much earlier, in the Ottonian empire, see K. Leyser, 'Ritual, Ceremony and Gesture', on pp. 189–213 of his book *Communications and Power in Medieval Europe: The Carolingian and Ottonian Centuries* (London, 1994), pp. 191–2. On gesture, see also pp. 208–9.

[16] Prose *Lancelot* 363.37–8. Also 10.1–2, 88.12–13, 160.12–13, 361.37–9. Also *Chevalier de la Charrete*, ll. 4965–6.

[17] *Raison des gestes*, p. 17. On the heading in the tapestry, 'Ubi Harold sacramentum fecit Willelmo duci', Schmitt observes: 'c'est-à-dire, ici, un acte qui engage les puissances du sacré. Un acte plein de risques, car le parjure déchaîne la vengeance divine' (p. 16). For other examples, see *OED Sanctuary* sb.[1], sense 3.

[18] *Le Roman de Perceval*, ed. W. Roach (Geneva, 1959), ll. 6194–6; *Yvain*, l. 6632.

[19] *Ywain and Gawain*, ed. A. B. Friedman and N. T. Harrington, EETS, 254 (1964), ll. 3904–5.

'book-oath', as they called it, was a serious matter. When Archbishop Arundel was interrogating the Lollard William Thorpe, he pressed him to swear by a Gospel book; but Thorpe persistently refused.[20] He refused, in fact, on principle, for he argued that it was not lawful to swear by any created thing. Orthodox writers did not, of course, share this Wycliffite scruple. In the treatise *Dives and Pauper*, Pauper is asked why men lay their hand on a sacred book when they swear before a judge, and offers an elaborate explanation for this still-current custom. It means, he says, that, if the sworn statement is false, the swearer 'forsakes', or abandons all claim on, Christianity, the prayers written in the book, the joys of heaven, and all his own good deeds.[21] In *Confessio Amantis*, Gower describes a deceitful lover running these risks:

> Anon he wole his hand doun lein
> Upon a bok, and swere and sein
> That he wole feith and trouthe bere.[22]

In Chaucer's Shipman's Tale, the lecherous monk swears secrecy to the merchant's wife on his breviary: 'on my portehors I make an ooth', and the wife reciprocates: 'By God and by this portehors I swere' (VII 131, 135). Their oaths are then sealed with a kiss. In the fabliau world of this tale, oaths are sworn, not on Gospels or missals, but on a light and portable breviary – a pocket-book, as it were – and confirmed by a distinctly equivocal kiss.

In the texts under consideration here, however, an even more common form of ritual behaviour is the gesture of submission. One does not have to be an ethologist to know that lowering of the body – crouching, slinking, and the like – marks the behaviour of many animals when they encounter a dominant other; and when human beings bow or kneel they exhibit the same response, no doubt phylogenetically determined.[23]

---

[20] *Two Wycliffite Texts*, ed. A. Hudson, EETS, 301 (1993), pp. 74–9.

[21] *Dives and Pauper*, ed. P. H. Barnum, EETS, 275, 280 (1976, 1980), Vol. I, Part I, p. 235.

[22] *Confessio Amantis* v 2889–91. For other examples, see *MED bok* n.(1) 3 a (d), and, for kissing, *kissen* v. 3 (b). In the *Life of the Black Prince*, ed. M. C. Pope and E. C. Lodge (Oxford, 1910), oaths are sworn 'sur le livre' (ll. 1569, 4145), as well as on the reserved host (ll. 1571, 2220).

[23] 'In species where social life is largely governed by dominance hierarchies, one would expect meetings between individuals to be marked by performance of the dominance-submission ritual or some version of it': H. Callan, *Ethology and Society: Towards an*

Gestures and looks in medieval narrative

Yet it is nurture rather than nature that determines the part played by such 'dominance–submission rituals' in any given human society. In the modern West, bowing generally survives only in the occasional deferential lowering of the head, and kneeling is confined to churches.[24] In the medieval West, on the other hand, bowing, kneeling, and even prostration served constantly to express and reinforce long-standing relations with dominant powers, from God and the king downwards. They also marked short-term relationships, as when benefits were sought or received. The performance of such acts (and also, on occasion, their pointed non-performance) conveyed a variety of messages not always easily read by those accustomed to the manners of the egalitarian West.

The general rule is that the more you lower your body, the more humbly you submit. Prostration marks the extreme form of such self-abasement; so it is appropriate that Pride, in Langland's confession of the Seven Deadly Sins, should express her contrition by flattening herself: 'Pernele proud-herte platte hire to þe erþe / And lay longe er she loked, and "lord, mercy!" cryde.'[25] Much more common, and also more varied in its significances, is the action of bowing. As in Japanese tradition, the depth of the bow can be adjusted to mark the degree of deference. Encounters with great men call for deep bows; slight bows can signify hostility or reserve; and failure to bow altogether will constitute a deliberate affront. All these three settings can be seen in Froissart's description of the encounter between the citizens of Ghent and their angry overlord, the Count of Flanders. As the Count approaches their town, the townsfolk 's'enclinoient tout bas à l'encontre de li et li faissoient toute l'onneur et reverence que il pooient' ['bowed very deeply before him and did him all the honour and reverence they could']. But the Count passes through them with no more than a slight inclination of the head:

Anthropological View (Oxford, 1970), p. 108. See generally Argyle, *Bodily Communication*, Chapter 13 'Posture'.

[24] On a quite different modern society, see H. Morsbach, 'Nonverbal Communication and Hierarchical Relationships: The Case of Bowing in Japan', in F. Poyatos, ed., *Cross-Cultural Perspectives in Nonverbal Communication* (Toronto, 1988), pp. 189–99.

[25] *Piers Plowman*, B V 62–3. Unless otherwise noted, all citations are from the edition of the B version by G. Kane and E. T. Donaldson (London, 1975). The A version will be cited from Kane's edition (London, 1960). Malory describes how the cowardly King Mark 'felle flatte to the erthe at kynge Arthurs feete, and put hym in his grace and mercy' (594.23–4).

'les enclinoit un petit dou chief'. Later, in the town market-place, the radical party of Ghent (the 'White Hats') express their hostility to the Count by an outright refusal to bow: 'ne le daignèrent onques encliner, dont il fu mout merancolieus' ['they did not deign ever to bow to him, at which he was very angry'].[26]

Kneeling also had its varieties. In its discussion of the first commandment, *Dives and Pauper* devotes a chapter to 'dedys of wurshepe and reverence', that is, 'tokenys of þe body, as be knelyngge, loutyngge, lyftyngge up of hondys, be bunchyngge on þe breist'. These gestures have different meanings, explains Pauper, according to whether they are directed at God or at 'resonable creaturys'; and, in the case of kneeling, they should be differently performed: 'as seyȝt a gret clerk, Doctor Halys, in Summa sua, to God men shuldyn knelyn wyt bothe knees in tokene þat in hym is al oure principal helpe, but to man only wyt þe to [one] knee'.[27] A fifteenth-century courtesy book makes the same distinction, between kneeling on two knees to God and on one to man:

> Be curtayse to God, and knele doun
> On bothe knees with grete devocioun.
> To mon þou shalle knele opon the ton,
> The toþer to þy self þou halde alon.[28]

A rather earlier English courtesy book explains that last line. By kneeling before one's lord on a single knee only, one reserves some honour for oneself: 'thy worshyp þou mayst save so'.[29] Yet in the English and French texts I have read, kneeling on both knees seems the more common form – certainly not confined to religious contexts – nor does kneeling on one knee often seem to imply any reservation. The matter might repay further investigation.[30]

---

[26] *Chroniques*, Vol. IX, ed. G. Raynaud (Paris, 1894), pp. 214, 217 (Book II, Section 129). I refer to this episode again in Chapter 3.
[27] *Dives and Pauper*, Vol. I, Part I, pp. 104–6.
[28] Ed. F. J. Furnivall, *The Babees Book*, EETS, 32 (1868), ll. 163–6 (p. 304). On the use of both knees in prayer, see Schmitt, *Raison des gestes*, pp. 295, 300, 306.
[29] *Urbanitatis*, ll. 9–10, in *Babees Book*, p. 13.
[30] J. Russell Major notices that, as gestural ceremonies of homage were scaled down in sixteenth-century France, vassals might be required to put only one knee, instead of the traditional two, on the ground: pp. 519 and 520 of the article cited below (n. 141).

Gestures and looks in medieval narrative

The act of submission itself most commonly, in the texts, takes the form of kneeling. Although much simpler than the elaborate ceremonies of homage and fealty, this action carries a full weight of meaning. In the Prose *Lancelot*, Galehot kneels and 'joins his hands' as he submits to King Arthur; and elsewhere a conquered knight, sent to a lady as her prisoner, dismounts and kneels to her with his helm in his hand.[31] In Malory, defeated knights kneel and yield up their swords to the victor (174.30–1, 178.16–17). However, when the two supreme knights Tristram and Lancelot have fought each other to a draw after four hours, each submits to the other with gestures of high courtesy: 'And therewyth sir Launcelott kneled adowne and yeldid hym up his swerde. And therewithall sir Trystram kneled adowne and yeldid hym up his swerde, and so aythir gaff other the gre' (569.31–4). Ceremonies of submission allow equality to be expressed only by such double, reciprocal performance. Another episode in Malory illustrates a different kind of awkwardness – arising, in this case, from a sudden shift in relationships. When the young Arthur has drawn the sword from the stone, his foster father and foster brother fall on their knees before him: 'And therwithalle syre Ector knelyd doune to the erthe and syre Kay. "Allas!" said Arthur, "myne own dere fader and broder, why knele ye to me?"' (14.32–5).

Bowing and kneeling also, of course, played a significant part in the regular social life of the times as courteous marks of respect and reverence. Indeed, to 'reverence' someone, in Middle English, commonly meant to bow to them, as when Abraham encounters God in *Piers Plowman*: 'I roos up and reverenced hym.'[32] The word 'courtesy', too, was moving towards its later gestural sense, as in 'curtsey': Malory's lady Lyones, seeing her rescuer Sir Gareth from an upper window, 'made curtesy to hym downe to the erth, holdynge up bothe her hondys'.[33] To be a king, in particular, meant to be knelt to. When Sir Orfeo abandons his throne and goes into the wilderness, the author of the Middle English poem characterises his previous royal state as one when he had 'kniȝtes

---

[31] Prose *Lancelot* 327.23–4, 391.10–12. In Chrétien's *Erec et Enide*, the defeated knight Ydiers falls at Guinevere's feet as her prisoner: ed. M. Roques (Paris, 1968), ll. 1179–84.

[32] B XVI 226. See *MED reverencen* v. (d), and *reverence* n. 2. Also *OED Worship* v., sense 2b: 'To treat with signs of honour or respect; to salute, bow down to'.

[33] *Works*, 321.31–2. A stage direction in Skelton's play *Magnificence* has one character 'doynge reverence and courtesy' as he approaches the king: John Skelton, *The Complete English Poems*, ed. J. Scattergood (Harmondsworth, 1983), after line 1514.

Gestures

of priis / Bifor him kneland, and levedis'.[34] On occasion, the ritual can be supercharged with meaning, as in Malory's scene of dumbshow towards the end of his *Morte Darthur*. Lancelot, having rescued Guinevere from the fire and carried her off to Joyous Gard, now returns her to an angry Arthur:

> So when sir Launcelot saw the kynge and sir Gawayne, than he lad the quene by the arme, and than he kneled downe and the quene bothe. Wyte you well, than was there many a bolde knyght wyth kynge Arthur that wepte as tendirly as they had seyne all their kynne dede afore them! So the kynge sate stylle and seyde no worde. And whan sir Launcelot saw hys countenaunce he arose up and pulled up the quene with hym.[35]

The weeping of the knights marks the significance of Lancelot's submission to Arthur; but the king responds with a pointed absence of movement or speech, where according to custom he would be expected to 'bid them arise'. So Lancelot's unbidden rising up, pulling the queen with him, speaks volumes, as a mute response to what he sees in Arthur's 'countenaunce'. There is a similar moment in the *Gest of Robyn Hode*, where the rich abbot of St Mary's York keeps a debtor knight on his knees for the space of twelve stanzas, until the knight rises unbidden: 'Up then stode that gentyll knyght, / To the abbot sayd he, / "To suffre a knyght to knele so longe, / Thou canst no curteysye."'[36]

Knights would kneel to kings, but they expected others lower down the social hierarchy to kneel to them. Langland has an extraordinary passage in *Piers Plowman* where Conscience 'proves' to Will that Jesus was in his life successively knight, king, and conqueror. Having observed that 'to be called a knyght is fair for men shul knele to hym' (B XIX 28), Conscience goes on to demonstrate the knighthood of the young Jesus by recalling that both kings and angels 'reverenced him' and knelt at his

---

[34] *Sir Orfeo*, ed. A. J. Bliss, 2nd edn (Oxford, 1966), Auchinleck Ms ll. 249–50. In *Sir Gawain and the Green Knight*, l. 248, Arthur is denoted by periphrasis simply as 'hym þat al shulde loute', that is, 'one to whom all should bow'.

[35] *Works*, 1196.31–1197.3. Malory seems to have expanded upon his sources here. Lancelot and Arthur meet without ceremony in the *Mort le Roi Artu*, ed. J. Frappier (Geneva, 1954), p. 157; and the English stanzaic *Morte Arthur* has only 'the kynge than salowes he full sone': ed. J. D. Bruce, EETS, E.S. 88 (1903), l. 2376.

[36] *Rymes of Robyn Hood*, ed. R. B. Dobson and J. Taylor (London, 1976), stanza 115.

birth, thus fulfilling the words of St Paul, 'that in the name of Jesus every knee should bow'.[37] It is as if the acts of bowing and kneeling here actually constitute knighthood or bestow it, albeit in a fanciful argument. The privilege is shared by other positions in the social hierarchy. Sons and daughters kneel to their fathers, as Galahad does to Lancelot in Malory and Constance does to the emperor her father in Chaucer's Man of Law's Tale.[38] Guests, too, might expect to be served on bended knee, as the valets serve Gawain 'a jenols' in Chrétien's *Perceval* (line 8242). Even a monk – though a proud and worldly monk – expects such service in Langland's satiric portrait: 'but if his knave knele þat shal his coppe brynge / He loureþ on hym and lakkeþ hym: who lered hym curteisie?'[39]

Kneeling was also, needless to say, the common form of submission to the lordship of God and the mysteries of religion. When a beautiful lady who appears to Will in *Piers Plowman* identifies herself as Holy Church, the dreamer immediately falls on his knees (B I 79); and he remains there throughout the rest of their encounter, for he is still on his knees at the beginning of the next passus ('Yet kneled I on my knees', II 1). Lady Mede kneels in confession to the friar (*Piers* B III 43), as Amans does to his confessor Genius in Gower's poem.[40] People also kneel or bow to sacred objects, even to a pardoner's bull, but especially to the cross.[41] At the end of Passus XVIII of *Piers Plowman*, Will and his family are commanded to honour Christ's resurrection by creeping on their knees to kiss the cross (B XVIII 427–8). In a remarkable imitation of

---

[37] Philippians 2.10, cited at XIX 80a. See J. F. G. Weldon, 'Gesture of Perception: The Pattern of Kneeling in *Piers Plowman* B.18–19', *Yearbook of Langland Studies*, 3 (1989), 49–66. English renderings of the Vulgate Bible are from the Douai version.

[38] Malory, *Works*, 1012.18; *Canterbury Tales* II 1152–3. Also, for example, *Confessio Amantis* I 3145. See *Dives and Pauper* on the Fourth Commandment: to 'worship' parents, 'we mon rysyn aȝenys hem, knelyn to hem and takyn her blissynge': Vol. 1, Part 1, p. 310.

[39] *Piers Plowman* B X 315–16. Failure to defer can anger an innkeeper's wife, as Chaucer's Host reports: '"And if that any neighebor of myne / Wol nat in chirche to my wyf enclyne, / Or be so hardy to hire to trespace, / Whan she comth hoom she rampeth in my face"' (*Canterbury Tales* VII 1901–4).

[40] *Confessio Amantis* I 212–13. Nature kneels to the same confessor, Genius, in the *Roman de la Rose*, ed. F. Lecoy, 3 vols. (Paris, 1965–70), ll. 16,688–9. Chaucer's Parson speaks of kneeling as 'signe outward' of inner humility before one's confessor: *Canterbury Tales* X 988–92. In the Prose *Lancelot*, a penitent Arthur appears before his bishops on his knees, as well as barefoot, stripped to the waist, and carrying rods in both hands – symbolic behaviour of a very elaborate kind: 284.30–2, 285.4.

[41] *Piers Plowman* B Prol. 73; Prose *Lancelot* 223.38, 383.36; Malory, *Works*, 928.23–4.

such adoration of sacred things, Chrétien's Lancelot bows to the bed in which Guinevere lies as to a reliquary, and he bows again to her chamber 'as if he were before an altar' on his departure.[42] Kneeling was also, as it is today, the regular gesture of petition and thanks to God or the gods, commonly with the hands joined and raised. In *Confessio Amantis*, even Nebuchadnezzar, degraded to a four-footed beast, bows, 'kneleth in his wise', and raises his front paws in humble petition to God (I 3022–30). Among medieval treatises on prayer, one in particular was concerned with its gestures and postures: the *De Modo Orandi Corporaliter* by an early follower of St Dominic.[43] This work lists no fewer than nine different corporal *modi* of prayer; but the texts considered here generally acknowledge only one, kneeling with hands raised. The sole exception I have noticed is in Gower's *Confessio*. When Solomon prays to his pagan goddess, 'he knelende hise armes spradde'; but here, for once, a medieval author appears to be imagining the body language of a culture other than his own.[44]

One of the chief functions of kneeling within human society was to seek or acknowledge a benefit.[45] The gesture was a formal, even an indispensable, mark of petitionary intention – to prompt or prevent some course of action, or to win pardon for some offence. Thus in the *Morte Darthur*: 'Whan sir Bors undirstode his brothirs wratth he kneled downe tofore hym to the erthe, and cryed hym mercy, holdyng up both hys hondis, and prayde hym to forgyff hym hys evyll wylle' (969.20–3). Where pardon was granted, courtesy required the injured party to give the offender permission to rise, as Erec does to the kneeling Guivret in

---

[42] *Chevalier de la Charrete*, ll. 4651–3, 4716–18. Compare *Cligés*, ed. A. Micha (Paris, 1982), ll. 1597–9.

[43] Ed. S. Tugwell, 'The Nine Ways of Prayer of St. Dominic: A Textual Study and Critical Edition', *Mediaeval Studies*, 47 (1985), 1–124. See Schmitt, *Raison des gestes*, pp. 309–13. His whole chapter has valuable discussion and references on gestures of prayer. See also his essay 'Between Text and Image: The Prayer Gestures of Saint Dominic', on pp. 127–62 of the special gestures number of *History and Anthropology*, Vol. 1, Part 1 (1984), and R. C. Trexler, 'Legitimating Prayer Gestures in the Twelfth Century. The *Penitentia* of Peter the Chanter', ibid., pp. 97–126.

[44] *Confessio* VII 4500. Compare the description of Aeneas at prayer in Gavin Douglas's *Aeneid*: 'Hys handis twa, as tho the custum was, / Towart the hevyn gan uplift', ed. D. F. C. Coldwell, STS, 4 vols. (1957–64), XIII ii 40–1 (from the Book XIII by Maphaeus Vegius).

[45] For a good study of supplication and its rituals, see G. Koziol, *Begging Pardon and Favor: Ritual and Political Order in Early Medieval France* (Ithaca, N.Y., 1992).

Gestures and looks in medieval narrative

Chrétien: '"Amis, relevez sus, / De cest forfet quites soiez"' ['"Friend, get up; you are forgiven for this offence"'].[46] On other occasions, a knight may actually raise petitioners from their knees because he cannot bear to see a lord or a great lady submitting to him in that way. So in the Prose *Lancelot*: 'Lors chiet la reine a monseignor Yvain as piez et li prie que il ait pitié de l'annor lo roi et de li. Et il l'an lieve contramont' ['Then the queen falls to Sir Ywain's feet, praying him to take pity on the king's honour and her. And he raised her up', 549.30–1]. In Malory's version of the episode of the poisoned apple, Queen Guinevere again kneels in supplication to one of her husband's knights:

> And therewith she kneled downe uppon both hir kneys and besought sir Bors to have mercy uppon her, 'other ellis I shall have a shamefull dethe, and thereto I never offended'. Ryght so cam kynge Arthure and founde the queene knelynge. And than sir Bors toke hir up and seyde, 'Madam, ye do me grete dishonoure.' (1052.19–24)

Bors finds himself in a false position in the eyes of his king; but it is more than that: '"Madam, ye do me grete dishonoure."' To kneel is to do honour to another person; but where a great lady is reduced by circumstances to honour one who should properly honour her – and on both her knees, too – then he cannot accept her submission without dishonouring himself.[47]

Kneeling also serves to express gratitude for benefits received. Here too conflicts can arise. Froissart describes how, in 1326, Sir John of Hainault offered to conduct Queen Isabella back to England. The queen goes to kneel before him in gratitude, 'mès li gentilz chevaliers ne l'euist jamais souffert; ains se leva moult apertement': God forbid that the queen of England should kneel to one of her own knights.[48] In *Ywain and Gawain*, again, the sister and niece of Sir Gawain fall at the feet of Ywain and thank him for his promise to defend them against a giant:

---

[46] *Erec et Enide*, ll. 5052–3.
[47] The kneeler may also be dishonoured. In *William of Palerne*, William reproaches the queen for kneeling to him, a simple soldier: 'ȝe don a gret deshonour wiþ þat to ȝou selve': ed. G. H. V. Bunt (Groningen, 1985), l. 3952.
[48] 'But the courteous knight would never have allowed her to do so, and he himself got up very deliberately', *Chroniques*, Vol. 1, p. 22 (Book I, Section 9).

Gestures

> 'A, God forbede', said Sir Ywain,
> 'Þat þe sister of Sir Gawayn
> Or any oþer of his blode born
> Sold on þis wise knel me byforn.'
> He toke þam up tyte both infere
> And prayd þam to amend þaire chere.
> (2323–8)

The French original, Chrétien's *Yvain*, has a rather more sophisticated version of this episode. The ladies are urged to kneel, but Yvain prevents them with these words:

> 'Des m'an deffande
> Qu'orguiauz an moi tant ne s'estande
> Que a mon pié venir les les!
> Voir, ja n'oblieroie mes
> La honte, que je an avroie.'

['God forbid that I should ever be so proud as to let them fall at my feet! Truly, I would never forget the shame of it', *Yvain*, 3983–7.]

Like Bors in Malory, Yvain sees nothing but shame in such incongruous honouring. It is in these same Yvain poems that one finds a remarkably elaborate description of grateful gesture – remarkable because the beneficiary is a lion. Animal communication attracted some attention from medieval writers. Augustine noted, 'Habent etiam bestiae quaedam inter se signa quibus produnt appetitum animi sui';[49] and later writers reflected on the semiotic nature of signs such as the dog's bark.[50] Modern ethologists pride themselves on avoiding anthropocentric readings of animal behaviour, but medieval writers readily interpreted beasts in human terms. So, since the lion was the king of beasts, it was natural for them to credit lions with noble gestures as well as sentiments.[51] In

---

[49] 'Some animals, too, have signs among themselves by which they show the desires of their minds': *De Doctrina*, pp. 58, 59.
[50] See Eco *et al.*, 'On Animal Language in the Medieval Classification of Signs'.
[51] In the Prose *Lancelot*, Galehot dreams of a lion kneeling to 'cry mercy' (578.16–18). In *An Alphabet of Tales*, Jerome's lion, apologising for failing in his duty, fawned and 'lowtid unto þe erþe, evyn as he had askid þaim forgyfnes': ed. M. M. Banks, EETS 126, 127 (1904–5), p. 301. Compare Gower's *Confessio* VII 3392–9, following the bestiary tradition that lions understand prostration and respond to the gesture with mercy: T. H. White, *The Book of Beasts* (London, 1954), p. 9.

25

Chrétien's poem, Yvain has killed a serpent that was attacking a lion, and the noble beast submits to him in gratitude. He stands on his hind legs and bows deeply, holding out his front paws joined together, whereupon he kneels down again, weeping tears of humility:

> il li comança a feire
> Sanblant, que a lui se randoit,
> Et ses piez joinz li estandoit
> Et vers terre ancline sa chiere,
> S'estut sor les deus piez deriere;
> Et puis si se ragenoilloit
> Et tote sa face moilloit
> De lermes par humilité.
>
> ['He began to make it appear that he was giving himself up to him. He stretched out his joined feet to him and bent his face towards the ground, standing on his two hind feet; and then he knelt and drenched his face in tears of humility', *Yvain*, 3394–401.]

The lion in the English version also abases himself and holds up his forefeet in thanks and admiration; but his behaviour has more of the feline about it: he makes 'grete fawnyng' and lies low to lick the knight's feet.[52]

Let me conclude these remarks about gestures of submission, however, with a very human instance, in an episode of Chrétien's *Perceval*.[53] The heroine of this lengthy episode, which takes place in Tintagel, is a little girl known as 'la Pucele as Mances Petites', or the Girl with the Little Sleeves. She has a crush on Sir Gawain, and she provokes her elder sister to slap her when she maintains that he is a finer knight than her sister's lover, Melians de Lis. This prompts her to approach Gawain in his lodgings and beg him to 'do her right' against her sister, making her sudden request wrapping her arms round Gawain's leg (lines 5334–5). Understandably puzzled, Gawain responds by silently laying a friendly hand upon her head, whereupon she impatiently tugs at him and repeats

---

[52] *Ywain and Gawain*, ll. 2001–8. Montaigne reflects on the mutual understanding of signs between men and beasts: 'We have some modest understanding of what they mean: they have the same of us, in about equal measure. They fawn on us and entreat us – as we do them': *The Complete Essays*, transl. M. A. Screech (London, 1991), pp. 505–7 (p. 506).

[53] *Roman de Perceval*, ll. 4824–5655.

Gestures

her appeal. Her father, who is present, finds his daughter's behaviour embarrassing – pay no attention, he says, she is only a child, a silly little thing ('niche chose fole') – but Gawain courteously grants her request: he will fight in the next day's tournament as her knight. The girl thanks him briefly, bows to the ground (5384), and goes home with her father, carried in his arms on the neck of his horse.[54] Gawain predictably vindicates Little Sleeves against her sister, unhorsing Melians to her great delight. As he is about to leave Tintagel, she takes hold of his foot and kisses it. Gawain is again puzzled by her irregular behaviour. What, he asks, does she mean? Her intention, she replies, is that he should never forget her (5638–48). These scenes derive some of their comic charm from the knight's amiable inability to read the girl's untutored gestures – a reminder of how clearly the normal repertoire of such expressive movements was prescribed and their meanings understood.

The same can be said of another kind of gesture-rich occasion, when people meet or receive others, and also when they part. The ritualisation of behaviour on these occasions has been much studied in modern times. The social anthropologist Raymond Firth, in a valuable survey, speaks of the expressive power of such conventional actions, and in particular stresses the way in which they indicate the status of the participants: 'Relative posture and gesture, especially as displayed in degree of bodily elevation, are used widely to indicate symbolically the relative status of the parties engaged ... a basic function of greeting and parting rituals is in creating occasion for establishment of relative status positions, or in providing a code (a "vocabulary") in which status relations can be expressed. These rituals too may provide conditions for exploration or assertion of changing status'.[55] Such rituals are, as Firth remarks, 'culture-specific, not universals', and they vary from place to place and from time to time; but I find little of this variation in the texts being considered here, for most of them observe a code of manners common

---

[54] Later in their ride, the girl enjoys what can only be called a cuddle: 'Einsi parlant entre ses bras / L'en porte, et s'a molt grant solas / De che que il l'acole et tient' ['As she talks thus in his arms she is carried off, much delighted by the fact that he holds and embraces her', ll. 5429–31].

[55] R. Firth, 'Verbal and Bodily Rituals of Greeting and Parting', in J. S. La Fontaine, ed., *The Interpretation of Ritual* (London, 1972), pp. 1–38 (pp. 31–2).

Gestures and looks in medieval narrative

to the politer worlds of medieval France, England, and Italy.[56] Their basic repertoire of meeting and parting gestures may be divided into two categories, according to the status relations they express. Some require that one of the participants should perform an act of deference before the other. These acts are: bowing, kneeling, doffing headgear, and rising from one's seat. The other person, meanwhile, may either acknowledge the salutation or do nothing at all – for in such hierarchical exchanges it is the party of lower status who does the moving.[57] Gestures of the second type, by contrast, directly involve both parties and, when they are fully reciprocal, indicate a relationship of equality, with any superiority of status disclaimed. The acts are: embracing, kissing, and joining hands. Quite often the gestures do no more – and no less – than endorse established and well-understood relationships, as when a valet kneels to a lord, or two brother knights embrace; but they may also carry more pointed messages. Gestures of greeting can be over- or under-performed, or not performed at all, with a variety of consequent messages (enthusiasm, hostility, etc.). Again, a submissive act of greeting may be met, and as it were corrected, by an embrace or a kiss; or it may prompt another submissive act in return, as between two great lords neither of whom wishes either to claim or concede the upper hand. Such gestural exchanges form part of a system of non-verbal communication highly sensitive to nuances which a modern reader may not always detect.[58]

Bowing and kneeling are the two acts of deference most commonly recorded in the French and English texts when people meet or part. These were gestures of courtesy and reverence which acknowledged one's inferiority to a king or queen, a great lord or lady, a knight, or a parent,

---

[56] Habicht, *Gebärde*, lists greeting gestures common to courtly manners in medieval English, French, and German texts: kneeling, bowing and baring the head, going to meet, leading by the hand, and kissing (p. 86, and see pp. 86–93). Texts concerned with less polite circles give less evidence for their manners; but see below, pp. 35–8, for discussion of the handshake.

[57] See E. Goody, '"Greeting", "Begging", and the Presentation of Respect', in La Fontaine, ed., *The Interpretation of Ritual*, pp. 39–71. She remarks that 'it is the inferior who moves towards, or into the presence of, the superior' (p. 40). So also Firth: 'the degree of disarrangement of the one party indicates the relative status of the other' (p. 20 in the same volume).

[58] Montaigne has some shrewd remarks about gestures of greeting, 'by which we acquire, as often as not wrongly, the honour of being thought humble and courteous: you can be humble out of pride!'. See pp. 719–20 in Screech's translation.

28

Gestures

as the case might be. Not to bow or kneel when the occasion required it commonly constituted a deliberate affront. It is as a malcontent, or satirist, that Will the dreamer says of himself in *Piers Plowman* that he is 'looþ to reverencen / Lordes or ladies or any lif ellis' (B xv 5–6); a hostile messenger does not bow to an emperor in Chrétien's *Cligés* ('il nel salue, ne ancline', 2442); and in the Prose *Lancelot*, when Lambegue comes before the tyrant Claudas to surrender, 'il ne s'agenoille pas' (127.21). Non-performance could also mark distinctions of status. When the great count of Foix, Gaston Phebus, entered the presence of the French king, the king's uncle, and other lords, Froissart makes it clear that he went down three times on one knee 'pour honorer le roi et non autrui' ['to honour the king *and no one else*'].[59] King Charles, acknowledging the correctness of his behaviour, responds with equally exact propriety, taking the count by the hand, embracing him, and raising him up. Gestures serve here to define power relationships, as elsewhere in Froissart's *Chronicles*. At the beginning of the Amiens peace conference in 1392, the leaders of the English delegation, the royal dukes of Lancaster and York, are conducted with great ceremony into the presence of the French king, led by three French dukes on their honorific right side. The French lords all kneel in the presence of their sovereign; but the two English dukes remain standing and bow 'only a little' before King Charles, to whom they owe no obedience. Though a slight bow can be offensive, on this occasion it makes a valid political point; and Charles courteously steps forward and takes the dukes by the hand.[60] Again, when two kings meet, gestures can express their equal dignities. When Richard II of England came to France in 1396 to marry princess Isabella, his meeting with King Charles was conducted with elaborate ceremony. At their first encounter, according to Froissart, both kings

---

[59] *Les Chroniques de Sire Jean Froissart*, ed. J. A. C. Buchon, 3 vols. (Paris, 1852–3), Vol. III, p. 29 (Book IV, Chap. 8). On the ceremony of three bows to a monarch, see J. Wildeblood, *The Polite World* (London, 1965), pp. 143, 276.

[60] 'Quand ils furent venus devers le roi, les trois ducs de France qui les adextroient, et les autres barons de France, s'agenouillèrent devant le roi. Mais les deux ducs d'Angleterre demeurèrent en leur estant; un seul petit s'inclinèrent pour honorer le roi. Le roi vint tantôt jusques à eux et les prit par les mains' ['When they had come before the king, the three French dukes who were leading them on their right hand, and the other French lords, knelt before him. But the two English dukes remained on their feet and bowed only a little to honour the king. The king at once came right up to them and took them by the hand']: *Chroniques*, ed. Buchon, Vol. III, p. 142 (Book IV, Chap. 27).

bared their heads, bowed 'a little', and took each other by the hand.[61] By exchanging underperformed bows, each monarch both reserved his own dignity and granted dignity to the other; so a gesture of submission acquires the same ability to symbolise equality of status as the fraternal handclasp by which it is followed.

When the dreamer in Chaucer's *Book of the Duchess* first approaches the solitary and grieving Black Knight, he doffs his hood and greets him as courteously as he knows how (lines 516–18). Removing of headgear, as a kind of body-lowering, commonly accompanies a verbal greeting, and sometimes a bow, in the texts. In the Prose *Lancelot*, for instance, a monk doffs his cowl to a lady and later approaches King Arthur uncovered (48.35, 54.8), and the knight Pharien removes his helmet as he enters the tent of Claudas (115.16). Sir Lamerok does the same in Malory: 'Whan he sawe the kynge he put of his helme and salewed hym' (608.1–2). One English courtesy book has this advice: 'When þou comeste before a lorde / In halle, yn bowre, or at þe borde, / Hoode or kappe þou of tho.'[62] A satirical poem, *Sir Penny*, sees the practice as evidence of the modern power of money: 'Sir Peny chaunges mans mode, / And gers þam oft do doun þaire hode, / And to rise him ogayne.'[63]

The gesture may be no more than a simple formality, as today; but on occasion it is charged with extra significance. When the dreamer in *Pearl* first encounters the queenly lady of his vision, she greets him by bowing deeply and taking off her crown: 'Enclynande lowe in womman lore, / Caȝte of her coroun of grete tresore' (lines 236–7). These gestures are quite unexpected in a crowned queen, and they mark her as what she once was, the dreamer's daughter. She acknowledges this relationship here, once for all, at their first meeting; but it is not long before she asserts her new royal status in heaven, straightening up from her bow and putting her crown back on (253–5).[64] The gesture functions quite

---

[61] 'Les deux rois à nud chef s'encontrèrent; si s'inclinèrent un petit et se prirent par les mains', ibid., p. 258 (Book IV, Chap. 51).

[62] *Urbanitatis*, ll. 3–5, in Furnivall, *Babees Book*, p. 13. Doffing is illustrated in Wildeblood, *The Polite World*, Plate VII.

[63] *Sir Penny II*, ll. 13–15, no. 58 in *Secular Lyrics of the XIVth and XVth Centuries*, ed. R. H. Robbins (Oxford, 1952).

[64] *Pearl*, ed. E. V. Gordon (Oxford, 1953). See J. Nicholls, *The Matter of Courtesy: Medieval Courtesy Books and the Gawain-Poet* (Woodbridge, 1985), p. 107. *The Life of St. Katherine of Alexandria*, by John Capgrave, has an exchange between the Virgin Mary and Christ

Gestures

differently in a scene between two cynical courtiers in John Skelton's play *Magnificence*.[65] One of the men enters singing a popular song, and the other, according to a stage direction, 'makes as if to doff his hat ironically' ('faciat tanquam exuat beretum ironice'). 'Ironice' is an editorial emendation for what seems a meaningless 'cronice' in the early prints. Schmitt cites a reference to gestural irony from the thirteenth-century *Rhetorica Antiqua* of Boncampagno da Signa, who speaks of 'gestus illorum qui subsannant et yronias proponunt' ['the gestures of those who sneer and deal in ironies'].[66] Gestures can be ironical, like words, as Andrea de Jorio observed in the early nineteenth century. In his encyclopaedic account of Neapolitan gesture, de Jorio has a section on Ironia.[67] A gesture will be read as ironical, he remarks, either when it cannot in the context carry its 'natural meaning', or else when, as again with verbal utterance, irony is suggested by some distinctive features in the performance of it. In Skelton's play, the newcomer responds to irony with vulgarity, producing a rude version of the Shakespearian 'Pray be covered': 'Decke your hofte and cover a lowce', roughly, 'Put your lid on and cover that louse.' Doffing, like bowing, can be underperformed, where relationships between the two persons call for something short of the full act. So, when the god Mercury has been elected speaker of the parliament of the gods in Robert Henryson's *Testament of Cresseid*, he addresses Cupid 'veiling his cap alyte'.[68] Failure to doff altogether might be a sign of hostility. As Ulysses says to Priam in the *Destruction of Troy* when he comes before him with a challenging message: 'an enmy to anoþer nothing it semys, / Hailsyng ne hynd speche with no hede bare.'[69] Otherwise the effect might simply be discourteous. The drunken Miller in the *Canterbury Tales* 'nolde avalen neither hood ne hat, / Ne abyde no man for his curteisie' (I 3122–3). Such failure to

---

where Mary first prostrates herself and takes off her crown before her enthroned son; but Christ shortly asks her to rise, and she resumes her crown: ed. C. Horstmann, EETS, 100 (1893), Book III, ll. 1175–6, 1184–5.
[65] In *The Complete English Poems*, ed. Scattergood, ll. 745–9.
[66] *Raison des gestes*, p. 401, n. 100.
[67] *La mimica degli antichi investigata nel gestire napoletano* (Naples, 1832), transl. and ed. A. Kendon as *Gesture in Naples and Gesture in Classical Antiquity* (Bloomington, Ind., 2000), pp. 256–7.
[68] *The Poems of Robert Henryson*, ed. D. Fox (Oxford, 1981), l. 271.
[69] *The Gest Hystoriale of the Destruction of Troy*, ed. G. A. Panton and D. Donaldson, EETS, 39, 56 (1869, 1874), ll. 4990–1.

doff plays a part in the comedy of the exchanges between the shepherd and the incognito king in the romance *King Edward and the Shepherd*. Not knowing who he is, the shepherd treats King Edward like a fellow shepherd, as when they first meet: 'þe scheperde lovyd his hatte so well, / He did hit of never a dele, / But seid, "Sir, gud-day."'[70] He goes on neglecting the courtesy, both to the king and to his lords, until a squire finally warns him of Edward's identity; whereupon he 'puts down his hood', falls to his knees, and begs forgiveness.

In the Second Book of Kings (2 Samuel), Absalom sets out to steal the hearts of the people of Israel in preparation for his rebellion against King David. When men came to the king for judgement, he talked with them, offered better justice than his father's, and also, 'when any man came to salute him, he put forth his hand, and took him, and kissed him'.[71] Where seekers for justice might expect to make obeisance, Absalom greets them with ingratiating familiarity. Unlike most submissive gestures, handclasps, embraces and kisses bring people into direct physical contact; and they carry implications of equality because, although one party most often takes the initiative, the participants commonly perform more or less the same physical act reciprocally.

Two foreign travellers to England in the later fifteenth century remarked on the frequency with which English people kissed when they met or parted. A Bohemian visitor in the 1460s observed: 'When the guests first arrive at an inn the hostess comes out with her whole household to receive them, and they have to kiss her and all the others. For with them, to offer a kiss is the same as to hold out the right hand; for they are not accustomed to hold out a hand.'[72] In a letter written in 1499, Erasmus makes a similar observation: 'When you arrive anywhere,

---

[70] *King Edward and the Shepherd*, in *Middle English Metrical Romances*, ed. W. H. French and C. B. Hale (reissue, New York, 1964), ll. 22–4. Cf. ll. 208–10, 626–8, 639–40, 693, 870, 1071. Also the *Gest of Robyn Hode*, stanzas 226–7.

[71] 2 Samuel 15.5: 'cum accederet ad eum homo ut salutaret illum, extendebat manum suam, et apprehendens osculabatur eum'. Cited by Wildeblood, *The Polite World*, p. 129.

[72] 'In primo hospitum in diversorium adventu hospita cum universa familia obviam egreditur hospites exceptura, quam caeterosque omnes deosculari necesse est. Apud eos namque idem est, si osculum tuleris, ac si manum dextram porrexeris; non enim manum porrigere consueverunt': *Commentarius Brevis et Jucundus Itineris atque Peregrinationis*, ed. K. Hrdina (Prague, 1951), p. 37. Translation adapted from M. Letts, *The Travels of Leo of Rozmital*, Hakluyt Society, 2nd Series, 108 (Cambridge, 1957), p. 54.

Gestures

you are received with kisses on all sides, and when you take your leave they speed you on your way with kisses ... The world is full of kisses'.[73] The kiss and embrace do indeed figure prominently among the greeting and parting rituals in the English texts, but they are equally prominent in the French. *Acoler* (embrace) and *baisier* are regularly coupled on such occasions there; and in the French texts, as in the English, kisses and embraces are exchanged between many different kinds of people.[74] These gestures marks meetings and partings between relatives, but also between knights. Men kiss ladies and ladies kiss men.[75] The actions were too ordinary to require much description; but, where writers do specify, kisses are said to be given mouth to mouth. Thus, in the Prose *Lancelot*, when Hervis recognises a fellow knight, 'mout doucement l'acola et besa en la boche mainte foiee' ['he embraced him very affectionately and kissed him many times on the mouth', 55.32–3]. In *Confessio Amantis*, again, when Apollonius returns home to Tyre with his family, 'Tho was ther many a mowth to kisse, / Echon welcometh other hom'.[76]

As in the exchange between Gaston Phebus and his king, considered above, courtesy may require that greetings of a submissive form should be countered by gestures which concede equality of status. Such gestures can also, conversely, be met with an act of submission, as if to repay an honour that has been conferred. There is an instance of such polite negotiation in Gower's account of the reception of Jason by King Oetes. The king comes to the palace gate to welcome Jason (itself an act of gracious condescension), takes him by the hand, and embraces him. Jason, however, responds to this 'gret worschipe' with the proper gesture of greeting to a superior, an obeisance:

---

[73] *The Correspondence, Letters 1 to 141*, transl. R. A. B. Mynors and D. F. S. Thomson (Toronto, 1974): Letter no. 103, to Fausto Andrelini, p. 193.

[74] The two actions commonly entail each other, though Malory once makes a distinction: 'Than the kynge and the quene kyssed, and sir Launcelot and sir Trystram enbraced aythir other in armys' (757.7–8: the king is Arthur, the queen Isode). On greetings and farewells in Chrétien, see Peil, *Gebärde*, pp. 31–72, 93–102.

[75] At one point in the *Confessio*, Gower recognises that it was not a universal custom for women to greet men with a kiss. When Jason returns from winning the golden fleece, Medea 'wolde have kist him wonder fayn, / Bot schame tornede hire agayn; / It was noght the manere as tho, / Forthi sche dorste noght do so' (v 3789–92).

[76] *Confessio* VIII 1894–5. Ladies kiss young people on the eyes or face, as well as on the mouth: Prose *Lancelot* 155.3; *Perceval*, l. 5254.

> And he, whom lacketh no manere,
> Whan he the king sih in presence,
> Yaf him ayein such reverence
> As to a kinges stat belongeth.
>
> (v 3332–5)

Elsewhere in the *Confessio*, Amans takes leave of his beloved with the usual parting kiss, but not without having first fallen to his knees before her. He then invents a reason to come back and so give occasion, he hopes, for a second parting kiss; for even social kisses, of course, carry added meaning for lovers (IV 2821–31).

The fifteenth-century Bohemian traveller said that the English 'are not accustomed to hold out a hand'. Yet expressions such as 'take by the hand' (corresponding to French 'prendre par le main') do occur not infrequently on occasions when people meet in Middle English texts. When these texts are translated, one has to reckon, of course, with the influence of the original. In Gavin Douglas's version of the *Aeneid*, people greet each other by clasping hands: 'Thai ionyt handis sone as thai war met.' But here as elsewhere, Douglas is following the Latin ('congressi iungunt dextras'); and, as we shall see shortly, the Scottish poet had another way of rendering such moments which perhaps corresponded better to his own general practice.[77] Elsewhere one may suspect the influence of a French original, as in this moment from Malory's Book of Tristram: 'So wyth this come kynge Arthure, and when he wyste sir Trystram was there, he yode unto hym, and toke hym by the honde, and seyde, "Sir Trystram, ye ar as wellcom as ony knyght that ever com unto this courte"' (570.20–4). Taking by the hand quite commonly marks such occasions in French writings, as in Froissart, where the young count of Flanders comes before Edward III: 'Li rois d'Engleterre prist le dit conte par le main droite moult doucement' ['The King of England took the said count by the right hand very affectionately'].[78] Yet, so far as English writers are concerned, at least, there is something to be said for the opinion of the scholar who observes that 'strictly speaking, the joining of right hands between two people should not be included

---

[77] Gavin Douglas, *Virgil's Aeneid*, ed. D. F. C. Coldwell, 4 vols., STS, 3rd series, 25, 27, 28, 30 (1957–64), VIII viii 27 (*Aeneid* VIII 467). Cf. I ix 57–9, II x 61, XIII vii 38. See below on Scottish handshaking.

[78] *Chroniques*, Vol. IV, ed. S. Luce (Paris, 1873), p. 35 (Book I, Section 302).

among the usual forms of salutation, for it was not a common form of greeting'.[79] Certainly the handclasp does figure rather less prominently among greetings of a reciprocal kind than do the embrace and the kiss; and on occasion its significance seems to be simply that the visitor is to be led somewhere by the hand, as guests commonly were.

When people 'hold out a hand' or 'take one another's hand', in these contexts, are they ever to be understood as 'shaking hands'? The question is not easy to answer. 'Shaking hands', in Modern English, denotes a quite clearly defined item in the gestural repertoire: the more or less vigorous and repeated moving of joined hands up and down. As such it is distinct both in form and function – at least according to the usage with which I am familiar – from the handclasp. On meeting a recently bereaved friend, one might clasp, but would surely not shake, hands. In the language of kinesics (borrowed from phonemics) the handclasp and the handshake are two distinct 'kinemes' in that usage.[80] Evidence for this distinction from antiquity or the Middle Ages, however, proves quite elusive. One may read that the handshake is an ancient gesture, going back at least to classical times: 'Romans became acquainted with the gesture in Greece and spread it throughout the Roman Empire.'[81] Yet the lexical evidence from Latin appears to show only expressions denoting the holding out or taking of hands. Thus, under *manus*, the great *Thesaurus Linguae Latinae* records nothing but 'manum prehendere', 'manum dare', or 'manum tenere'.[82] Scholars who take such expressions as referring specifically to the shaking of hands simply beg the present question.

Lexical evidence from medieval England and France is equally unhelpful. I find nothing to the purpose in Tobler-Lommatzsch,[83] nor does *MED* have any examples of *shaken* in the relevant sense. *OED*, conformably, gives no citations earlier than the sixteenth century, its

---

[79] Wildeblood, *The Polite World*, p. 137.
[80] On kinemes and their 'allokines', see Birdwhistell, *Kinesics and Context*.
[81] B. J. and F. H. Bäuml, *Dictionary of Worldwide Gestures*, 2nd edn (Lanham, Md., 1997), p. 285. Morsbach also traces the custom back to ancient Rome: 'Nonverbal Communication', pp. 191–3.
[82] *Thesaurus Linguae Latinae*, under *manus*, I A 1 (b).
[83] I refer to the Tobler–Lommatzsch *Altfranzösisches Wörterbuch*. Professor Frank Shaw kindly informs me that he finds no evidence for handshaking as a form of salutation in Middle High German dictionaries either.

earliest coming from Coverdale's Bible in 1535 (*Shake* v., sense 9). The *Dictionary of the Older Scottish Tongue* antedates this by only a very little. It gives three examples of 'to schake handis' from Douglas's *Aeneid* (1513), in each case rendering Latin '(con)iungere dextras'.[84] This provides the earliest evidence of what James Cleland, writing in 1607, called the 'good olde Scottish shaking of the two right hands togethir at meeting'.[85] Yet by Cleland's time the gesture was evidently familiar also in England. In his book on 'the natural language of the hand' entitled *Chirologia*, published in 1644, John Bulwer declares that 'to shake the given hand is an expression usual in *friendship, peaceful love, benevolence, salutation, entertainment*, and *bidding welcome, reconciliation, congratulation, giving thanks, valediction*, and *well-wishing*'.[86] It may be hoped that someone will attempt a history of the handshake in modern times, for the gesture has evidently been subject to many vagaries of fashion and custom since the sixteenth century. A good start has been made by H. Roodenburg in his essay entitled 'The "Hand of Friendship": Shaking Hands and Other Gestures in the Dutch Republic'. After reviewing the Early Modern evidence, Roodenburg hazards the following tentative conclusion:

> Shaking hands, then, has been rightly called a 'traditional' gesture; it clearly goes back to the sixteenth century at least. But its history is far from linear; from that century on an intriguing development ensued. The gesture was gradually displaced by more hierarchic ways of greeting or taking leave and even became a polemical instrument in the hands of the Quakers against all deference and worldly vanity. Then, as manners were relaxed, the handshake became popular again: first in England and probably also in the Dutch Republic, spreading later to France and later still to Russia.[87]

---

[84] *Dictionary of the Older Scottish Tongue*, under *S(c)hake* v. 8, citing Douglas's *Aeneid*, I viii 37, III ii 28, and VI xi 39.
[85] Cited by Roodenburg, 'The "Hand of Friendship"', p. 178.
[86] Cited from p. 88 of the modern-spelling edition by J. W. Cleary. Bulwer's many examples, from classical and biblical sources, confuse handshakes with handclasps: *Chirologia*, pp. 88–93.
[87] 'The "Hand of Friendship"', pp. 178–9. It may be noticed that, as late as the time of Jane Austen, 'handshaking had not yet universally supplanted the bow and the curtsey, but was a mark of intimacy or affability': R. W. Chapman, ed., *The Novels of Jane Austen*, 3rd edn (Oxford, 1933), Vol. IV, p. 508. For a miscellaneous gathering of instances, see Bäuml and Bäuml, *Dictionary of Worldwide Gestures*, pp. 285–9.

Gestures

It is hard to imagine that medievalists would ever be able to produce the kind of nuanced historical study of an individual gesture suggested by Roodenburg's essay. The evidence would probably be insufficient, and certainly so in the case of shaking hands. The depth of our ignorance was brought home to me when, quite accidentally, I came upon one indubitable example of the handshake in medieval England, the only such example known to me. This occurs in the fourteenth-century *Anonimalle Chronicle*, written in French at St Mary's Abbey, York. The chronicler gives what appears to be an eyewitness account of the events of the Great Revolt of 1381, including the encounter at Smithfield between Richard II and the leader of the rebels, Wat Tyler. Summoned into his presence by Richard, Tyler approaches him on a little horse and dismounts. Then:

> Quaunt il fuist descendu il prist le roy par la mayne dimy genolaunt et schaka sa brace durement et fortement dissaunt a luy: 'Frer, soiez de bone comforte et lee.'

> ['When he had dismounted, he half bent his knee and took the king by the hand, shaking his arm forcefully and roughly, saying to him, "Brother, be of good comfort and joyful."'][88]

The point of these details was to display the shockingly free and familiar way in which Wat greeted Richard – a king particularly insistent on deep deference from his subjects.[89] Tyler underperforms his kneeling, grasps the king's hand and shakes his arm, and goes on to address him without further ceremony as 'brother' (later promising that 'we will be good companions'). In describing what must be some kind of handshake, the chronicler first employs the customary French formula for a handclasp, 'il prist le roy par la mayne', and then reveals the full extent of the rebel's effrontery: 'et schaka sa brace durement et fortement'. It is significant that the writer's French evidently had no customary formula for the handshake and also that, in his improvised description, he had to resort to the word 'schaka'. This is a Frenchified version of the English word, recorded only here in Anglo-Norman. It was taken over, most probably,

---

[88] *The Anonimalle Chronicle, 1333 to 1381*, ed. V. H. Galbraith (Manchester, 1927), p. 147; translation from R. B. Dobson, *The Peasants' Revolt of 1381*, 2nd edn (London, 1983), p. 164.
[89] See N. Saul, *Richard II* (New Haven, Conn., 1997), pp. 342f.

from the eyewitness account in English upon which the chronicle is here thought to be drawing.[90]

The availability of that term, in default of a French one, must imply that, in England if not in France, there were people who did 'shake' hands. One can only speculate, in the absence of other evidence at present, that the gesture may have been a form of popular greeting not practised in polite society. Perhaps the common people 'shook' hands where gentlefolk 'took' them? If this is so, then Wat's handshake, so offensive to Richard, would represent a custom familiar among the rebels themselves – employed on this occasion, it may be, as a defiantly egalitarian gesture, rather in the manner of those later anti-deferential Quakers of whom Roodenburg speaks.[91] Such a supposition would go some way to explain why the narrative texts under consideration here make no other reference to the shaking of hands; for these texts are, of course, heavily biased towards those upper reaches of medieval society where hands were apparently clasped, not shaken. Yet it remains odd that, in their much more comprehensive materials, English and French dictionaries have failed to record any clear evidence for the custom, apart from 'schaka' in the *Anonimalle Chronicle*.

The gestures so far considered in this chapter have all formed part of rituals and social ceremonies. Handshakes apart, these are quite generously represented in the texts. Indeed, so far as polite society is concerned, the record may be considered not far from complete. For less formal gestures, on the other hand, evidence of the repertoire is much more patchy. This is not surprising. Even modern novelists, even Laurence Sterne or James Joyce, record only a fraction of the many things people continuously do with their bodies to communicate their feelings and attitudes, or else to convey (by gestures such as beckoning or pointing) other kinds of message. Many of these movements, mainly of the head or hands, lack a name; and many can be passed over by story-tellers as

---

[90] Galbraith notes the admixture of English words in this part of the chronicle (p. xli of his edition). The *Anglo-Norman Dictionary* records only this occurrence, under *schaker* 'to shake'.

[91] 'For the Quakers this particular gesture connoted friendship and brotherhood, just as they addressed each other as "friends" thereby eliminating all hierarchy and class distinctions among themselves': 'The "Hand of Friendship"', p. 176.

Gestures

inconsequential. Yet medieval narratives do find some room for gestures of this less formal kind, and it is to them that the rest of this chapter will be devoted.

The writers pay most attention, as one might expect, to gestures expressing the emotions of characters and their attitudes to others. The face was, and is, the part of the body most expressive of feeling; but the hands also play a role. Where medieval hand-gestures still figure in the modern Western repertoire, they may yet differ in the range of emotions they express. Clapping is a small example. When a group of spectators clap their hands at the success of Lybeaus Desconus in a joust, their behaviour happens to conform to modern conventions of applause: 'Every man toke othir by the lappe / And low3en and couthe her handis clappe'.[92] But clapping in fact functioned more generally, as an all-purpose gesture of delight or surprise. In Malory, when Meliot's sister meets Lancelot, 'she clapped hir hondys and wepte for joy' (281.30–31); and when, in the Southern *Octovian*, Florence learns of the wherabouts of her lost son, 'Tho gan Florence her hondys clappe.'[93] In his version of the *Aeneid*, Gavin Douglas describes Ganymede's companions 'clappand thar lufis and thar handis' in amazement as he is snatched up to heaven (v v 24), where Virgil has a different gesture (hands raised to heaven, v 256). Clapping would no longer seem appropriate on occasions such as these.

It is grief or distress, however, that hand gestures most commonly express.[94] In Malory, the 'woeful knight' Palomydes is observed by Tristram: 'And than he gate his swerde in hys honde and made many straunge sygnes and tokyns, and so thorow the rageynge he threw hys swerde in that fountayne. Than sir Palomydes wayled and wrange hys hondys' (528.33–6). To wring one's hands is a common gesture of distress in English and also in French texts ('tordre ses poinz');[95] but other 'signs and tokens' involve more violent forms of self-touching. Women,

---

[92] *Lybeaus Desconus*, Lambeth Ms, ll. 1686–7.
[93] *Octovian Imperator*, ed. F. McSparran (Heidelburg, 1979), ll. 569–70. In the *Alphabet of Tales*, little devils express their *exultacio* by clapping their hands (ed. Banks, p. 395).
[94] On gestures of distress and lamentation in Middle English, see Habicht, *Gebärde*, pp. 94, 103, 126–8; and for Chrétien, as well as Hartmann and Wolfram, see Peil, *Gebärde*, pp. 108–47, 325–6.
[95] Some English examples: *Piers* B II 239 (Mede 'wepte and wrong'); stanzaic *Morte Arthur*, ll. 1173, 3916; *Ywain and Gawain*, l. 2773; *Confessio Amantis* III 1426; *House of Fame*, l. 299. In French: *Perceval*, l. 760; *Cligés*, l. 5739 ('Tordent lor poinz, batent lor paumes').

Gestures and looks in medieval narrative

and occasionally men, pull and tear at their hair. The betrayed Ariadne, in Chaucer's *Legend of Good Women*, 'hire her torente' (line 2188), and in Gower 'hire faire tresces sche todrouh' (*Confessio Amantis*, V 5464). In Chrétien's *Perceval*, Gawain comes upon a grieving maiden who 'ot ses dois en sa trece / Fichiez por ses chaveus detraire' ['had fixed her fingers in her tresses so as to tear her hair', 6544–5].[96] Men and women both will also on occasion tear their clothes. Chaucer's Melibee 'lyk a mad man, rentynge his clothes, gan to wepe and crie' (*Canterbury Tales* VII 973); and Chrétien's Enide, crying out and wringing her hands, leaves no clothes on her breast to be torn ('De robe ne li remest poinz / Devant le piz a dessirier', *Erec et Enide*, 4576–7). But the most extreme of these signs and tokens of grief take the form of physical violence upon one's own flesh, most commonly by scratching the face or striking the breast. Such gestures occur rather more frequently in French texts than in English, and they are generally performed by women. As Trevisa's version of the *De Proprietatibus Rerum* puts it: 'It is the maner of wymmen to cracche her chekis in sorowe.'[97] So, in Chrétien's *Erec et Enide*, the heroine 'tears her tender face' (4579, also 4305–7); and in his *Cligés*, ladies and damsels 'Batent lor piz et lor memeles' ['strike their chests and breasts', 6050].[98] Breast-beating takes its most fully ritualised form as the prescribed gesture of contrition. The treatise *Dives and Pauper* explains: 'Qhanne we bunchyn oure breistys we knowlechyn us gylty aȝens hym [God] in herte and in dede ... Also we bunchyn oureself on þe breist in tokene of sorwe of herte for oure mysdedys.'[99]

Some of these gestures might nowadays be regarded as signs of mental illness. Medieval people evidently did on occasion indulge in such extravagances; yet literary convention also plays a part in these descriptions of grieving behaviour, especially where several of the gestures are

---

[96] To have the hair down and in disorder ('dischevele') was a further ritual sign of female grief: *Legend of Good Women*, l. 1829; *Confessio Amantis* VII 5006, 5023. Men sometimes tear their hair, e.g. *Cligés*, l. 2054, *Perceval*, l. 2372, Prose *Lancelot* 417.20.
[97] Cited by *MED* under *cracchen* v. (a).
[98] In the Prose *Lancelot*, ladies and knights express grief by striking one hand or fist on the other: 368.14, 381.29, 391.5, 417.12, 436.25. In *La Mort le Roi Artu*, Arthur grieves and 'fiert ses meins ensemble qui encore estoient armees' ['strikes his hands together still in their gauntlets': ed. J. Frappier, Geneva, 1954, p. 129].
[99] Vol. I, Part 1, p. 105. In the *Purgatorio*, a penitent Dante strikes himself on the breast three times (as in 'mea culpa, mea culpa, mea maxima culpa'): *Purg.* IX 111. Cf. *Purg.* VII 106, X 120.

40

Gestures

combined to form set pieces. When Guillaume de Lorris describes the picture of Tristesse on the outer wall of the garden of the Rose, he exploits the whole repertoire of non-verbal signs: face-scratching, clothes-ripping, hair-tearing, self-beating, and knocking hands together.[100] In the Prose *Lancelot*, the knight Pharien manifests his sorrow with similar extravagance:

> Il detort ses poinz et fiert ensenble li un en l'autre menuement. Il arrache ses chevox a granz poigniees, il deront sa robe si durement que les pieces en gisent environ lui et loign et pres, il esgratine sa face et son col, si que li sans vermaux en degote aval son cors jusq'a la terre.
>
> ['He wrings his hands and strikes one constantly into the other. He tears his hair out in great handfuls, rips up his clothes so violently that the pieces lie scattered far and near around him, and scratches his face and his neck so that the red blood runs down his body right to the ground', 80.30–4.]

Such set pieces occur more rarely in the English texts. *Sir Orfeo* has a three-line version, perhaps derived from a French original.[101] The English version of Chrétien's *Yvain* reduces the French poet's notations of Laudine's grief for her dead husband almost to nothing. Chrétien says in one place that Laudine tears herself, her hair, and her clothes (1157–9); in another, that she strikes and tears herself (1300); in another, that she clasps her neck, wrings her hands, and beats them together (1412–13); and in yet another, that she clutches her throat, wrings her hands, and strikes and scratches her breast (1479–87). Of these four passages, all that remains in the English poem are the following lines (corresponding to lines 1157–9 in the French):

> Sho wrang hir fingers, outbrast þe blode,
> For mekyl wa sho was nere wode.
> Hir fayre hare scho al todrogh.
> (821–3)

Hanging the head is another gesture of sorrow, less autistic than those just considered since it commonly takes account of the presence of others by the very act of declining to meet their eyes. This is one of the

---

[100] Ed. Lecoy, ll. 313–28; *Romaunt of the Rose*, ll. 321–38.
[101] Heurodis wakes from her dream of the faery: 'Sche froted hir honden & hir fet, / & crached hir visage – it bled wete; / Hir riche robe hye al torett', Auchinleck Ms, ll. 79–81.

41

Gestures and looks in medieval narrative

most natural of gestures – Darwin observed that his dog drooped its head when dejected[102] – and an image such as that of Tristesse gazing at the ground, in an illustrated manuscript of the *Roman de la Rose*, requires no scholarly gloss.[103] The captive maidens in Chrétien's *Yvain* 'all bow their heads... nor can they withdraw their eyes from the ground' ['S'anbrunchent totes... Ne lor iaux ne pueent retraire / De terre'].[104] Again, Malory's grieving lover Palomydes, when addressed, 'wolde answere no wordys but syghed wondirly sore, and hongynge downe his hede, takynge no hyde to his wordys' (590.9–11). The same 'lumpish' gesture expresses bashfulness and shame.[105] When the young Enide is first brought to the court of Arthur and sees the knights gazing at her, 'Son chief ancline contre val; / Vergoigne an ot, ne fu mervoille, / La face l'an devint vermoille' ['She bends her head down; she is abashed, not surprisingly, and her face becomes red', *Erec et Enide*, 1710–12]. Even a young knight may find his first sight of Arthur too much for him. In the Prose *Lancelot*, Banyn 'mot ne dist et tint la teste basse, si sanbla qu'il fust esbahiz de ce qu'il estoit devant persone a si haut home com estoit li rois Arthus' ['said not a word and kept his head down, seeming to be abashed at finding himself in the presence of so exalted a person as King Arthur', 136.29–31]. Elsewhere the gesture expresses shame rather than abashment or shyness. In *Ywain and Gawain*, Alundyne is ashamed of her recent behaviour, and her maiden finds her 'Hingand hir hevyd ful drerily' (1036). In the French original, she 'tint le chief beissié, / Qui a mesfeite se savoit' ['held her head down, knowing she had done wrong', 1788–9].

Because heads can make fewer distinct movements than hands can, individual head-movements tend to carry a wider range of possible meanings than hand-gestures. Thus, lowering the head is not only a sign of grief or shame; it can also, by virtue of cutting off eye contact,

---

[102] *Expression of the Emotions in Man and Animals*, pp. 57–60.
[103] Illustration no. 158 in F. Garnier, *Le langage de l'image au moyen âge: signification et symbolique* (Paris, 1982).
[104] See the entry in Tobler–Lommatzsch for *embronchier*, 'bow the head', listing the meanings of the gesture: weariness, thought, dejection, grief, shame, and displeasure.
[105] The courtesy book *Stans Puer ad Mensam* has: 'Whoso speke to þee in ony maner place, / Lumpischli caste not þin heed adoun, / But with a sad cheer loke hem in þe face': ll. 15–17, in Furnivall, *Babees Book*, p. 27.

signify anger. Guinevere expresses her displeasure at Lancelot in this way, as will be noticed in the next chapter. Angry or scornful feelings are more commonly expressed, however, by the shaking of the head: 'croller le chief' in French, 'shake the head' or 'wag the head' in English.[106] These expressions fail to make clear the distinction, critical in modern times, between the positive vertical movement ('nod' in Modern English) and the negative horizontal one (to which the term 'shake' is now arbitrarily confined). I shall return to this problem later. For the moment it is enough to note that, among the various meanings of medieval 'headshaking', anger and scorn figure prominently. In *Piers Plowman*, Will expresses his indignation at a friar's love of silver with an abrupt movement of the head: '"Ouh!" quod y tho and myn heved waggede' (C XII 18, not in B); and in *Arthour and Merlin*, Merlin shakes his head in anger, even as a baby, at his midwife: 'lodly on hire gon loke / And his hed on hire he schok.'[107] King Arthur, angered by Kay in Chrétien's *Perceval*, 'crolle le chief' at him (line 2877); and a similar expression, 'croler la tete', is used by Froissart of the Black Prince in his anger.[108] Such head movement can also express scorn. In the Latin Bible 'movere caput' is a gesture of contempt, both in the Old Testament and in the Gospels. Verse 8 of the twenty-first psalm has, 'All they that saw me have laughed me to scorn: they have spoken with the lips *et moverunt caput*', where the last phrase is rendered 'wagid the heved' in one Middle English version.[109] In their account of the crucifixion, Matthew and Mark both echo this psalm when they describe scornful bystanders 'moventes capita sua' (Matthew 27.39, Mark 15.29), and Middle English writers follow.[110]

---

[106] See Tobler–Lommatzsch, under *croler* vb.; *OED*, under *Shake* v. 6b, and *Wag* v. 11 c; *MED*, under *waggen* v. 1 (b), and *shaken* v. 3 (b); *DOST*, under *S(c)hake* v. 7b.

[107] Ed. O. D. Macrae-Gibson, EETS, 268, 279 (1973, 1979), Lincoln's Inn Ms, ll. 1037–8. At l. 1232 in the same copy, an angry man 'on his modur schok his hed'; and at l. 1214 in the Auchinleck Ms, Merlin 'schoke his heved and louȝ' in both anger and confidence.

[108] 'Quant li princes de Galles ot oy lire ceste lettre, si fu plus esmervilliés que devant, et crole la tieste et regarda de costé sur les dessus dis François' ['When the Prince of Wales had heard this letter read, he was more amazed than ever, and he shook his head and looked askance at the abovementioned Frenchmen']: *Chroniques*, Vol. VII, ed. S. Luce (Paris, 1878), p. 96 (Book 1, Section 606). See also ibid., Vol. VI, p. 232, and Vol. IX, p. 78. In the *Roman de la Rose*, the churl Dangier 'crolle la teste' at the lover and (with the same meaning) 'croule sa hure' at Franchise (ed. Lecoy, ll. 2932, 15,355).

[109] Quoted by *OED* under *Wag* 11 c.

[110] *MED*, *shaken* 3 (b), cites *Ancrene Wisse*: 'Hore heaved schakinge up on him'.

Gestures and looks in medieval narrative

Gestures of scorn are multiplied in the treatise *A Talking of the Love of God*, where the buffeting of Christ is accompanied by grimacing, headwagging, and the sticking out of tongues: 'þei grenneden uppon þe and waggeden heor hevedes and blatten out heore tonges.'[111]

The tormentors of Christ also spit at him (Matthew 26.67, 27.30). Spitting is among the most drastic acts of scorn and contempt found in the texts.[112] Even knights and ladies may do it. In the *Wars of Alexander*, the proud king Nicholas confronts Alexander and 'spittis in his face' (line 868); and twelve fair damsels in Malory, somewhat more decorously, spit and throw mud at the shield of a knight who, they say, hates ladies (158.27–8). A more churlish action is to fart in someone's face (Latin *oppedere*), as Nicholas does to Absolon in Chaucer's Miller's Tale (*Canterbury Tales* I 3806–8). His fart, like that delivered by Thomas to the friar in the Summoner's Tale (III 2149–51), is a recognised sign of contempt ('I fart at thee'). So too, of course, is baring the buttocks ('kiss my arse'), as both Alison and Nicholas do in the Miller's story.[113] Froissart reports a striking example. The Frisians are under attack from the Hainaulters and others. As the enemy ships approach, a 'foolish and enraged' Frisian woman rushes out to within a bowshot of them: 'elle se tourna, et leva ses draps, c'est à savoir sa robe et sa chemise, et montra son derrière aux Hainuyers, Hollandois et Zélandois' ['she turned round and lifted her clothes, that is to say her robe and chemise, and showed her backside to the men of Hainault, Holland, and Zeeland']. 'Take that as your welcome,' she cries. This 'unhappy woman', says Froissart, was first riddled with arrows and bolts 'par les fesses et par les jambes' and later hacked to pieces.[114]

The texts also record a few postures which, by their deliberate insouciance, can express a scornful sense of superiority. In Skelton's *Bowge of*

---

[111] Ed. C. Horstman, *Yorkshire Writers*, Vol. II (London, 1896), p. 359. On sticking out the tongue, see Garnier, *Le langage de l'image*, pp. 136–9.

[112] See *MED*, *spitten* v.(1) 2(a) and (b), for biblical and other examples.

[113] For further instances of '"bum baring" as a comic insult', from textual and pictorial sources, see V. A. Kolve, *Chaucer and the Imagery of Narrative: The First Five Canterbury Tales* (London, 1984), pp. 191–7.

[114] *Chroniques*, ed. Buchon, Vol. III, pp. 253–4 (Book IV, Chap. 50). Shooting at bared buttocks may be seen illustrated in M. Camille, *Image on the Edge: The Margins of Medieval Art* (London, 1992), Illustrations nos. 50 and 55, with discussion on p. 106. See also the scornfully bared buttocks in Illustration no. 9 there.

Courte, the narrator says of Disdain: 'He set the arme proudly under the syde.'[115] To hold the arm akimbo in this way commonly signifies a position of power, being a posture which casually extends the amount of space claimed by a body. The art historian Joaneath Spicer demonstrates this in her study of Renaissance portraits, in which husbands, for example, commonly adopt the position, while wives do not. In medieval pictures, too, the posture is associated with men of power.[116] The earliest recorded instance of the term 'akimbo' shows how aggressive the gesture can be. In the *Tale of Beryn*, a deceitful bourgeois threatens and bullies the hero: 'set his hond in kenebowe ... "Wenyst þowe", seid he to Beryn, "for to scorne me?"'[117] Power can also find expression in an akimbo posture marked by confident and relaxed ease. Chrétien's *Chevalier de la Charrete* describes a happy scene of young knights and damsels in a meadow. To one side sits on horseback an older knight, father of one of the young people. Since the weather is fine, he is lightly dressed, and he has one hand on his hip: 'Une main a l'un de ses lez / Avoit par contenance mise' ['He had rested a hand on one of his hips *par contenance*', 1654–5]. The phrase 'par contenance' means something like 'to give himself airs'.[118] It occurs again later in the same poem, when an armed knight approaches to provoke and challenge Lancelot:

> De l'une janbe an son estrier
> Fu afichiez, et l'autre ot mise
> Par contenance et par cointise
> Sor le col del destrier crenu.

---

[115] Ed. Scattergood, l. 321. The whole description of Disdain (ll. 284–322) is rich in non-verbal signs: he looks scornful, bites his lip, frowns, stares, and stamps.

[116] 'The Renaissance Elbow', in Bremmer and Roodenburg, eds., *A Cultural History of Gesture*, pp. 84–128. On p. 95, Spicer quotes John Bulwer's observation in 1644: 'to set the arms agambo or aprank ... is an action of pride and ostentation'. See also Garnier, *Le langage de l'image*, pp. 185, 188–9, and plates. Also de Jorio, transl. Kendon, *Gesture*, pp. 262–6 ('Mano in Fianco').

[117] *The Tale of Beryn*, ed. F. J. Furnivall and W. G. Stone, Chaucer Society Publications, 2nd Series, 17, 24 (1876, 1887), ll. 1838–9. On 'kenebowe', see *MED s.v.*

[118] The editor of Chrétien's *Perceval* glosses the phrase 'pour se donner un air' in a similar context: young Perceval first encounters Gornemans strolling at leisure and holding a cane in his hand 'par contenance' (ll. 1356–7). Tobler-Lommatzsch glosses the phrase with 'um sich eine Haltung zu geben' (under *contenance*). The corresponding English expression is 'for (a) contenaunce': see *MED contenaunce* n. 3 (c), and *OED Countenance* sb. 2c.

['He was secured by one leg in his stirrup, and he had put the other on the thick-maned neck of his warhorse, to give himself airs and look good', 2572–5.]

The body language here expresses the arrogance of a knight who is described as 'orguelleus'. Somewhat less acrobatic versions of the proud leg are to be found elsewhere. In his study of the language of medieval art, Garnier observes that, increasingly in the later Middle Ages, persons of power and authority are represented with their legs crossed.[119] So Froissart describes the 'manière orgueilleuse et présomptueuse' of the duke of Bourbon, who, at a siege in Africa, sits all day outside his tent with 'jambes croisées', requiring the utmost deference from anyone who would speak with him.[120] The posture expresses a cooler kind of self-possession in the French fabliau *Le foteor* ('The Fucker'). A lady sees a beautiful young man sitting outside her house. His legs are crossed (no doubt partly to show one off): 'Janbe sor autre iluec se seoit.' When asked by a damsel who or what he is, he announces himself as a 'fouteur'.[121] These passages illustrate the expressive power of bodily posture, which is part of what Middle English refers to as 'port'. The texts are rarely so specific, however, commonly contenting themselves with such general expressions as 'high port' or 'humble port'.[122]

Crossing the legs figures again in a remarkable passage of the early Middle English *Ancrene Wisse*, a passage headed in the Latin translation of that work with the words 'nutus superbie', that is, the gestures or bodily signs of pride.[123] The author of this guide for anchoresses

---

[119] Garnier, *Le langage de l'image*, p. 229 and Plates 93 and 111.
[120] *Chroniques*, ed. Buchon, Vol. III, p. 88 (Book IV, Chap. 15). In the English *Kyng Alisaunder*, Darius crosses his legs in fury: 'He þroweþ legges overe oþer': ed. G. V. Smithers, EETS, 227, 237 (1952, 1957), l. 1807.
[121] *Nouveau receuil complet des fabliaux*, ed. W. Noomen, Vol. VI (Assen/Maastricht, 1991), 104.5.
[122] For examples, see *MED port* n.(4), sense 1 (a): 'Bearing, demeanor, deportment'. See the chapter 'Posture' in Argyle, *Bodily Communication*, pp. 203–13, noting that 'posture plays an important role for many animals in signalling dominance, threat, submission, and other interpersonal attitudes' (p. 203).
[123] The English original is on pp. 102–3 of *Ancrene Wisse*, ed. J. R. R. Tolkien, EETS, 249 (1962); the Latin is on p. 69 of *The Latin Text of the Ancrene Riwle*, ed. C. D'Evelyn, EETS, 216 (1944). I am indebted to Bella Millett for help with this passage. It may be compared with the self-description by Pride in *The Pilgrimage of the Lyfe of the Manhode*: 'Asquynt I biholde þe folk, and for feerstee I strecche my nekke and heve up þe brouwen

warns his readers against a whole catalogue of telltale postural, gestural, and paralinguistic expressions of the sin. He calls them 'semblanz' and 'sines', using the Latin loanword 'sign', here and elsewhere in the treatise, for the first recorded time in English. The passage is worth quoting at length, as the testimony of a learned and observant moralist on the non-verbal behaviour of proud or affected women:

> Beoren on heh þet heaved, crenge wiþ swire, lokin o siden, bihalden on hokere, winche mid ehe, binde seode mid te muþ, wiþ hond oþer wiþ heaved makie scuter signe, warpe schonke over schench, sitten oþer gan stif as ha istaket were, luve lokin o mon, speoken as an innocent, ant wlispin for þen anes.
>
> ['Holding the head high, arching the neck, looking askance, gazing scornfully, closing the eye, pursing the lips, making taunting signs with hand or head, throwing leg over leg, sitting or walking stiffly as if tied to a stake, looking amorously at a man, speaking like an innocent, and deliberately lisping.']

Some of these behaviours can readily be recognised today as arrogant or superior: holding the head high, scornful looks, very upright bearing, and (perhaps) pursing the lips.[124] Others, like crossing the legs, require some explanation. It is not clear to me what 'crenge wiþ swire' ('collum curvare' in the Latin version) exactly denotes: *MED* has 'to bend haughtily, condescend' for *crenge*. Also, the author might have been more specific about the 'taunting signs with hand or head'. 'Lokin o siden' suggests a scornfully indirect glance, and 'winche mid ehe' may indicate a brief closing of the eyes in weary contempt. In the last three items, the author seems to have had worldly and affected ladies in mind, rather than proud ones: shooting flirtatious glances, talking like an ingénue, and lisping on purpose, like Chaucer's Friar, to make their English sweet upon the tongue. Here, as elsewhere, one has of course to reckon with textual traditions, going back in this case to the Old Testament;[125] but

---

and þe chin, makinge þe countenaunce of þe lyoun': ed. A. Henry, EETS, 288, 292 (1985, 1988), ll. 4086–89.

[124] See *MED seode* n., 'a purse'.

[125] Isaiah 3.16: 'the daughters of Sion are haughty, and have walked with stretched out necks and wanton glances of their eyes'. Hugh of St Victor cites this passage in his *De Institutione Novitiorum, Patrologia Latina*, Vol. CLXXVI, Col. 939. It may be Isaiah's reference to wanton glances ('nutus oculorum' in the Vulgate) that prompted the reference to amorous looking in *Ancrene Wisse*.

the passage does offer one of the fullest accounts of non-verbal behaviour to be found in Middle English, and what one sees there, so far as one can make it out, is a not uncharacteristic mixture of the strange and the perfectly familiar.

These gestures of pride, like those of scorn and anger, stand aloof from any touching of other persons. By contrast, gestures of friendship, sexual feeling, and the like regularly involve body contact – holding hands, embracing, kissing.[126] Taking these into account, as well as the more formal acts considered earlier, a modern anthropologist who classified societies as 'contact' and 'non-contact' types would no doubt assign medieval England and France to the contact type. Modern readers who, like the present writer, belong to non-contact cultures will not fail to be struck by the frequency with which people kiss, embrace and hold each others' hands in the medieval texts.[127]

The holding of hands takes two generally distinct forms. Either one person leads another 'by the hand', or two people walk together 'hand in hand'. These actions differ in their significance. To lead someone by the hand is an act of courtesy by which the leader bestows honour on the led, most often when the leader is on his or her home ground and so can take the initiative with newly arrived guests and the like. So in Chrétien's *Erec*, the father of the young heroine tells her to receive their new guest Erec courteously:

> 'Ma fille chiere,
> Prenez par la main ce seignor,
> Si li portez molt grant enor'.
> La pucele ne tarda plus,
> Par la main l'an mainne leissus,
> Qu'ele n'estoit mie vilainne;
> Par la main contre mont l'an mainne.
>
> ['"My dear daughter, take this gentleman by the hand and do him very great honour." The maiden without delay led him in by the hand, for she was in no way ill-bred; she led him up by the hand', *Erec*, 470–6.]

---

[126] See Argyle, *Bodily Communication*, Chapter 14, 'Touch and Bodily Contact'.
[127] On the 'great cultural differences in the amount and type of touching', see ibid., pp. 60–1. Among modern 'contact cultures', Argyle lists Arabs, Latin Americans, southern Europeans (Greeks, Turks), and some African nations.

Gestures

Similarly, when Enide herself is received by a king later in the poem, he leads her by the hand up into his hall, 'si con franchise le semont' ['as good breeding requires of him', *Erec*, 5512].[128] Where the writers specify which hand is used by the leader, as they sometimes do, this affects the meaning of the gesture. What anthropologists call 'lateral symbolism' commonly favours the right-hand side.[129] Accordingly, when people are said to lead others on their right, this emphasises the honour they do. An English courtesy book advises, 'Ever on thi ryght hond take thou thy better.'[130] Medieval French has a verb *adestrer*, the primary meaning of which is defined in Tobler–Lommatzsch as 'to escort on the right side'. This verb is used in the Anglo-Norman romance *Ipomedon*, in which the hero, travelling with his lady cousin, conducts her on his right: 'Il meisme adestra sa cusine.'[131] To lead a lady on one's left side, by contrast, can only be a mark of diminished respect. In Chrétien's *Chevalier de la Charrete*, Lancelot looks out of a window and sees 'uns granz chevaliers qui menoit/ Une bele dame a senestre' (558–9). But the knight in question is the dastardly Meleagant, leading the lady whom he has abducted, Guinevere.[132]

Polite leading commonly involves some advantage, enjoyed by the leader but courteously yielded to the led. To go 'hand in hand' has a different significance, for the phrase implies no advantage on either side. The two parties treat each other as equals. In the modern West, public handholding is rather uncommon, especially among adult pairs of the same sex;[133] but medieval texts show a very much wider distribution of the gesture. As today, it can imply amorous feelings – on the part of Edward III, for instance, when he enters the castle of the countess of

---

[128] Two other examples: in the *Roman de la Rose*, Bel Acueil greets the lover and leads him 'par la main' (ed. Lecoy, ll. 3331–2); and in the *Gest of Robyn Hode*, Robin leads a guest to dinner in the greenwood 'full fayre by the honde' (*Rymes of Robyn Hood*, stanza 388).

[129] See R. Needham, ed., *Right and Left: Essays on Dual Symbolic Classification* (Chicago, 1973), and especially the essay by R. Hertz there, pp. 3–31.

[130] *Stans Puer ad Mensam*, l. 195, in the Ashmole version, ed. F. J. Furnivall, *Queene Elizabethes Achademy*, EETS, E.S. 8 (1869), pp. 56–64.

[131] *Ipomedon*, ed. A. J. Holden (Paris, 1979), l. 2726. The English version has: 'on his righte hond he here ledde', *Ipomadon*, ed. R. Purdie, EETS, 316 (2001), l. 2469. Cf. Froissart's use of 'adextroient' (n. 60 above).

[132] For further discussion, see below, pp. 145–6. There is a verb *senestrer*, meaning 'to lead on the left side': Thomas's *Tristan*, ed. F. Lecoy (Paris, 1991), l. 1141.

[133] E. Goffman discusses handholding in his *Relations in Public* (London, 1971), pp. 226–37.

Gestures and looks in medieval narrative

Salisbury hand in hand with her.[134] More common, however, is same-sex handholding, between friends, colleagues, siblings, and the like. Men hold hands in a variety of circumstances. In *Kyng Alisaunder*, thirteen dukes, sent with messages from Darius, appear before Alexander 'alle honde in honde';[135] in Chrétien's *Perceval*, Gornemans and the hero 'main a main andui se tienent' (line 1550); and at the grand meeting between Richard II and Charles VI of France, already referred to, as Charles leads Richard by the hand to his tent, they are followed by the dukes of both nations hand in hand.[136] Ladies do the same. In *Perceval*, Guinevere's damsels accompany her all holding hands ('Main a main trestoutes se tienent', 4042), and later in the same poem, two queens hold hands (8102). In Chrétien's *Erec*, again, when Erec and Enide take leave of their two hostesses, they pair off and hold hands with each, 'tout main a main antre tenu' (*Erec*, 5262).

Kissing is a more complex contact-gesture than handholding. It takes a variety of physical forms and carries a variety of significances. The twelfth-century English monk Aelred of Rievaulx distinguished four types of physical kiss sanctioned by the 'lex naturalis'.[137] A kiss may properly be given, he says, 'as a sign of reconciliation [*in signum reconciliationis*]', when enemies become friends; 'as a sign of peace', as when those about to communicate in church manifest their inner peace by an external kiss; 'as a sign of love', permissible between husband and wife, or between friends after long separation; and 'as a sign of catholic unity [*in signum catholicae unitatis*]', as when a guest is received. Aelred writes as a moralist, and his scheme allows amorous kisses only within marriage. Some three hundred years later, the great French prince Charles d'Orléans offers a different classification, in one of the English poems that he wrote during his long captivity in England.[138] Charles

---

[134] Froissart, *Chroniques*, Vol. II, ed. S. Luce (Paris, 1870), p. 132 (Book I, Section 157).
[135] *Kyng Alisaunder*, Laud Ms, l. 1699; cf. l. 1782. For other English examples, see *MED hond(e* n. 1 b (a).
[136] *Chroniques*, ed. Buchon, Vol. III, p. 258 (Book IV, Chap. 51).
[137] *De Spirituali Amicitia*, *Patrologia Latina*, Vol. CXCV, Col. 673. The *osculum corporale*, performed by the pressing of lips, is itself distinguished by Aelred from the *osculum spirituale* and the *osculum intellectuale*, neither of which takes a physical form.
[138] *Fortunes Stabilnes: Charles of Orleans's English Book of Love*, ed. M.-J. Arn (Binghamton, N.Y., 1994), ll. 3657–70. The French version is Chanson XXXVII in Charles d'Orléans, *Poésies*, ed. P. Champion, 2 vols. (Paris, 1982–3).

distinguishes public from private kisses. It is the latter that he values. These are 'the prive cossis of plesaunce', or, in his French version, 'les privez, venans par plaisance'. Kisses of the other type, he says, are exchanged merely out of politeness ('for a countenaunce'), with acquaintances and strangers, and these can be had for nothing. Curiously enough, in the English but not in the French, Charles characterises these valueless public kisses as 'cossis Dowche', that is, 'Teutonic' kisses (not Dutch, specifically).[139] Whether or not he had his English hosts in mind, the epithet testifies to an awareness that conventions of kissing differed from country to country – to the advantage, perhaps, of the amorous French.

So far as public kissing is concerned, there can be no doubt that conventions did indeed vary from country to country in the Middle Ages as they do today; and one also has to reckon with changes over time (as customs have changed in England during my own lifetime), as well as with variations according to circumstance and social class. The matter is very complex, and little secure information is at present available. In the most substantial study known to me, entitled 'Le rôle juridique de l'*osculum* dans l'ancien droit français', Emile Chénon argues that the mouth kiss ceased to be used to seal contracts in France during the thirteenth century, though it continued thereafter to play a part in ceremonies of homage.[140] In a study of those ceremonies, J. Russell Major suggests that there was a general move away from public kissing in the thirteenth century. He cites Chénon and adds that the English in that century began to abandon the kiss of peace in church, replacing it with a tablet (the 'pax') which was passed round to be kissed.[141] Such developments are in keeping, certainly, with the idea put forward by Norbert

---

[139] See *OED* Dutch a., sb., headnote and sense 1. Also Arn's note to l. 3657.

[140] *Mémoires de la Société des Antiquaires de France*, 6 (1919–23), 124–55. 'Ce rite de l' *osculum* dans les contrats semble avoir disparu dans le courant du xiiie siècle. Il se maintint plus longtemps dans l'hommage féodal' (p. 136).

[141] J. Russell Major, '"Bastard Feudalism" and the Kiss: Changing Social Mores in Late Medieval and Early Modern France', *Journal of Interdisciplinary History*, 17 (1987), 509–35. On the 'new attitude toward kissing', see pp. 514–5. Major's evidence for the obsolescence of the kiss in homage hardly antedates 1500; but see K. M. Phillips, 'Bodily Walls, Windows, and Doors: The Politics of Gesture in Late Fifteenth-Century Books for Women', in J. Wogan-Brown *et al.*, eds., *Medieval Women: Texts and Contexts in Late Medieval Britain, Essays for Felicity Riddy* (Turnhout, 2000), pp. 185–98.

Elias, that the 'civilising process' entailed an increase in squeamishness about the body – a raising of the 'thresholds of embarrassment and shame', as he puts it.[142] But Elias himself dates these changes back no further than the time of Erasmus, and in this he is followed by Willem Frijhoff, who remarks that 'after the kissing-eager Middle Ages all kinds of public kissing have been gradually banished, to be readmitted only recently'.[143]

Frijhoff rightly observes that 'kissing is an extremely difficult subject for historical study'; and the present discussion cannot claim to throw much light upon it. For what it is worth, the texts under consideration here present no challenge to the testimony of Erasmus (himself a 'Dowche' observer): that as late as 1499 there were 'kisses in abundance' in English public life. I have already had occasion to notice public kissing in ceremonies of homage and of greeting. Another common type is that identified by Aelred of Rievaulx as the 'osculum in signum reconciliationis'. In the English and French romances alike, knights kiss and make up after fighting each other. Chrétien writes of Erec and Guivret that 'Li uns l'autre beise et acole' (*Erec*, 3900), and of Gawain and Yvain that 'Les braz au col, si s'antrebeisent' (*Yvain*, 6311). The English version of the latter poem follows, with 'aiþer oþer in armes toke / And kissed so ful fele sithe' (*Ywain and Gawain*, 3672–3); and Malory has several instances of the same kind, as when Gawain and Marhaus 'toke of her helmys and eyther kyssed other'.[144] Kisses seal reconciliations at other times too. Froissart tells how the duke of Juliers, having offended the emperor, kneels before him and confesses his fault; whereupon the emperor takes him by the hand, 'et me fut dit que, par confirmation d'amour, il baisa le duc de Julliers, quand il fut levé, en la bouche' ['and I was told that, to confirm his love, he kissed the duke of Juliers, when he had risen, on the mouth'].[145] At a much humbler social level, Chaucer's

---

[142] N. Elias, *The Civilizing Process: The History of Manners*, transl. E. Jephcott (Oxford, 1978), p. 70. Also p. 204.
[143] W. Frijhoff, 'The Kiss Sacred and Profane: Reflections on a Cross-Cultural Confrontation', in Bremmer and Roodenburg, eds., *A Cultural History of Gesture*, pp. 210–36 (p. 213).
[144] *Works*, 161.17–18. So also 451.22–3, 570.1–2, 773.18–19. Cf. the stanzaic *Morte Arthur*, ed. Bruce, ll. 1622–3.
[145] *Chroniques*, ed. Buchon, Vol. II, p. 658 (Book III, Chap. 93).

Gestures

Knight persuades the Host and the Pardoner to give up their quarrel and kiss, which they do: 'Anon they kiste, and ryden forth hir weye.'[146]

There are other forms of public kissing still more remote from the modern West, for in these the gesture is directed either to the lower parts of another's body or else to some object. To kiss someone's hand, leg, or foot evidently humbles the kisser and signifies respect.[147] In Gower's story of the trump of death, a king shows extreme and exemplary humility when, encountering two ancient pilgrims, he jumps down from his carriage, embraces them and kisses them 'bothe fot and hond'.[148] More conventional is the behaviour of Charles VI on entering the chamber of pope Clement. According to Froissart, Charles bowed, Clement rose, Charles kissed his hand and his mouth, and Clement gave the king a seat at his side.[149] The balance of power between the two dignitaries emerges nicely from this exchange of gestures, including the French king's two kisses – one for submission and one for fraternity. Kissing the foot or leg also signifies a petitionary intention, as when the Theban ladies kneel before Theseus at the beginning of Chaucer's Knight's Tale and 'wolde have kist his feet ther as he stood' (*Canterbury Tales* I 1759). Or it may express gratitude for a favour received, as in the Prose *Lancelot*, where Synados goes to kiss Hestor's feet (though Hestor courteously does not allow him to do so, 439.26–9). Again in the *Lancelot*, a grateful lady falls at Gawain's feet and kisses both his leg-armour and his spurs (389.21–2). People also signify deference by kissing an object which stands as a surrogate for some higher power. Sacred objects may be kissed, liturgically in the case of the cross on Good Friday or, in *Piers Plowman*, at Easter:

---

[146] *Canterbury Tales* VI 968. Langland derives the kiss of reconciliation between the Four Daughters of God (B XVIII 417–21) from psalm 84.11 (AV 85.10); but he himself invents those at IV 3 and XX 353.

[147] For examples, see *MED kissen* v. 1 (d). Koziol observes: 'Every ritual action is capable of conveying several possible meanings, many of them contradictory. A kiss, for example, was usually a sign of friendship (*amicitia*) or brotherhood (*fraternitas*), and therefore an acknowledgement of a rough parity between two parties. But kissing a reliquary was a sign of reverence, as was kissing the king's foot': *Begging Pardon and Favor*, p. 308.

[148] *Confessio Amantis* I 2053. In the *Roman de la Rose*, the lover wishes to kiss the feet of Amors (l. 1924), but the god takes him by the hand and allows his mouth to be kissed as acts of favour (ll. 1925, 1933–4). Images of saints might be kissed on the feet: *Dives and Pauper*, Vol. I, Part I, p. 101.

[149] *Chroniques*, ed. Buchon, Vol. III, p. 15 (Book IV, Chap. 4): 'Le roi de France le baisa en la main et en la bouche. Le pape s'assit et fit séoir le roi delez lui sur un siége.'

'Crepeþ to þe cros on knees and kisseþ it for a iuwel'.[150] In Malory's book of the Grail, Lancelot has a vision of a wounded knight kissing both the cross and the grail vessel itself.[151] Simple people kiss the pardoner's bull in *Piers Plowman* (Prologue 73), and an equally unscrupulous pardoner in the *Canterbury Tales* invites the Host to kiss his relics (VI 944). In secular life, deference can be signified by similar gestures. Messengers from King Arthur kiss his letters before delivering them (Malory, 21.30), and Guinevere, in the Prose *Lancelot*, kisses and embraces Gawain's shield when it is brought to court.[152] Lovers also engage in such vicarious kissing. In Chrétien's *Cligés*, Alexander kisses the shirt into which are woven strands of his mistress's hair (line 1612). Chaucer's *Legend of Good Women* has several instances of such behaviour. Pyramus and Thisbe both kiss the wall that divides them (768); Pyramus kisses Thisbe's abandoned wimple (846); Dido kisses a cloth left behind by Aeneas (1337); and Ariadne kisses the footprints of the departed Theseus (2208–9).

These last examples lead on to a consideration of those 'privy kisses of pleasance' which Charles d'Orléans valued so highly. Little need be said here about the embraces and kisses to which English and French writers commonly confine themselves when they have occasion to describe the private sexual activity of lovers. When Lancelot goes to bed with Elayne, believing her to be Guinevere, Malory passes to other matters with the words, 'Now leve we them kyssynge and clyppynge as was a kyndely thynge' (804.36–805.1). Chrétien also draws back from any further description of these 'natural things'. After an unusually long passage on the joy which Lancelot and Guinevere take in their mutual embraces and kisses, he remarks: 'Mes toz jorz iert par moi teue, / Qu'an conte ne doit estre dite' ['But I will never speak about that, for it ought not to be described in a story', *Chevalier de la Charrete*, 4680–1]. More interesting, for present purposes, are those kisses that are exchanged not in the bedchamber but in public, where they exploit an uncertainty

---

[150] *Piers Plowman* B XVIII 428. Compare Robert Manning (Robert of Brunne), *Handlyng Synne*, ed. F. J. Furnivall, EETS, 119, 123 (1901, 1903), ll. 3867–70. Further examples of such kissing of material objects in *MED*, *kissen* v. 3(a) and (b).

[151] *Works*, 894.30, 895.3–4. In the French *Queste*, the knight kisses the cross, but is allowed to kiss only the silver table upon which the grail stands: *La Queste del Saint Graal*, ed. A. Pauphilet (Paris, 1949), p. 59.

[152] 'Et la reine ... prant l'escu, si lo baise et anbrace et en fait autretel joie com ele feist do prodome qui la portoit', 408.24–6.

which may exist between the two types so sharply distinguished by Charles d'Orléans. Public kisses between men and women always carry at least the possibility of erotic implication. As Raymond Firth observes: 'The kiss is susceptible of a great many modifications. Linked with the sensitivity of the lips is their function in erotic contact, which introduces a possible ambiguity in gestures that are intended to signalize social but non-erotic greeting.'[153] Such ambiguity can be exploited quite grossly, as by the friar in Chaucer's Summoner's Tale – friars being notorious for their equivocal relations with prosperous housewives. Visiting a sick man in his room, the friar rises to greet the wife as she enters:

> The frere ariseth up ful curteisly,
> And hire embraceth in his armes narwe,
> And kiste hire sweete, and chirketh as a sparwe
> With his lyppes.
> (*Canterbury Tales* III 1802–5)

By overperforming his gestures of greeting, the friar alters their significance – but without giving the husband any good grounds to object.

In politer circles, such equivocal kisses were performed more discreetly. They formed, in fact, the non-verbal equivalent of the flirtatious verbal 'dalliaunce' in which gentlemen often engaged with ladies. The Anglo-Norman romance *Ipomedon*, written about 1180, provides an early example. King Meleager wants to retain the hero, and Ipomedon agrees to stay, on condition that he is accepted as the queen's 'dru' (something like a *cavaliere servente*). As her 'servant', he will have the right to lead the queen to and from her chamber and also to kiss her once 'doucement' on each occasion.[154] The king grants this rather peculiar request, and the hero acts accordingly (kisses at lines 3477, 4471, 5512, and 6576). Whereas Ipomedon has his own reasons for that arrangement, the queen rather fancies him and is ready, says the poet, to love him 'de amor fine'; but she has to remain content with nothing more than 'sweet' kisses of greeting and parting. Chrétien's *Erec* has another public kiss whose erotic value remains intriguingly vague, the Kiss of the White Stag. According to an old custom, whoever kills a white

---

[153] 'Greeting and Parting', p. 24.
[154] *Ipomedon*, ed. Holden, ll. 3006–31; the English version, *Ipomadon*, ed. R. Purdie, EETS, 316 (2001), ll. 2732–49.

stag can claim a kiss from the most beautiful woman at Arthur's court. Arthur himself has made the kill; and in a scene of high ceremony, with which the first section of the poem concludes, the king kisses Enide:

> Beisiee l'a come cortois,
> Veant toz ses barons, li rois,
> Et si li dist: 'Ma dolce amie,
> M'amor vos doing sanz vilenie.'

> ['The king kissed her courteously, in the sight of all his lords, and said to her: "My sweet friend, I give you my love in all honour"', *Erec et Enide*, 1787–90.]

Different issues arise when the man and woman who exchange public kisses are in reality lovers – especially when, as in the case of Lancelot and Guinevere, their love is secret. In the Prose *Lancelot*, when Lancelot is arming for battle, the queen takes him in her arms and kisses him. This might pass for an ordinary leavetaking, were it not that she kisses him 'au plus doucement que ele puet' ['as tenderly as she could', 560.19–20, cf. 606.14–15]. Elsewhere, Guinevere is said to take leave of Lancelot with a kiss 'in the sight of all who choose to see' ('voiant toz cels qui veoir lo vuelent', 604.8). Her purpose is not, of course, to flaunt her adulterous affair in the presence of Arthur and the rest. Rather, the kiss declares that she has nothing to hide. The author makes this intention clear in another place, where Guinevere publicly welcomes her lover back after a victorious campaign:

> Et ele laisse toz les autres, si giete les braz a Lancelot au col, si lo baise voiant toz cels qui laianz estoient, por ce que toz les an voloit decevoir et que nuns n'i pansast ce qu'i est.

> ['And she left all the others to throw her arms round Lancelot's neck, and she kissed him in the sight of everyone there, for she wished to deceive them all so that none might guess what was going on', *Lancelot*, 569.6–8.]

These are lover's gestures masquerading as gestures of welcome, covered by the consideration that no mistress would surely dare to welcome her secret lover so tenderly in public. In Malory, Lancelot outfaces criticism more directly. In the highly charged scene when he returns Guinevere to her husband and takes what is virtually his final leave of both, he kisses the queen;

> and than he seyde all opynly, 'Now lat se whatsomever he be in thys place that dare sey the quene ys nat trew unto my lorde Arthur, lat se who woll speke and he dare speke.' And therewith he brought the quene to the kynge, and than sir Launcelot toke hys leve and departed. (1202.17–23)

Honi soit qui mal y pense. It is a moment of great pathos and tension, not least because Lancelot knows very well that the queen is indeed *not* true to his lord Arthur.

Modern writers on gesture have as yet arrived at no agreed classification of its constituent types. The present chapter assumes a threefold distinction, for which I claim only that it accommodates most of the evidence under consideration. Gestures of the third and last type, to which I now turn, neither contribute to ceremonies nor (primarily, at least) express emotions or attitudes. These belong to the category of what are sometimes called 'emblems'. Argyle describes them as follows: 'Emblems are gestures which have a direct verbal translation, like head-nods, beckoning, and pointing.'[155] The emphasis here must fall upon 'direct'. All gestures, presumably, convey messages which could be rendered verbally; but the three actions given as examples by Argyle function just like the simple verbal utterances which they may replace: 'yes', 'come here', and 'over there'. There are many such small behaviours in modern use, and no doubt the same was true in the Middle Ages; but texts understandably pay less attention to them than to the weightier gestures of ceremony or emotion. Medieval writers do on occasion refer to them, however; and most often, as it happens, they record the emblems suggested by just those terms that Argyle employs by way of illustration: 'beckoning', 'pointing', and 'headnods'.

The modern word *beckon* goes back to the Old English *becnan*, a verb which also gave rise in Middle English to a shorter verb form *beck* and thence to a noun *beck* (as in later 'beck and call'). Whereas 'beckon'

---

[155] *Bodily Communication*, p. 52 (on emblems, see pp. 52–4, 191–4). Kendon defines an emblem as 'a class of gestural action in which the gesture can stand by itself as a single act, is recognized as a standard item within the community that uses it, and can be given a verbal gloss with comparative ease', 'Geography of Gesture', p. 135. See also P. Ekman and W. V. Friesen, 'The Repertoire of Nonverbal Behavior: Categories, Origins, Usage, and Coding', *Semiotica*, 1 (1969), 49–98 (pp. 63–8).

Gestures and looks in medieval narrative

nowadays refers only to a 'come here' gesture, the three Middle English words shared a much wider field of application. Indeed, in their range of meanings they come close to matching the modern *gesture* – a word hardly found in Middle English.[156] *OED* defines the main medieval sense of *beckon* as 'To make a mute signal or significant gesture with the head, hand, finger, etc.', and offers equally broad definitions for *beck* as both verb and noun.[157] Thus, Trevisa can use the noun *beck* to render the general Latin gesture-word *nutus* in his translations, writing 'with signes and bekkes' for 'signis et nutibus'.[158] Given such very wide application, individual becks and beckonings will vary considerably both in their physical form and also in their intended significance. Chaucer's Manciple reports his mother as warning him to keep his mouth shut: 'My sone, spek nat, but with thyn heed thou bekke' (*Canterbury Tales* IX 346). The mother's point is that becks are more non-committal than words (as lawyers also noticed); and the customary editorial gloss 'nod' obscures that point, since a nod in modern use signifies a definite 'yes'. 'Nod' may also be too specific a gloss for the Pardoner's use of the verb, in describing his technique as a preacher:

> Thanne peyne I me to strecche forth the nekke,
> And est and west upon the peple I bekke,
> As dooth a dowve sittynge on a berne.
> (VI 395–7)

These extravagant gestures, being unregulated by any rational principle, like those of a dove, would fall under the general medieval condemnation

---

[156] 'Gesture' (Medieval Latin *gestura*) occurs first in English about 1400 in the more general sense 'deportment, bearing' (*MED gesture* n. (a), *OED Gesture* sb. 1). *MED* has just one example of what appears to be the modern sense: Pecock (c. 1454) allows that preachers may legitimately use certain 'wordis, countenauncis, gesturis, and uttrauncis'.

[157] *OED Beckon* v. 1 and 2, *Beck* v. 1, *Beck* sb.² 1. Similarly, *MED bekenen* v. 1 (a), *bekken*, v. (a), *bek* n.(2) (a). 'Beckon' is related to 'beacon' (in Old English, a sign, portent, or ensign).

[158] The translation of Higden's *Polychronicon*, cited by *MED* under *bek* n.(2). The early English–Latin dictionaries commonly offer forms of *nutus* and *nutare* as equivalents for 'beck' or 'beckon'. *Catholicon Anglicum* has: 'to *Bekyn*; Annuere, nuere, innuere, nutum facere, nutare': ed. S. J. H. Herrtage and H. B. Wheatley, EETS, 75 (1881), p. 26. Similarly, *Promptorium Parvulorum*, ed. A. J. Mayhew, EETS, E.S. 102 (1908), col. 57: '*Bekenyn*: anuo ... nuto', and '*Bekenyn* with eye: nuto ... anuto'.

Gestures

of such *gesticulatio*.[159] On occasion, 'beck' can refer to a bow of the head. In Robert Henryson's *Fables*, when the Fox encounters Friar Wolf, he falls to his knees, doffs his hood, and greets his confessor 'with mony binge and mony bek'.[160] Or a 'beck' can be a simple glance of the eye. In the Latin Isaiah, the haughty daughters of Sion walk with stretched-out necks and 'nutibus oculorum', a phrase rendered in the Wycliffite Bible as 'in beckes of eȝen'.[161] More commonly it is the hand that becks or beckons. It can signal silence, as when, in a rendering of Acts 12.17, St Peter 'bekkende unto hem wiþ hise honde, þat þei schulde holde þem stille'.[162] The hand can also, however, beckon in the modern sense. When Paris and Helen first set eyes on each other in a temple, according to one English poet, they exchanged both looks and 'signs', and Helen 'beckonet' Paris to come over to where she was.[163] In *Handlyng Synne*, a dying miser calls for money to be brought to his bedside with a gesture: he 'sette hym up yn hys bedde, / And bekened þeraftyr with hys hand'.[164] The dictionaries record other places where the modern application of the gesture can be seen; for example, 'He se the ship . . . and bekened theim to come toward the land' (*MED bekenen* v. 1 (a)). This is also presumably a hand-gesture, though not necessarily in just the modern form.[165] It is usages such as these which give rise to the modern *beckon*, a word which preserves only a fraction of its medieval English applications.

The Middle English word can also refer to that other hand-emblem now known as pointing. In *Wynnere and Wastoure*, the king tells Waster

---

[159] Schmitt, *La raison des gestes*, passim, especially p. 282 on *modestia* in the movements of a preacher's body.
[160] *Poems*, ed. Fox, l. 673. See also l. 1961. *OED Beck* sb.² 3 and *MED bek* n.(2) (c) both cite *Promptorium Parvulorum* glossing 'Bek or lowte' with forms of the Latin *conquiniscere*, to stoop or bow.
[161] Cited by *MED* under *bek* n.(2): Isaiah 3.16 (see above, n. 125). In psalm 34.19, 'annuunt oculis' is rendered 'beckes with þaire eghen': *MED bekken* v.
[162] *MED* under *bekken* v., rendering the Vulgate 'annuens autem eis manu ut tacerent'.
[163] *The Gest Hystoriale of the Destruction of Troy*, ed. G. A. Panton and D. Donaldson, EETS, 39, 56 (1869, 1874), l. 3112.
[164] *Handlyng Synne*, ll. 6204–5.
[165] Even in modern Europe, come-here beckoning takes differing physical forms. In Mediterranean countries the hand turns downwards, not upwards as elsewhere in Europe (though with the palm turned inwards to the waver in both cases). See D. McNeill, *Hand and Mind: What Gestures Reveal about Thought* (Chicago, 1992), pp. 62–3; and Morris *et al.*, *Gestures*, pp. 241–6.

Gestures and looks in medieval narrative

to encourage simple newcomers to London in extravagance by, among other things, pointing out to them fat shoulders of lamb for sale: 'bikken þi fynger, / Schew hym of fatt chepe scholdirs ynewe'.[166] Pointing was a form of *gesticulatio* quite widely condemned, then as now. The word 'point' itself, in the relevant sense, appears first in a passage condemning the 'nice corious contenaunces' of bogus contemplatives, in *The Cloud of Unknowing*: 'Som, when þei schulen speke, poynten wiþ here fyngres, or on þeire fyngres, or on þeire owne brestes, or on þeires þat þei speke to.'[167] English courtesy books advise young people not to point: 'With þi fyngris marke not þi tale'; 'With þi fynger schew þou no thynge'; 'Bekenyng, fynguryng, non þou use.'[168] Yet pointing is such an expressive gesture – universal among human beings, we are told, and practised even by chimpanzees – that it cannot be suppressed by rules of politeness. In the Anglo-Norman *Ipomedon*, Ismeine points out the Black Knight to her mistress ('li mustre al dei', line 5928); and the god Seraphis points out a mountain to Alexander in a dream: 'Toward a miȝti montayne him myntis with his fyngir'.[169] Secret and silent pointings are more questionable. In the nightmare world of Skelton's *Bowge of Courte*, the narrator sees Disdain and Dissimulation in conversation: 'there was poyntynge and noddynge with the hede, / And many wordes sayde in secrete wyse' (lines 421–2). Elsewhere, in his play *Magnificence*, Skelton writes of how Crafty Conveyance offends another courtier by an imperious summons to his side, 'poyntyng with his fynger' and clearing his throat significantly.[170]

Argyle's remaining example of an emblem, the 'headnod', refers of course to that up-and-down movement which acts, as a positive sign,

---

[166] Ed. S. Trigg, EETS, 297 (1990), ll. 480–1. *MED bekenen* v. 1 (c) has another example. An Anglo-Saxon glossary gives 'becnend' for the index or forefinger: *Supplement to An Anglo-Saxon Dictionary*, ed. T. N. Toller (Oxford, 1921), under *bicnend*.

[167] *The Cloud of Unknowing*, ed. P. Hodgson, EETS, 218 (1944), p. 99. 'Point', in this sense, is rare in Middle English: see *OED Point* v.¹ 9, 10, and *MED pointen* v.(1) 2(c).

[168] All in *The Babees Book*, ed. Furnivall: *Stans Puer ad Mensam*, Lambeth Ms, l. 71 (p. 31); *The Young Children's Book*, l. 69 (p. 21); *The Boke of Curtasye*, l. 249 (p. 306). 'Showing with one's finger', a common expression for pointing, corresponds to 'monstrare digito' in Latin and 'mostrer al dei' in French: see *OED Show* v. 14 and *MED sheuen* v.(1) 5 (a). The *MED* entry gives examples of the expression 'showing finger' for the index finger in Middle English.

[169] *Wars of Alexander*, l. 1213. See *OED Mint* v.¹, *MED minten* v. 3 (c).

[170] Stage direction after l. 778, and l. 779. For examples of pointing in medieval pictures, see Garnier, *Le langage de l'image*, pp. 165–7 and 169.

Gestures

in direct and formal contrast to the negative, side-to-side, headshake in many modern societies. Charles Darwin discussed this pair of gestures in his book on the expression of emotions.[171] At first Darwin was inclined to regard them as 'innate or instinctive' and therefore probably universal. He saw the origins of the headshake in the fact that infants 'withdraw their heads laterally from the breast' when refusing to suck. But the answers he received when he sent questionnaires to correspondents in various parts of the world revealed considerable cultural diversity; and he could only conclude, doubtfully, that nodding and shaking of the head 'are not universal, yet seem too general to have been independently acquired by all the individuals of so many races' (p. 352). In 1970 Roman Jakobson published an essay on the same subject, in which he argued that the affirmative nod was not a purely arbitrary sign, given its analogues in rituals of welcome and submission: 'The movement of the head forward and down is an obvious visual representation of bowing before the demand, wish, suggestion or opinion of the other participant in the conversation'.[172] Like Darwin, however, Jakobson recognised the existence of other systems with other rationales – including that variant found in Greece and Southern Italy to which I shall allude in my last chapter. These and other studies suggest, in fact, that one cannot simply take it for granted that the widespread modern usage of lateral and vertical head-movements necessarily formed part of the medieval gestural repertoire. It may well have done, but it also may not.[173]

Jakobson observed that, in the study of contemporary gesture, 'the linguist ought to take into account the highly instructive indigenous terminology' (p. 95); and the same consideration applies *a fortiori* to studies of past usage, where no direct observation is possible. Unfortunately, the record of medieval English terminology leaves much to be desired, so far as nodding and headshaking are concerned. *Nod* is a

---

[171] Darwin, *Expression of the Emotions*, pp. 272–7.
[172] R. Jakobson, 'Motor Signs for "Yes" and "No"', *Language in Society*, 1 (1972), 91–6 (p. 92), an essay first published in Russian. Jakobson sees the lateral headshake as a secondary form, being a clear-cut opposite to the nod, though with a certain iconicity of its own because the face is turned away from the addressee. His essay shows how the principles of structural linguistics, in particular the principle of binary opposition, can be applied to gesture.
[173] The ethologist Eibl-Eibesfeldt discusses cultural variations in modern yes/no gestures: Hinde, *Non-Verbal Communication*, pp. 303–4.

word of obscure etymology, though it has always, seemingly, denoted a vertical head-movement of one sort or another.[174] The noun is not recorded in Middle English, and the first record of the verb comes as late as Chaucer's *Canterbury Tales*. In the Manciple's Prologue there, the Manciple has deliberately provoked the Cook, who is dozing drunkenly on his horse:

> And with this speche the Cook wax wrooth and wraw,
> And on the Manciple he gan nodde faste
> For lakke of speche, and doun the hors hym caste.
> (IX 46–8)

OED cites this as its first instance of the main modern sense, 'To make a quick inclination of the head, especially in salutation, assent, or command' (sense 1). But, although the Cook does indeed intend something by his nod 'for lakke of speche', his is certainly not an affirmative sign of the kind indicated by the *OED*'s definition. The *MED* is nearer the mark when it cites the passage, along with three from Lydgate, under the definition, 'To nod the head in drunkenness, sleepiness, gloominess, etc.' In fact, it is not until the sixteenth century that one can confidently identify examples of nodding as a positive sign of 'salutation, assent, or command'.[175] It may well be that the custom antedates 1500, but I have been unable to discover earlier evidence.

Middle English writings speak more often of 'shaking', or 'wagging', the head than of nodding it. The gestures which these words denote had a range of negative meanings, including, as has already been noticed, feelings of anger and scorn. They can also express distress or sorrow, as when the Virgin Mary shakes her head over the dead Christ, or Aesop laments the foolish obstinacy of humanity 'schaikand his heid'.[176] On occasion, too, a 'shake' of the head may accompany and colour a verbal

---

[174] *OED Nod* v., *Nodding* vbl. sb.; *MED nodden* v., *nodding(e* ger. I know of no alternative to 'nod' in this sense.

[175] The earliest example of a positive nod is the devil's nod of approval in Dunbar: *OED Nod* v. (read 'cowld' for 'qwoth' there).

[176] *OED Shake* v. cites the Virgin's words, 'On him mi hefd I scock' (*Cursor Mundi*), as its earliest example of sense 6b: '*To shake one's head*: to turn the head slightly to one side and the other in sorrow or scorn, or to express disapproval, dissent or doubt.' For Aesop, see *Fables*, l. 1388. 'Wagging' can also express sorrow. In *Partonope of Blois*, the grieving heroine 'piteously ... wagged hir hede': ed. A. T. Bödtker, EETS, 109 (1912), l. 8564.

negative. In Chaucer's *Shipman's Tale*, the merchant's wife 'shakes her head' over the poor performance of her husband in bed:

> This faire wyf gan for to shake hir heed
> And sayde thus, 'Ye, God woot al,' quod she.
> 'Nay, cosyn myn, it stant nat so with me.'
> (VII 112–14)

Similarly, in the *Seven Sages of Rome*, a doctor expresses his doubts about a queen's claim that her son is legitimate: '"Par foi, dame," he saide, "no",/ And schok his heved upon the queen.'[177] The dictionaries, understandably enough, take all such uses as referring to the familiar side-to-side movements of the head, but this would be hard to prove. The only actual description of a negative head-gesture known to me in medieval English is as unspecific as the word 'shake' itself. In Manning's *Handlyng Synne* a dead man rejects the offer of masses sung for him by priests of unclean life: 'þe dede mevede hys hede to and fro, / For he was payd of noun of þo.'[178] And there is another difficulty. In the case of 'wag', one finds occasions where the gesture can only have some kind of positive significance. The dying Philip, in the *Wars of Alexander*, accompanies his blessing of his son with a wag of the head: '"A! wele be þe, my wale son!" & waged with his hede'. The context here might seem to exclude a lateral movement of the head; so the editors offer the gloss 'nodded'.[179] But all such inferences rest on the unsafe assumption that medieval Englishmen must always have moved their heads up and down or from side to side according to the same (perhaps natural?) principles that are familiar today. A headwag in Malory illustrates the same obstinate problem. Lancelot is fighting as Guinevere's champion against her accuser, Meleagant. Having Meleagant at his mercy, he turns to the queen, who is looking on, for guidance on what to do: 'So sir Launcelot loked upon the quene, gyff he myght aspye by ony sygne or countenaunce what she wolde have done. And anone the quene wagged hir hede upon sir Launcelot, as ho seyth "sle hym". And full well knew sir Launcelot by her sygnys that she wolde have hym dede'

---

[177] *The Seven Sages of Rome*, ed. K. Brunner, EETS, 191 (1933), ll. 1058–9.
[178] *Handlyng Synne*, ll. 2291–2. Manning's French source, as printed by Furnivall, has 'la teste escut', with 'croulout' reported as a variant for 'escut' (which also means 'shook').
[179] *Wars of Alexander*, l. 1092. *MED waggen* v. 1 (b) also glosses with 'nod'.

Gestures and looks in medieval narrative

(1138.29–1139.3). Guinevere's 'sign' is as good as a word for Lancelot ('as ho seyth'); but what did she actually do?[180] What Jakobson calls the indigenous terminology proves less than instructive in such cases.

Guinevere responded to Lancelot's inquiring look with a sign, evidently, because she was too far off to be heard. This is one of those times when signs are the only possible mode of communication. Quite a full list of such occasions is given by the Italian rhetorician Boncampagno da Signa, in a passage from his *Rhetorica Novissima* cited by Jean-Claude Schmitt:

> Muti, naufragi a litore vel portu distantes, egri qui loqui non possunt, captivi et amatores qui loqui non audent, obsessi et religiosi, per gestus vel indicia seu nutus suos effectus transumunt.
>
> ['Those incapable of speech, those shipwrecked far from shore or port, sick people who cannot speak, captives and lovers who dare not speak, besieged persons and those in religious orders, all these convey their sentiments by gestures, tokens, or signs.'][181]

In such cases, authors commonly speak only of 'signs' or, in English, 'tokens', without specifying any particular emblematic gesture. May, in Chaucer's Merchant's Tale, is one of those 'amatores qui loqui non audent'; so she uses 'privee signes' to communicate with her lover, both before and after they enter January's garden.[182] Of the lecherous Hawkyn in *Piers Plowman*, Langland says that 'ech a maide þat he mette he made hire a signe / Semynge to synneward' (B XIII 344–5). There are also 'muti', those who simply cannot speak for one reason or another. After her tongue has been cut out, Philomela complains to her sister 'with

---

[180] OED thinks she shook her head from side to side (under sense 11 c). MED, more cautiously, cites the instance under sense 2(a): 'To move (something), especially back and forth or up and down, shake'. The French original does not help: 'la royne li fait signes quil li cope la teste', *The Vulgate Version of the Arthurian Romances*, ed. H. O. Sommer, 7 vols. (Washington, 1909–13), Vol. IV, p. 225.

[181] *Rhetorica Novissima*, ed. A. Gaudentius, Biblioteca Iuridica Medii Aevi, Vol. II (Bologna, 1892), pp. 249–97, cited from p. 284. On Boncampagno, see Schmitt, *Raison des gestes*, pp. 285–8, noting that he also wrote a 'librum de gestibus et motibus corporum humanorum', now apparently lost. On sign-languages of *religiosi*, not considered in this book, see ibid., pp. 255–7 and the references given there.

[182] *Canterbury Tales* IV 2105, 2150, 2209, 2213. Because her husband is blind, he cannot protect her as thoroughly as can the guardian of Bel Acueil in the *Roman de la Rose*: 'Nus ne la poroit enginier / De seignier ne de guignier' ['No one could deceive her, either with signing or with winking': ed. Lecoy, ll. 3907–8].

Gestures

signes' in *Confessio Amantis* (v 5868); and in Chaucer's version of the same story, she both makes requests and even swears 'by signes'.[183] In the prose romance *Valentine and Orson*, Orson has been reared from infancy by a bear, and when he first meets his brother, 'he made hym sygnes with his handes and heed that he would pull him in peces'. Thereafter – until he finally, as an adult, manages to speak – communication with him is conducted entirely by 'sygnes' (or on occasion 'geastes').[184] In *William of Palerne*, the werewolf is said to express himself by 'signes', 'tokene', or 'contenaunce'.[185] Monsters have a similar problem. In his travels, Alexander comes upon a race of strange people without mouths or noses: 'Tunge ne have hii non, iwis, / To speken Latyn oiþer Englissh. / Everyche oþere understonde / By þe toknes of þe honde.'[186] Trevisa's translation of the encyclopaedia of Bartholomeus Anglicus refers to the same creatures: 'þese beþ acounted tongeles and useþ signes and bekkes in stede of spekynge.'[187] When Boncampagno speaks also of 'obsessi', he refers (*pace* Schmitt, who translates the word as 'possédés') to exchanges between besieged people and their besiegers. Froissart in his *Chronicles* describes several such occasions, where warriors communicate with signs across the intervening space. Thus, the captain of French forces besieged in the castle of Le Riolle sticks his head out of a lower window in the tower, wishing to surrender: 'et fist signe qu'il voloit parler à qui que fust de l'ost' ['and made a sign that he wished to speak to someone from the army'].[188] Captains of besieging forces also use signs to attract the attention of the enemy garrison, as Sir John Chandos does before Romorentin: 's'en vint devant les barrières, et fist signe que il voloit parlementer d'aucune cose' ['he went out before the barriers and made

---

[183] In the source followed by both poets, Ovid's *Metamorphoses*, Philomela makes her request 'gestu' (VI 579) and, when she complains to her sister, 'the hand served for voice' ('pro voce manus fuit', VI 609). On signing by the deaf and dumb, see Schmitt, *Raison des gestes*, pp. 253–4.

[184] *Valentine and Orson*, ed. A. Dickson, EETS, 204 (1937), pp. 68, 70, 71, 72, 74, 75, etc. In Spenser's *Faerie Queene*, the wild or 'salvage' man communicates 'by signes, by lookes, and all his other gests': Book VI, Canto iv, Stanza 14 (also Stanza 11).

[185] *William of Palerne*, ed. Bunt, ll. 2740, 3489, 3494 ('signes'); 3086 ('tokene'); 2209, 4378 ('contenaunce').

[186] *Kyng Alisaunder*, Laud Ms, ll. 6426–9.

[187] *On the Properties of Things: John Trevisa's Translation of Bartholomaeus Anglicus De Proprietatibus Rerum*, ed. M. C. Seymour *et al.*, 3 vols. (Oxford, 1975, 1988), p. 1200.

[188] *Chroniques*, Vol. III, ed. S. Luce (Paris, 1872), p. 88 (Book I, Section 232).

a sign that he wished to parley about a certain matter'].[189] Perhaps Froissart's original readers would have known what these signs were.

To conclude this chapter, let me notice two anecdotes current in the Middle Ages, both of which turn on unusual employments of gesture – understood in one case, but not in the other. In his *Confessio Amantis*, Gower tells a story about Tarquinius Superbus. His son has inveigled his way into a position of power in the city of their enemies, the Gabii, and he sends a message to his father asking how they might now win the town. When he received the message, Tarquinius was in a garden. He then

> tok in honde a yerde,
> And in the gardin as thei gon,
> The lilie croppes on and on,
> Wher that thei weren sprongen oute,
> He smot of, as thei stode aboute,
> And seide unto the messager:
> 'Lo, this thing, which I do nou hier,
> Schal ben in stede of thin ansuere;
> And in this wise as I me bere,
> Thou schalt unto mi sone telle.'
> (VII 4676–85)

The son understands his father's expressive action, and has the princes of the Gabii beheaded. Gower took the story, as his editor points out, from Ovid's *Fasti* (V 687–710). Livy in his *History* (I 54) describes the same events (though with poppies rather than lilies), adding that Tarquinius responded to his son wordlessly because he did not trust the messenger. Herodotus and Aristotle have much the same story, though in a different context. In both, a tyrant is consulted by another tyrant about the best way to govern, and he responds by taking the messenger out into a field and cutting off the tallest ears of corn. The messenger does not understand, but his master does and acts accordingly.[190] It is this anecdote

---

[189] *Chroniques*, Vol. V, ed. S. Luce (Paris, 1874), p. 7 (Book I, Section 3730). For examples of 'signes' used on other occasions in Froissart, see Vol. XIV, pp. 55–6, and Vol. XV, p. 183. Margery Kempe, when travelling in Italy, communicated 'be syngnys er tokenys and in fewe comown wordys': *The Book of Margery Kempe*, ed. S. B. Meech, EETS, 212 (1940), p. 93 (see also p. 99).

[190] Herodotus, *History*, V 92; Aristotle, *Politics*, III 13, 1284a (and see 1311a).

Gestures

that Francis Bacon selected as his example of signification by gesture, in *The Advancement of Learning* (1605). Bacon there distinguishes words, which are arbitrary signs (*ad placitum*), from the two sorts of sign that have 'some similitude or congruity' with what they represent. These are hieroglyphics (as in Egyptian picture-writing) and gestures. Of the latter, he writes:

> And as for Gestures, they are as transitory Hieroglyphics, and are to Hieroglyphics as words spoken are to words written, in that they abide not; but they have evermore, as well as the other, an affinity with the things signified: as Periander, being consulted with how to preserve a tyranny newly usurped, bid the messenger attend and report what he saw him do; and went into his garden and topped all the highest flowers; signifying, that it consisted in the cutting off and keeping low of the nobility and grandees.[191]

Francis Bacon was not the first to use this incident to illustrate the efficacy of communication by gesture. In the Fourth Book of the *Gargantua and Pantagruel* of François Rabelais, published in 1552, Pantagruel promises to answer questions put to him by his companions in the most satisfactory way, not 'par longs ambages et discours de parolles', but 'par signes, gestes et effectz'.[192] By way of explanation, he narrates the story of Tarquinius answering his son 'par signes', as told by Livy. Like his contemporary Montaigne, Rabelais took an interest in non-verbal communication. As M. A. Screech observes, 'repeatedly in *Pantagruel*, *Gargantua*, and the *Tiers Livre* deceptive or deliberately ambiguous use of words is contrasted with concrete gestures'.[193] Yet in his first volume, *Pantagruel*, Rabelais also has a comic set piece which illustrates the misunderstanding of ambiguous gestures.[194] Panurge manages to impress a great English scholar, Thaumaste, with his wisdom, in a disputation between them conducted 'par signes seulement'. He responds to Thaumaste's cabbalistic hand-signs (whose deep, esoteric meaning

---

[191] *Francis Bacon: A Critical Edition of the Major Works*, ed. B. Vickers (Oxford, 1996), p. 231. Since it is in the *Politics* that Periander is consulted (in Herodotus he is the consulter), Aristotle is evidently the main source; but the lopping of flowers in a garden must go back to Ovid or Livy.

[192] Book Four, Chapter 63: p. 255 in *Le Quart Livre*, ed. R. Marichal (Geneva, 1947).

[193] M. A. Screech, *Rabelais* (London, 1979), p. 413. In Book Three, Panurge receives advice on marriage by gestures and signs from a deaf and dumb man (Chapters 19–20).

[194] Chapters 17 and 18 in the 1534 *Pantagruel*, ed. G. Defaux (Paris, 1994).

is never explained) with a series of very vulgar gestures – obscene, insulting, and threatening – which nevertheless impress the Englishman by the profound significance he sees in them. 'Behold, a greater than Solomon is here', he cries. Screech compares this episode with a story narrated by the thirteenth-century jurist Accursius. In his commentary on the *Pandects*, Accursius sets out to explain how the civilised Greeks came to satisfy themselves that the barbarous Romans were yet worthy of being instructed in the mysteries of the law.[195] The fourteenth-century Spanish poet, Juan Ruiz, took the same story from Accursius, at the beginning of his *Libro de Buen Amor*, using it as a warning to readers not to misinterpret his work.[196] In two exchanges of gesture, 'por signos e por señas de letrado' ('by means of gesture and the signs used by the learned'), both the Greek emissary and the crude Roman 'ribald' misread the other's meaning. Thus, in the first exchange, the Greek holds out his index finger, meaning, as he later explains, that there is but one God; but the Roman takes this to mean 'I'll poke your eye out'; and in response he threatens to poke both the Greek's eyes out and knock his teeth in as well, by holding out two fingers and a thumb. The Greek, however, understands this gesture as a sign of the three Persons of the one God, and is duly impressed. This story, for all its comic absurdity, stands as a salutary warning for studies such as the present one. Gestures, like words, are often uncertain or ambiguous in meaning; and their interpretation may depend as much upon the expectations of the observer as upon the intentions of the signer.

[195] Screech, *Rabelais*, pp. 88–9, summarising the Accursius story. Screech has many valuable observations on Rabelais's interest in 'the linguistic, legal and philosophical theories applied to signs' (p. 412). He notices, for instance, the disputes of medieval lawyers over the legal force of gesture (*gestus*) when unsupported by speech (pp. 411–13, 433–5).

[196] Juan Ruiz, *Libro de Buen Amor*, ed. and transl. R. S. Willis (Princeton, N.J., 1972), Stanzas 46–64. On Accursius as source, see references in V. Marmo, *Dalle Fonti alle Forme: Studi sul Libro de Buen Amor* (Naples, 1983), p. 41.

3

Looks

Classical manuals of rhetoric and medieval arts of poetry alike recommend speakers or reciters to support their words with appropriate behaviour of the body, and they distinguish in this connection between *vultus* and *gestus*. So, in his *Poetria Nova*, Geoffrey of Vinsauf writes:

> In recitante sonent tres linguae: prima sit oris,
> Altera rhetorici vultus, et tertia gestus.[1]
>
> ['In reciting let three tongues speak: first, that of the mouth, second, that of the speaker's face, and third, that of his gesture.']

Geoffrey here rates the expressive face and the gesturing body on a par with the speaking mouth in a reciter's performance: all three are equally *linguae*, tongues, instruments of communication. In the present chapter I turn from *gestus* to *vultus*.

As everyone knows, and as infants very early discover, there is more to be learned about what other people are thinking and feeling from their faces than from any other part of the body. The complex structure of facial muscles makes possible a very wide range of subtly varied expressions — some ten thousand, it is said — and the eyes play a special part also by the direction, duration, and intensity of a glance or a gaze.[2] Not all facial activity, of course, entails any *voluntas significandi*. The primary

---

[1] *Poetria Nova*, ll. 2031–2, ed. E. Faral, *Les arts poétiques du XIIe et du XIIIe siècle* (Paris, 1924), p. 259. In Geoffrey's *Documentum de Arte Versificandi* (ed. Faral, p. 318), he cites *Ad Herennium* on the fifth branch of rhetoric, *pronunciatio* or delivery: 'Pronunciatio est vocis, vultus, gestus moderatio cum venustate' ['Delivery is the graceful regulation of voice, countenance, and gesture'], ed. and transl. H. Caplan (Cambridge, Mass., 1954), I ii 3.

[2] The social psychologist Michael Argyle surveys modern discussions in his *Bodily Communication*, Chapters 8 ('Facial Expression') and 10 ('Gaze'). See also S. Weitz, 'Facial

purpose of the eyes is to receive information, not to convey it; yet they also serve to transmit 'speaking looks', actively intended by the gazer to communicate information to others. Again, facial expressions may, as Augustine noticed, be no more than 'natural signs' or involuntary symptoms of some inner condition; yet they are also commonly directed at others with the more or less distinct intention that they should be read as signs of what we think or feel. Since the present study concerns only non-verbal communication – as against non-verbal behaviour generally – this chapter will concentrate on those instances of facial expression and gaze which offer themselves to be read as signals. I take the face first, and then the eyes.

As noticed in the introductory chapter, cross-cultural studies of contemporary practice tend to suggest that facial expressions exhibit less variation than do gestures. P. Ekman states his own conclusion firmly enough: 'The same facial expressions are associated with the same emotions, regardless of culture or language.' And again, rather less sweepingly: 'There are some facial expressions of emotion that are universally characteristic of the human species.' This state of affairs is due, according to Ekman, in part to those innate or genetic factors already identified by Charles Darwin, and in part to what he calls the common 'learning experiences' of all human beings.[3] Cultural differences, where they exist, may be referred either to differing 'display rules' (encouraging or discouraging facial expressiveness) or to differing 'elicitors' (the same emotion with its associated expression being elicited by different circumstances).[4] Not all the experts would go as far as Ekman does, by any means; but I have found little, in the present diachronic study, to challenge his general position. If there were differences in physical form between facial expressions then and now, the texts do not allow them to appear; for the writers most commonly content themselves with a simple verb ('smile') or noun phrase ('sad visage'). Yet the texts do give

Expression and Visual Interaction', in Weitz, ed., *Nonverbal Communication: Readings with Commentary*, 2nd edn (New York, 1979), pp. 17–36.
[3] P. Ekman, 'Cross-Cultural Studies of Facial Expression', in Ekman, ed., *Darwin and Facial Expression*, pp. 169–222 (p. 219). See also Chapter XIX in Ekman *et al.*, *Emotion in the Human Face*.
[4] Ibid. Other experts are more impressed by the cultural differences: for example, Birdwhistell in his essay on smiles, cited below (n. 11).

Looks

evidence of what Ekman calls the 'elicitors' and 'display rules' – why and when one might be expected to laugh, for instance – and here I shall have occasion to notice some points on which medieval usage differs from our own.

Middle English appears, on the surviving evidence, to have been distinctly less rich than the English of today in terms distinguishing varieties of facial expression. It did have some words lacking in Modern English, such as *mowen*, meaning to make a derisive face;[5] but more numerous are the cases of words which came into the language later and had no close medieval equivalents – words such as *glower*, *grimace*, or *sneer*. Older speakers, however, did not lack terms for the basic opposition between smiling and frowning, even though those particular verbs, *smile* and *frown*, prove to have been quite late borrowings from other languages. So far as concerns frowning, to take that first, the older and more common word in Middle English was *louren*. *Frown* itself is a late Middle English loanword, from the French *froignier*. The dictionaries record it first in Chaucer's Clerk's Tale, with only a scattering of other instances to follow.[6] It is not inappropriate that the word should make its first appearance where it does, for, of all Chaucer's Canterbury stories, it is the Clerk's that shows most interest in facial expressions. Proposing marriage to Griselda there, Walter the marquis requires that she should submit to his will in all things:

> 'And eek whan I sey "ye", ne sey nat "nay",
> Neither by word ne frownyng contenance.'
> (IV 355–6)

At this point, Petrarch's Latin original has 'sine ulla frontis aut verbi repugnancia' ['without any opposition of either brow or word'].[7] Chaucer preserves this coupling of verbal and non-verbal, rendering Petrarch's *frons* with a more specific expression. It is by 'frownyng contenance' that a refractory wife might say 'nay' to a husband, quite as distinctly as by words.

---

[5] See *MED mouen* v.(2) and especially *moue* n.(2). Professor C. J. Kay has kindly made available to me the relevant material from the *Historical Thesaurus of English*.
[6] See *MED frounen* v. and *louren* v.
[7] Petrarch is quoted from the edition in W. F. Bryan and G. Dempster, eds., *Sources and Analogues of Chaucer's Canterbury Tales* (London, 1958), pp. 296–330; here from p. 306.

Walter's use of 'frown' fits comfortably with the *OED*'s prime definition of the word, as it is understood today: 'To knit the brows, especially by way of expressing displeasure' (*Frown* v. 1). So also do many occurrences of the more common 'louren'. In modern use, 'lour' may suggest a blacker look than 'frown' – more like a scowl, perhaps – but it is not easy to distinguish in Middle English between the two. Elsewhere in the *Canterbury Tales*, the Friar lours at his enemy the Summoner while the Wife of Bath is telling her tale:

> This worthy lymytour, this noble Frere,
> He made alwey a maner louryng chiere
> Upon the Somonour, but for honestee
> No vileyns word as yet to hym spak he.
> (III 1265–8)

'A kind of louring expression'. What kind? Although the text does not specify, the meaning of the look is clear enough. It carries the same message as would the use of a 'vileyns word' if the Friar were not concerned to preserve decency and dignity ('honestee'). Such was one of the functions, then as now, of silent looks. The Friar's frown belongs to a type commonly attributed by moralists to personifications of ill-will. In Langland's *Piers Plowman*, Envy 'lours' at a rival London trader (B V 133); and in the *Romaunt of the Rose*, Hate wears a permanent frown: 'Frounced foule was hir visage.'[8] In Gower's *Confessio Amantis*, again, Melancholy 'wol as an angri beste loure', and Malebouche cannot say a good word about anyone 'withoute frounce / Awher behinde a mannes bak' (III 30, II 392–3).

Frowns are not, of course, confined to such malignant powers. Where other personifications are concerned, a frown may express the disapproval of some higher power. When Amans first encounters Venus in the *Confessio*, he claims to be her man, but the goddess responds with a lour:

> And sche began to loure tho,
> And seide, 'ther is manye of yow
> Faitours...'
> (I 172–4)

---

[8] Line 155. See *MED frouncen* v., sense 1 (b). The verb derives from French *froncier*, used in the original *Roman* here. An old hag 'frounceth up the browe' in *Confessio Amantis* I 1589.

Langland has a somewhat similar exchange in *Piers Plowman*, prompted there by a rash pronouncement from the dreamer on a point of theology: '"*Contra!*" quod Ymaginatif þo and comsed to loure' (B XII 280). Perhaps surprisingly, Langland's personification allegories rely quite heavily on showing the expressions and looks exchanged between his dream-persons. So, in another passage involving a lour, Long Will, having just spoken in reproach of an avaricious friar, is checked by Lewty (representing justice or fair judgement here):

> And Lewte louʒ on me for I loured on þe frere;
> 'Wherfore lourestow?' quod Lewtee, and loked on me harde.
> (B XI 84–5)

Will's frown might have been taken simply as a quite proper expression of righteous indignation, given the character of the friar in question. But it turns out to prompt both a 'laugh' and a hard look from Lewty. What kind of 'laugh' is this?[9] And why the hard look? Since Lewty goes on to encourage Will to publish his anti-fraternal sentiments, the 'laugh' may be read as supportive; but the hard look seems to recognise that Will's louring indignation, here as elsewhere in the poem, is not without its admixture of unworthy feelings. Taken together, the lour, the laugh and the look serve as a reminder that non-verbal signals do not necessarily carry only simple messages. They may contribute to quite complex and subtle relationships.

Smiles belong with frowns as a contrasting pair, negative and positive. Human smiles are held to have developed from the playface, an expression very common in primates, observable in monkeys; and some such phylogenetic origin probably accounts for the fact that smiles can be said to go along with pleasure, friendliness and the like in all human societies.[10] Nevertheless, the smile can exhibit quite a wide range both of physical forms ('broad', 'thin', etc.) and of significances. As one authority

---

[9] It may be a smile rather than a laugh (see below, pp. 76–8). At l. 84, Kane and Donaldson read 'louʒ' with the C text (XII 23), preferring this more difficult reading to the 'loked' of B manuscripts (see p. 90 of their edition). See further J. A. Burrow, 'Gestures and Looks in *Piers Plowman*', *Yearbook of Langland Studies*, 14 (2000), pp. 75–83.

[10] For the 'playface', see Argyle, *Bodily Communication*, p. 37 and Plate 3. For a somewhat different account, see J. A. R. A. M. van Hooff, 'A Comparative Approach to the Phylogeny of Laughter and Smiling', in Hinde, ed., *Non-Verbal Communication*, pp. 209–38.

Gestures and looks in medieval narrative

observes: 'A "smile" in one society portrays friendliness, in another embarrassment, and in still another may contain a warning that, unless tension is reduced, hostility and attack will follow.'[11]

In Middle English, the vocabulary of this important facial expression is not rich. The word 'smile' itself appears in the dictionaries no earlier than about 1300, apparently as a borrowing from Old Norse. The verb for smiling in Old English was *smearcian*. This is recorded only once in Middle English, in that older general sense, and thereafter it does not appear until the sixteenth century, where it is already restricted to the modern specialised meaning of 'smirk'. The only alternative available to Middle English writers, it seems, was *grennen* (Modern *grin*); but that word more often denotes a grimace than a smile ('Of persons or animals: To draw back the lips and display the teeth', *OED Grin* v.[2] 1). Modern English, admittedly, is not much better off, so far as basic vocabulary is concerned; but, unlike many later writers, medieval story-tellers rarely attempt to remedy the deficiency by description. Only occasionally, in the texts under consideration here, are people said to smile 'a litel', and in French 'un peu' or 'durement'. There is hardly more than that.[12]

Yet smiles do not need to be directly characterised for their significance to be divined from the context in which they occur. Sometimes smiling simply expresses amicable feelings, as when Malory's Sir Tristram recognises Lamorak and 'smyled uppon hym and knew hym well' (443.1). On occasion such friendliness is touched with condescension, as when, again in Malory, Tristram thanks Dynadan with a smile for an unnecessary offer of help (532.26). Equally familiar today are quiet smiles of private satisfaction. In *Confessio Amantis*, Gower's Amans 'in my self... gan to smyle' as he reflects upon the black beads given him by Venus; and old people there, happy to join in the dance of love, 'With sobre chier

---

[11] Birdwhistell, *Kinesics and Context*, p. 34, in the essay 'There are Smiles...'. On the physical form of smiles, see pp. 34–7 of that essay, and also van Hooff, 'A Comparative Approach', pp. 231–5, with illustrations.

[12] Examples of such epithets may be found in *MED* under *smilen* v. and *smiling(e* ger. Ménard, *Le rire et le sourire*, p. 442, notices 'sozrire un pou'; but he observes that 'la plupart du temps les romanciers courtois se contentent de dire qu'un personnage rit, sans apporter d'autres précisions' (p. 439). On the 'smooth' smiling of the hero in *Sir Gawain and the Green Knight*, see below, pp. 149–50. Another interesting case is Chaucer's Prioress, 'that of hir smylyng was ful symple and coy'. An elaborate modern characterisation of a smile is quoted from John Updike by S. A. Portch, *Literature's Silent Language: Nonverbal Communication* (New York, 1985), p. 24.

among thei smyle, / For laghtre was ther non on hyh' (VIII 2958, 2684–5). A more striking feature of the texts is the frequency with which smiles there conform to the type well defined by *MED* as sense (c) of the verb: 'to assume or wear an expression of ironic amusement or satisfaction, usually because of secret knowledge'. Chivalric narratives in both French and English have many knowing smiles of this kind. The 'secret knowledge' in question often concerns the identity or whereabouts of that elusive hero, Lancelot. Malory's King Arthur declines to tell his knights that Lancelot, whom he has spotted in a neighbouring garden, will be coming to the tournament: '"At thys tyme ye shall nat wyte for me!" seyde the kynge and smyled, and wente to hys lodgynge' (1067.1–2). In the French Prose *Lancelot*, the Dame de Malohaut, who is secretly holding Lancelot in prison, smiles when she hears that Arthur has sent out to search for him, 'por que il chaçoient la folie' ['because they were on a fool's errand'].[13] Similar smiles occur rather frequently also in the French *Mort le Roi Artu*. Twice Arthur 'commence a sozrire' as he conceals his knowledge of Lancelot's identity, and the knowing smile of a squire sent by the hero to Arthur's court provokes Gawain's curiosity: 'Je te demant, fet messire Gauvains, por quoi tu commenças ore a sozrire.'[14]

Smiles that speak of superior knowledge can elsewhere be positively scornful. In Chaucer's Reeve's Tale the miller, seeing through the tricks of his two undergraduate customers, 'smyled of hir nycetee'; and in the Friar's Tale, when the summoner asks the name of his 'yeoman' companion – who is in fact a devil – 'this yeman gan a litel for to smyle' (*Canterbury Tales* I 4046, III 1446). In the Prose *Lancelot*, a damsel smiles enigmatically and, in answer to Gawain's question, explains that she is reflecting upon the follies of the world, 'les folies do siegle' (419.36–9). Smiling expresses a scornful sense of social superiority in Froissart's account of the reaction of the English lords to a Flemish embassy. In 1382, a party of Flemish citizens came to London seeking English support against the French, while demanding at the same time that an English

---

[13] *Lancelot do Lac: The Non-Cyclic Old French Prose Romance*, ed. E. Kennedy, 2 vols. (Oxford, 1980), 301.28–9. Malohaut smiles again 'mout durement' for a similar reason at 313.19. When Gawain identifies a recent giant-killer as Lancelot, he lowers his head and smiles, prompting Guinevere to ask what he meant by it (272.4).

[14] *La Mort le Roi Artu*, pp. 16, 20, 46. Gawain smiles on p. 34. See D. Lateiner, *Sardonic Smile: Nonverbal Behavior in Homeric Epic* (Ann Arbor, Mich., 1995), on the 'sardonic smiles' of Odysseus, especially pp. 42 and 193–5.

Gestures and looks in medieval narrative

debt, incurred long ago by Edward III, should be repaid to them. The diplomatic amateurishness of this demand, coupled as it was with such a request, strikes the English lords as ridiculous: 'Quant li signeur eurent oi ceste parolle et requeste, il regardèrent l'un l'autre et commenchièrent li aucun à sousrire' ['When the lords heard this statement and this request, they looked at each other and some of them began to smile'].[15] While the Flemings are still in the room, the lords content themselves with looks and smiles; but once the embassy has left, they break out in contemptuous laughter.

This is a painfully familiar kind of laugh, clearly distinguished by Froissart from the earlier smiles: *rire* as against *sourire*. Yet the distinction between these two French verbs was not always so clear, as Philippe Ménard shows in his massive study entitled *Le rire et le sourire dans le roman courtois en France au moyen âge (1150–1250)*. *Sourire* (Latin *sub*ridere) becomes common only towards the end of Ménard's period, and he argues that 'il n'y a pas dans le vocabulaire médiéval d'opposition de sens entre rire et sourire... l'aire sémantique du mot rire englobe le sourire'.[16] In other words, although *sourire* always refers to smiles ('*sub*ridere'), where it occurs, *rire* can refer to smiles as well as laughs. One piece of evidence for this is that *rire* on occasion refers back to an event previously denoted by *sourire*; but Ménard is otherwise forced to rely on the argument that *rire* sometimes will occur in contexts where we today would expect not a laugh but a smile. The problem with this argument lies in the assumption, commonly made, that changes of meaning are to be looked for in words but not in non-verbal signs. But what if medieval people actually laughed on occasions when we would only smile? Maybe they had different 'display rules'. This is the problem of what I call 'double signification' in NVC words, which I shall address in connection with 'winks' later in this chapter. The same problem arises with the corresponding English words, *smile* and *laugh*. Like *sourire* in French, *smile* is a latecomer in English; and the dictionaries claim that its meaning would also have been covered in the semantic field of *laughen*: *OED Laugh* v. sense 4, and *MED laughen* v., senses 1(a), 1(d), and 3(a). But it is difficult to determine in which particular cases smiles may be

---

[15] *Chroniques*, Vol. x, ed. G. Raynaud (Paris, 1897), p. 268 (Book II, Section 297).
[16] *Le rire et le sourire*, p. 31; see also pp. 430–1.

meant rather than laughs. The reasoning will beg the question of double signification: is it the word that has changed its meaning since medieval times, or rather the action which the word signifies?

Certainly there are not a few cases in the texts, French and English, where *rire* or *laughen* occurs in contexts where modern Western usage leads us to expect a smile. It is understandable that, when the lady approaches the hero in *Sir Gawain and the Green Knight* 'wyth lyppez smal laȝande', the editor should gloss the word by 'smile'.[17] Another kind of context where we would expect something more subdued than a laugh can be illustrated from the stanzaic *Morte Arthur*. Bors and Lionel are sharing their secret knowledge that Lancelot is to come in disguise as the queen's champion: 'Bors than loughe on Lyonelle, / Wyste no man of here hertys worde.'[18] This is exactly the context in which, as we have seen, knights commonly smile (knowing about Lancelot). In French, there are questionable cases of *rire* in the romances of Chrétien – a poet who, according to Ménard (*Le rire et le sourire*, p. 426), never uses the word *sourire*. In his *Chevalier de la Charrete*, Lancelot, accompanied by a damsel in his quest for Guinevere, comes upon an ivory comb with blond hair caught in its teeth. He picks it up and gazes at it, whereupon the damsel, recognizing it as Guinevere's, gives what seems to be a knowing smile:

> Et cele an comança a rire.
> Et quant il la voit, se li prie
> Por qu'ele a ris, qu'ele li die.
>
> ['And she began to smile (?) at that, and he, noticing what she did, asked her to tell him why she was smiling.'][19]

In a scene already referred to from Chrétien's *Cligés*, a smile (or a laugh) takes its place, along with speaking looks and actions, in an exemplary sequence of high courtly manners. Alexander is sitting with Guinevere in her chamber, together with her damsel Soredamors, whom he loves.

---

[17] Line 1207, as glossed in the Tolkien–Gordon–Davis edition (Oxford, 1967). See also below, p. 149.

[18] *Le Morte Arthur*, ll. 1536–7. *OED* admits the sense 'smile' for the verb only in the expressions 'laugh *on, upon* (rarely *up, to*)', distinguishing these from 'laugh *at*' and the like. Cf. *MED laughen* v., sense 3.

[19] Ed. Roques, ll. 1394–6.

Gestures and looks in medieval narrative

He wears a silk shirt into which, unknown to him, Soredamors has woven strands of her blond hair. Guinevere, taking Alexander by the hand and gazing at his shirt, recalls that Soredamors had a hand in it:

> et si s'an rist.
> Alixandres garde s'an prist
> Et li prie, s'il fet a dire,
> Qu'el li die qui la fet rire.

> ['And so she smiled (?). Alexander noticed this and asked her to tell him, if she would, who was making her smile.'][20]

My criterion of intentionality or *voluntas significandi* comes to seem a bit gross in this context. Guinevere's smile (if that is what it was) might be considered as nothing but an involuntary adjunct of amused recollection; but in such company as queens keep, smiles form part of the vocabulary of silent expression; and Alexander commits no unmannerly intrusion upon her privacy in asking what she meant by it.

Most of the contexts in which *laughen* and *rire* occur, however, coincide comfortably enough with those in which a modern English or French person might be expected to laugh rather than smile. As Ménard remarks: 'D'une manière générale on rit au Moyen Age pour les mêmes raisons qu'aujourdhui' (*Le rire et le sourire*, p. 432). Like Ménard, accordingly, I confine myself here to a few of the more interesting cases. Leaving aside the many occasions where people simply laugh for joy at some happy outcome or the like, I notice a place in the stanzaic *Morte Arthur* where such laughter goes along with tears. When the alarming episode of the poisoned apple has turned out well, 'The knyghtis all wepte and loughe, / For ioye as thay togedyr spake.'[21] Laughter may be a conventional sign of joy, but tears are not. John Barbour has a remarkable passage in his *Bruce* where he takes occasion to explain why, when Bruce and his men are reunited with the Earl of Lennox, they all wept – instead of laughing, as one might have expected. This was not 'properly' weeping, he says, because proper tears have their cause in suffering (except, he adds, with some women, who can 'wet their cheeks' at will!). On occasion, though, great joy can cause the heart to

---

[20] Ed. Micha, ll. 1553–6.
[21] Ed. Bruce, ll. 1636–7. On laughter with weeping in French, see Ménard, *Le rire et le sourire*, pp. 445–6.

open, allowing water to rise from it and 'wet the eyes so that they seem to be weeping, though it is no such thing'.[22] So tears are involuntary physiological symptoms, to be explained and not, like signs, to be interpreted. Laughter is such a sign, but weeping is not.[23]

More often – indeed, surprisingly often – writers speak of laughter as a sign of that more general and diffused kind of joy that courtly society in particular valued when people met together. In *Sir Gawain and the Green Knight*, one mark of an evening's festivities is 'laȝyng of ladies' (l. 1954); and in Chaucer's *Troilus*, a distressed Criseyde is said to have lost 'the pleye, the laughter, men was wont to fynde / On hire, and ek hire joies everichone' (IV 866–7). Pandarus makes Criseyde laugh a lot in their scenes together in Book II, as when he

> gan his beste japes forth to caste,
> And made hire so to laughe at his folye,
> That she for laughter wende for to dye.
> (II 1167–9)

It was evidently not thought at all impolite to indulge in such immoderate laughter; and this was often prompted by japes less subtle than those of Pandarus. Malory's Sir Dynadan, a 'grete bourder' or jester, as well as a 'passynge good knyght' (615.7–8), is unhorsed by Lancelot and brought back dressed in women's clothes: 'and whan quene Gwenyver sawe sir Dynadan ibrought in so amonge them all, than she lowghe, that she fell downe; and so dede all that there was'.[24] Elsewhere, laughter strikes a note of amused condescension, more or less friendly in character. In Chrétien's *Perceval*, Yvonet laughs at the young Perceval's blundering attempts to strip the armour off a knight he has just killed (l. 1130); and the Friar in the *Canterbury Tales* laughs at the Wife of

---

[22] *Barbour's 'Bruce'*, ed. M. P. McDiarmid and J. A. C. Stevenson, 3 vols, Scottish Text Society, 4th Series, 12, 13, 15 (1980–5), III 506–34.

[23] It is for this reason that I have excluded weeping from the present study (in the absence of examples of women deliberately 'wetting their cheeks'). I might have excluded laughter also, since it is not always marked by a *voluntas significandi* as clearly as are smiles; for it can be an uncontrolled physical reaction – arising, according to medieval authorities, from the spleen (see *MED splen(e* n. (c) and *OED Spleen* sb. 1c). Yet the texts mostly represent laughter as a deliberately significant act.

[24] *Works*, 669.36–670.2. Elsewhere, Dynadan's jokes make Guinevere and her companion laugh so much 'that they myght nat sytte at their table' (668.26–7). Arthur's fool, Dagonet, makes knights laugh 'as they were wylde' at 588.24.

Bath's 'long preamble' to her tale (III 829). From such condescension it is a short step to actual contempt, as in the expression 'laugh to scorn', quite common in Middle English.[25] In *Piers Plowman*, Love takes a low view of Lady Mede and 'louȝ hire to scorne' (A IV 137). In the French Prose *Lancelot*, a knight laughs as he watches Sir Gawain defending himself against several adversaries whom he describes as 'those cowardly whoresons that cannot overcome this single knight' ('ces filz a putain failliz qui ne puent ce seul chevalier comquerre', 415.3–4). Chaucer's Troilus gives the grandest of scornful laughs, from the spheres after his death, when 'in hymself he lough right at the wo / Of hem that wepten for his deth so faste' (*Troilus* V 1821–2).

There remains a more singular species of laugh, noticed in French by Ménard and found also in English texts. This is the 'prophetic laugh', associated particularly with the Arthurian seer Merlin. After an unnamed knight has failed, in Malory, to handle Balyn's sword, 'than Merlion lowghe. "Why lawghe ye?" seyde the knyght. "Thys ys the cause," seyde Merlion: "there shall never man handyll thys swerde but the beste knyght of the worlde, and that shall be sir Launcelot other ellis Galahad, hys sonne"' (91.25–31). The English poem *Arthour and Merlin* has a sequence of four laughs of this kind, each of them a sign of Merlin's knowledge of 'all that is done on earth and all that will be done', even at the age of only five.[26] He laughs first when he divines that three men have been sent by King Vortigern to find him (l. 1214). Then, as he accompanies them to the king, the child shows his powers with three strange laughs: first, when shoes are being bought by a man who, Merlin knows, will very shortly die (l. 1299); second, when they see a man grieving for his dead son, not knowing that the child's actual father was the priest who is burying him ('swiþe schille and loude he louȝ', l. 1320); and finally, when he sends a message to Vortigern warning him of his wife's treachery ('þo louȝ Merlin þe þridde time', l. 1342).[27] In his discussion of the corresponding laughs in the Vulgate *Merlin* (the English poet's source)

---

[25] *MED laughen* v. 2(e). On biblical laughing to scorn, see M. A. Screech, *Laughter at the Foot of the Cross* (London, 1997).
[26] *Of Arthour and of Merlin*, Auchinleck Ms, ll. 1251–2.
[27] Lewis Thorpe, 'Merlin's Sardonic Laughter', in W. Rothwell *et al.*, eds, *Studies in Medieval Literature and Languages in Memory of Frederick Whitehead* (Manchester, 1973), pp. 323–39; Ménard, *Le rire et le sourire*, pp. 436–9.

and also in Geoffrey of Monmouth's *Vita Merlini*, Lewis Thorpe dubs them 'sardonic'; but they are better described by Ménard, as 'magique', 'divinatoire', and 'prophétique'. They may be touched with scorn for those who do not know, but that is not their primary meaning. Scorn is quite absent in two other examples of such laughter. According to John Gower, the mage Zoroaster laughed the moment he was born as a 'tokne' of his own unhappy end.[28] In Chrétien's *Perceval*, again, a strange damsel, who has not previously laughed for more than six years, laughs when she first sees Perceval, prophesying that he will, if he lives, prove to be the best knight in the world.[29] One might look to anthropologists for an account of such uncanny laughs, whose archaic character sets them apart from everyday expressive behaviour, medieval or modern.[30]

Three terms much favoured by Middle English writers when they notice body-language are *chere*, *countenaunce*, and *semblant*. In English, as in the French from which each is borrowed, the behaviour to which these words refer regularly involves facial expression; but, unlike the modern term 'expression' (first recorded by *OED*, in the relevant sense, as late as 1830), they do not clearly single out the face. Their range of meaning is broader and most often, for a student of NVC, tantalisingly indistinct. *Chere* derives, through French, from the Latin *cara* 'face'. This meaning is found early in Middle English: *OED Cheer* sb., sense 1; *MED chere* n.(1), sense 1; both noting places where the word renders Latin *vultus*. From 'face' the meaning relevant here easily derives: 'The look or expression of the face; countenance, aspect, visage, mien' (*OED*, sense 2). Yet, as the tail of that definition suggests, 'chere' came to refer also to more general features of expressive behaviour. Nor can the word's application to facial expression or to 'mien' always be distinguished from *OED* sense 3: 'Disposition, frame of mind, mood, especially as showing itself by external demeanour, *etc.*'. Equally broad is the range of possible meanings for *countenaunce*. Its primary meaning, as in French, was

---

[28] *Confessio Amantis* VI 2370–1. The editor's note to l. 2368 cites Pliny and Augustine. The latter connects Zoroaster's 'monstrosus risus' with his subsequent invention of the arts of magic: *De Civitate Dei*, Book XXI, Chapter xiv.

[29] Ed. Roach, ll. 1037–48. See Ménard, *Le rire et le sourire*, p. 438.

[30] Merlin might be considered along with those 'ritual jokers' discussed by Mary Douglas, as 'one of those people who pass beyond the bounds of reason and society': *Implicit Meanings: Essays in Anthropology* (London, 1975), p. 108. See also Ménard, *Le rire et le sourire*, pp. 437–8.

'bearing, demeanour, comportment' (*OED*, sense 1), whence it came to denote all kinds of NVC: 'Any indicative or expressive movement, such as a salute, wink, nod, smile, glance, etc.; a sign, gesture, facial expression; also gesturing' (*MED contenaunce* n., sense 4). It was only in the Early Modern period, according to Werner Habicht, that the word began to be restricted in its application, to the expressive face.[31] *Semblant*, again, refers only loosely to varieties of expressive behaviour. It has a primary meaning of a very general kind, 'external appearance' ('seeming'); and its secondary meanings include 'demeanour' (*OED*, sense 1b), as well as 'facial expression, mien; an expression, a look' (*MED*, sense 2(b)).

The frequent use of these terms contributes to the difficulty of finding distinct or interesting representations of facial expression in English and French narratives. Even when writers single out the face or 'visage', they rarely characterise its expression with more than one general epithet. Typical is the 'glad visage' with which a warrior responds to a good omen in Gower's *Confessio* (II 1789). One should not, however, expect too much from medieval narratives, for even modern novelists give only occasional satisfaction. The truth is that the many nuances of facial behaviour, although their varying meanings speak with great clarity to the eye, cannot easily be caught in words at any time. So one has in general to rest content, in the old texts, with such unspecific phrases as 'glad semblant' and 'hevy chiere'. Only rarely does a writer linger even briefly over a play of expression, as in Malory's sketch of Arthur's angry reaction to an insulting message from the emperor of Rome: 'Whan kynge Arthure wyste what they mente he loked up with his gray yghen and angred at the messyngers passyng sore. Than were this messyngers aferde and knelyd stylle and durste nat aryse, they were so aferde of his grymme countenaunce' (185.11–15). It is not difficult, for once, to picture this 'grymme countenaunce'. Occasionally, too, writers will pay some attention to changes of expression. In Chrétien's *Perceval*, Gawain has been angered by his host, and he accordingly sits in his chamber 'a chiere molt dolente et morne' ['with a very sad and gloomy expression', l. 8037]. So a damsel is surprised to find that this previously genial guest has changed 'la parole et la contenance':

---

[31] W. Habicht, 'Zur Bedeutungsgeschichte des englischen Wortes *Countenance*', *Archiv für das Studium der Neueren Sprachen und Literaturen*, 203 (1966), 32–51. On 'contenance' in Chrétien, see Peil, *Gebärde*, pp. 27–8.

> S'aperçoit bien assa samblance
> Qu'il est iriez d'aucune chose,
> Mais samblant fere ne l'en ose.
>
> ['She could well see from his look that he was angry about something, but she did not dare show any sign of knowing', ll. 8046–8.]

This damsel's polite concealment of her surprise at the change in Gawain serves to introduce a matter in which medieval writers did take considerable interest. Faces do not always tell the truth. Their expressions may be designed to carry misleading messages for a variety of reasons, some good and some bad. Once upon a time, according to Gower, 'Of mannes herte the corage / Was schewed thanne in the visage' (*Confessio*, Prologue 111–12); but nowadays relationships between 'herte' and 'visage' prove more uncertain and questionable. The damsel in Chrétien's poem has one of the good reasons for such concealment, for hers is a case of what Erving Goffman calls 'civil inattention', where courtesy requires that a blind eye should be turned. In the scene already referred to in *Cligés*, Guinevere divines from their 'contenance' that Alexander and Soredamors are in love, but she conceals her knowledge, not wishing to distress or embarrass the young people:

> Mes ne lor an vialt feire angoisse,
> Ne fet sanblant qu'ele conoisse
> Rien nule de quanqu'ele voit.
> Bien fist ce que ele devoit,
> Que chiere ne sanblant n'an fist.
>
> ['But she did not wish to cause them pain or give any sign that she understood anything of what she had seen. She did exactly as she ought and gave nothing away by expression or manner', ll. 1581–5.]

In Chrétien's *Yvain*, again, after the hero has been discovered asleep and naked by three ladies and cured by them of his madness, one of them spares his blushes by politely pretending, when they meet, that she has never seen him before:

> Cuidier li fist par tel sanblant,
> Qu'ele de lui rien ne savoit,
> N'onques mes veu ne l'avoit;
> Et san et corteisie fist.

['She led him to believe by her demeanour that she knew nothing of him and had never seen him before, and behaved with good sense and consideration', ll. 3060–3.]

Malory has a charming instance of a similar 'san et corteisie', displayed in this case specifically by direction of gaze. Balyn comes upon a stranger knight sitting under a tree and making moan. He asks what is wrong, but the knight declines to say. Whereupon, 'Balyn went a litill frome hym and loked on hys horse' (86.27–8).[32]

There are a number of good reasons why one's face should on occasion not reflect one's feelings – 'display rules' dictated again, in part at least, by courtesy to others. Manifestations of grief or anxiety are to be suppressed on social occasions. So when Gower's Apollonius, believing his wife to be dead, is royally received by the people of Tharsis,

> thogh he were in his corage
> Desesed, yit with glad visage
> He made hem chiere.
> (VIII 1283–5)

Courteous receptions are among those occasions which demand a 'glad visage', however distressed the 'corage'. The rule applies to hosts as well as guests. In *Ywain and Gawain*, Gawain arrives at a castle oppressed by a murderous giant, but the household labours to show the appropriate 'fair semblant' in his honour:

> But ofttymes changed þaire chere;
> Sum tyme, he saw, þai weped all
> Als þai wold to water fall;
> þai made slike murnyng and slik mane
> þat gretter saw he never nane;
> þai feynyd þam oft for hys sake
> Fayre semblant forto make.
> (ll. 2234–40)

---

[32] The principle of civil inattention may explain a difficulty in Chaucer's *Book of the Duchess*. Why, having overheard the Black Knight plainly lamenting the death of his mistress, does the dreamer there fail to admit his knowledge of the fact in their subsequent conversation? Readers might have understood his behaviour as dictated by civil 'san et corteisie' towards a distressed stranger.

It is not easy to describe behaviours that combine both joy and sorrow, and the medieval poet here resolves the complex into alternations of the two: 'ofttymes changed þaire chere'.

Medieval narratives have many examples of such 'feigning'. People suppress symptoms of sorrow and the like on a variety of occasions, offering instead signs of equanimity or even joy. When Constance, the heroine of Chaucer's Man of Law's Tale, is being shipped off against her will to marry the Sowdan of Syria, she 'peyneth hire to make good contenance' (*Canterbury Tales* II 320). Gower has a similar phrase, applied in this case to kings:

> Of Aristotles lore I finde,
> A king schal make good visage,
> That noman knowe of his corage
> But al honour and worthinesse.[33]

Love-sorrows will often call for such putting on, or 'making', of a good face.[34] Malory's Guinevere conceals her feelings effectively when, after quarrelling with Lancelot and banishing him from court, she preserves a haughty expression: 'So whan sir Launcelot was departed the quene outewarde made no maner of sorow in shewyng... but wyte ye well, inwardely, as the booke seythe, she took grete thought; but she bare it oute with a proude countenaunce, as thoughe she felte no thought nother daungere.'[35] Lovers do not always succeed, however, in 'bearing it out' like this. In *Cligés*, Soredamors tries to conceal her grief for Alexander, whom she supposes dead; but she cannot control her 'contenance' or her 'sanblant':

> Et se nus garde s'an preist,
> A sa contenance veist
> Con grant destrece avoit el cors
> Au sanblant qui paroit defors.

---

[33] *Confessio* VII 3544–7. In Chrétien's *Erec*, the hero shows no semblance of grief for his dead father, since 'diaus de roi n'est mie genz / N'a roi n'avient qu'il face duel' ['it is not polite or fitting for a king to give vent to his grief', ll. 6468–9].

[34] The corresponding French expression was 'bele chiere faire', as in the Prose *Lancelot*, 331.14, 579.36–7, 598.14.

[35] *Works*, 1048.4–10. Compare Guinevere's 'sanblant de passejoie' in *Chevalier de la Charrete*, l. 5201.

['And anyone observing her would have seen from her expression and from other outward signs what great distress she was suffering inwardly', ll. 2093–6.]

Most interesting of all the texts, in this connection, is Chaucer's Clerk's Tale. Following and sometimes going beyond its sources – Petrarch's Latin and the French translation of that – this story pays constant attention to 'chere' and to its varying relationships with feeling and intention. To begin with, the relationship is simple and straightforward. Walter first chooses Griselda for his wife after long observation of her 'chere', in which he reads, quite correctly, 'hir wommanhede / And eek hir virtu' (*Canterbury Tales* IV 237–41). As Petrarch puts it, he penetrates to the inner truth with his sharp gaze: 'acri penetrarat intuitu'.[36] Griselda responds according to her nature, kneeling to Walter with 'sad contenance' (the epithet means 'settled, constant', l. 293) and 'humble cheere' (l. 298). Then it is with 'a ful sobre cheere' that Walter announces his unlikely choice to his followers (l. 366). Yet once Walter, no longer relying on his 'acer intuitus', embarks on his outrageous series of tests, his external behaviour parts company with his intentions and feelings. When he first threatens their daughter, he enters Griselda's bedroom 'with stierne face and with ful trouble cheere' (l. 465, 'turbida fronte' in Petrarch, p. 310); and when he leaves the room, 'Al drery was his cheere and his lookyng', concealing his actual satisfaction at Griselda's response.[37] Keeping up the charade, his servant takes the child 'and gan a cheere make / As though he wolde han slayn it er he wente' (ll. 535–6). So also later, after telling Griselda that her son too must die, Walter assumes a grim expression, while yet rejoicing inwardly at her behaviour: 'And forth he goth with drery contenance, / But to his herte it was ful greet plesance' (ll. 671–2).

Griselda, for her part, suffers the cruellest of assaults on her feelings as a mother (twice) and as a wife; yet the poem persistently asserts that her face and demeanour remained unchanged. She 'noght ameved / Neither in word, or chiere, or contenaunce' (ll. 498–9); and so in Petrarch, she is 'nec verbo mota, nec vultu' ['unmoved either in word or face', p. 312].

[36] Cited from Bryan and Dempster, *Sources and Analogues*, p. 302. Quotations from the French translation are taken from the same.
[37] He is 'glad' (l. 512), and, in Petrarch, 'letus... sed dissimulans visu mestus' ['happy, but assuming sorrow in his look', p. 312].

This extraordinary claim is repeated throughout, much as in the Latin and French sources. Griselda gives up her daughter 'with ful sad face' (l. 552, where the epithet renders 'tranquilla' in Petrarch, p. 312), and she suffers that loss with 'cheere' and 'word' unaltered (ll. 598–602).[38] When she has to give up her son, 'she no chiere maade of hevynesse' (l. 678), and endures this second loss 'with sad visage':

> He waiteth if by word or contenance
> That she to hym was changed of corage,
> But nevere koude he fynde variance.
> (708–10)

Finally, when rejected as a wife, she once more gives no sign of distress, 'neither by hire wordes ne hire face' (l. 920), preserving her 'glad visage' and welcoming the supposed new bride with 'glad cheere' (949, 1013, 1016, 1045). What is the reader to make of such insistence? Surely her behaviour, like Walter's, must be belying her inner feelings. Yet the poem resolutely sets its face against any such conclusion. It asserts that 'she was ay oon in herte and in visage' (l. 711). What the unchanging 'visage' shows is, in her case, truly what the heart constantly feels. Chaucer even cuts out the one place where Petrarch and his French translator both distinctly suggest the contrary. Where Chaucer says simply 'she no chiere maade of hevynesse' (l. 678), Petrarch has 'illa eodem quo semper vultu, qualicunque animo . . .', that is, 'she with the same countenance as ever, whatever she may have thought . . .' (p. 316). The French draws out the implication of that last phrase: 'elle respondy de bonne chiere, ja fust ce que bien estoit courroucee en cuer', that is, 'she replied with an untroubled face, even though she was surely angered at heart' (p. 317). It seems then that Chaucer, or his Clerk, means us to take seriously his heroine's claim: 'naught greveth me at al, / Though that my doughter and my sone be slayn' (ll. 647–8). Such impassivity could be understood, if at all, only were one prepared to grant the even more extraordinary claim made elsewhere, that Walter and Griselda share one single will (which is, of course, Walter's):

---

[38] Here Petrarch has: 'Valterius interea, sepe vultum coniugis ac verba considerans, nullum unquam mutati animi perpendit indicium' ['Walter meanwhile, always alert to his wife's face and words, saw no sign at all of any change in her mind', p. 314]. The French expands the customary coupling of *vultus* and *verba* here to 'la chiere, les parolles, le semblant, et le maintien' (p. 315).

> For which it semed thus: that of hem two
> Ther nas but o wyl, for as Walter leste,
> The same lust was hire plesance also.
> (715–17)

So also Petrarch: 'duorum non nisi unus animus videretur' ['there seemed to be but a single mind in the two of them', p. 318]. What we are offered, it would seem, is an extreme and absolute example of the virtue for which Griselda stands, patience. For patience was held to require much more than control of external behaviours. It involved, according to the most demanding interpretations, complete control over the will, a radical redirection of one's innermost feelings and wishes.[39] So it seems that readers are invited to believe that Griselda really does, inwardly as well as outwardly, go along with all that her husband demands of her. Her 'visage' does not belie her 'herte'.

The strangeness of the Clerk's story makes it hard to know what to think about Walter; but there are many clearer cases in the texts where such behaviour is condemned as hypocrisy, treachery, or deceit. Lying is not confined to the tongue. In his treatise *Destructorium Viciorum*, the fourteenth-century moralist Alexander Carpenter has a section on lying, *mendacium*, in which he takes a broad view of human communication, following and citing Augustine's discussion of signs in the *De Doctrina*. He is concerned with 'every sign, however it may be produced, by which truth or falsehood may be conveyed' ('omne signum quo signari potest verum vel falsum quocunque modo fiat'). So Carpenter can speak of lying in NVC: 'ille qui intendit significare aliquod falsum nutibus non est immunis a mendacio', that is, 'one who sets out to convey a falsehood by bodily signs is guilty of lying'.[40] A modern expert on NVC makes a similar observation, referring specifically to the face: 'The face appears

---

[39] As another poet points out, patience requires one to 'steer the heart': *Patience*, in *The Poems of the Pearl Manuscript*, ed. M. Andrew and R. Waldron (London, 1978), l. 27. Cf. Proverbs 16.32: 'The patient man is better than the valiant: and he that ruleth his spirit [*dominatur animo suo*] than he that taketh cities.'

[40] Alexander Carpenter, *Destructorium Viciorum* (Paris, 1516), fol. eii, referred to by E. D. Craun, *Lies, Slander, and Obscenity in Medieval English Literature* (Cambridge, 1997), p. 39. Augustine, cited by Craun, sanctions this extended notion of lying: 'a person is lying when he thinks one thing and expresses another, either in words or by any other kind of signifying': *De Mendacio*, in *Corpus Scriptorum Ecclesiasticorum Latinorum*, Vol. XLI (1900), p. 415 (my translation).

to be the most skilled nonverbal communicator and perhaps for that reason the best "nonverbal liar", capable not only of withholding information but of simulating the facial behaviour associated with a feeling which the person in no way is experiencing.'[41] Such parallels between verbal and non-verbal communication would not have seemed strange in a period when 'word' and 'chere' were so commonly coupled together; and Middle English does, in fact, on occasion apply the term 'lie' to non-verbal signals. In Laȝamon's *Brut*, the treacherous Vortigern pretends to be grieved by the decapitation of King Constance:

> þa Vortiger þis hæved isæh, þa hælde he to grunde ful neh,
> Swulc he hafvede mod-kare, mest of alre monne;
> Mid his lechen he gon liȝen, his heorte wes ful bliþe.
>
> ['When Vortigern saw this head, he bent almost to the ground as if he were suffering the greatest of sorrows; with his looks he was lying, for his heart was full of joy'.][42]

In *Guy of Warwick*, again, a lady is conducted to a treacherous appointment by a man 'wiþ leyȝeand cher'.[43] Gower's Amans, on the other hand, can deny that he has ever misled his mistress by 'feigned chiere': 'God wot wel there I lye noght, / My chiere hath be such as my thoght' (1 725–6).

'Non-verbal liars' may be represented, as a general type, by Falssemblant in Gower's *Confessio Amantis*:

> For whan his semblant is most clier,
> Thanne is he most derk in his thoght,
> Thogh men him se, they knowe him noght;
> Bot as it scheweth in the glas
> Thing which therinne nevere was,
> So scheweth it in his visage
> That nevere was in his corage.
> (II 1918–24)

---

[41] Ekman, Friesen, and Ellsworth, *Emotion in the Human Face*, p. 23.
[42] Laȝamon, *Brut*, ed. G. L. Brook and R. F. Leslie, EETS, 250, 277 (1963, 1978), Caligula Ms, ll. 6836–8. For 'lechen', see *MED leches* n. pl. The passage is referred to by Habicht, *Gebärde*, in his discussion of Vortigern as an instance of 'gesture as deceit' (pp. 63–8).
[43] Ed. J. Zupitza, EETS, E.S. 42, 49, 59 (1883–91), Auchinleck Ms, l. 5632. In Bokenham's *Legendys of Hooly Wummen*, a cruel pagan officer addresses a saint 'wyth chere symulat, / And half smylyng as hym had lyst to playe': ed. M. S. Serjeantson, EETS, 206 (1938), ll. 3678–9.

Like a mirror, the face of Falssemblant has things in it which are not really there – not in the heart, that is. Gower's favourite rhyming contrast between 'visage' and 'corage' figures again in his description of a typical villain, the False Bachelor, who

> thoghte more than he seide,
> And feigneth with a fals visage
> That he was glad, but his corage
> Was al set in an other wise.
> (II 2670–3)

Non-verbal (as well as verbal) lying is a particular speciality of lovers. Among those who help the lover in his quest for the rose in the *Roman de la Rose* is Faus Semblant: 'La chiere ot mout simple et piteuse, / Ne regardeure orgueilleuse / N'ot il pas, mes douce et pesible' ['He has a very honest and sympathetic countenance, with no proud looks, but all sweet and docile'].[44] The function of Faus Semblant in the *Rose* is to deceive Male Bouche or 'malicious talk' (Wicked Tongue in the English version); and deceit of this kind, practised on others by lovers such as Troilus or Lancelot in the interests of secrecy, commonly passes without criticism in romances.[45] Deceit practised by false lovers on their ladies is quite another matter, condemned by writers of all kinds. In his section devoted to *Ipocrisis* in the *Confessio*, Gower passes straight from the hypocrisy of churchmen to that of lovers, 'que sub amoris facie fraudulenter latitando mulieres ipsius ficticiis credulas sepissime decipit innocentes' ['which, lurking deceitfully under a face of love, very often deceives credulous and innocent women with its lies'].[46] Lovers of this kind 'feignen hem an humble port' (I 674) and employ 'fals pitous lokynge' as well as softspoken lies (I 679–80). Chaucer's *Legend of Good Woman* has several such. Theseus deceives Ariadne with 'his hertely wordes and his chere' (ll. 2124); and Jason is addressed as 'the root of false lovers':

---

[44] *Le Roman de la Rose*, ed. Lecoy, ll. 12055–7. Faus Semblant is elsewhere referred to as a robber 'who has the face of treachery, white without and black within' (ll. 11982–3).

[45] Perhaps it is for this reason that Jean de Meun has Faus Semblant speak of himself chiefly as a hypocrite not in love but in religion – like his descendants, Chaucer's Friar and Pardoner.

[46] Sidenote to I 672. The case of Diomede in Chaucer's *Troilus* is referred to below, pp. 132–3.

> Thow madest thy recleymyng and thy lures
> To ladyes of thy statly aparaunce,
> And of thy wordes farced with plesaunce,
> And of thy feyned trouthe and thy manere,
> With thy obesaunce and humble cheere,
> And with thy contrefeted peyne and wo.
> (1371–6)

Such men ensnare women, not only by words, but also by 'aparaunce', 'manere', and 'cheere'.

'Ut imago est animi vultus sic indices oculi': 'As the face is the image of the soul, so are the eyes its interpreters.'[47] Although eyes play a big part in facial expressions, they also have their own distinctive functions as *indices animi*. Modern students of NVC devote considerable attention to what they call visual interaction, or simply 'gaze':

> Gaze is perhaps the most deceptively simple nonverbal signal, but one which arouses a complexity of responses, depending on the context and perhaps on subtle differences in the type of look. No other human signal can be so closely associated with both positive and negative feelings. It acts as an affective signal for both dominance and affiliation.[48]

Gaze has the special capacity to single out a particular object, and those who find themselves the object of another's gaze commonly wonder what it may mean. Speaking looks of this kind get recorded quite frequently in medieval texts. One may guess that writers were encouraged to think of the eye as an active communicator in part by the classical theory of optics, still current at the time. This theory held that sight depended on visual rays emitted by the eye itself and striking the object seen: 'The lookynge, by castynge of his bemys, waiteth and seeth fro afer al the body togidre.'[49] Although the modern view of the eye as a passive receptor of

---

[47] Cicero's *Orator*, ed. and transl. H. M. Hubbell (Cambridge, Mass., 1942), xviii 60.
[48] Weitz, 'Facial Expression and Visual Interaction', p. 33. See also Argyle, *Bodily Communication*, Chapter 10, and M. Argyle and M. Cook, *Gaze and Mutual Gaze* (Cambridge, 1976), especially Chapter 3, 'Gaze as a Signal for Interpersonal Attitudes and Emotions'.
[49] Chaucer's *Boece*, Book v, Prosa 4, ll. 145–7, rendering the Latin, 'Ille [i.e. visus] eminus manens totum simul iactis radiis intuetur.'

Gestures and looks in medieval narrative

beams of light had already emerged (in tenth-century Cairo, we are told), the older theory of the beam of sight (*radius visibilis*) still held the field.[50]

Men and women in love are among those who have particular occasion to communicate by glance or gaze. This is 'the language of the eyes'.[51] From the point of view of a moralist, such love-looks are nothing but provocations to sin. In *Piers Plowman*, the Lordship of Lechery deals in 'werkes and in wordes and waityng with ei3es'.[52] Most other writers, though, take gaze to be a necessary and proper activity in amorous relations: Sweet Looking is a close companion of the God of Love in the *Roman de la Rose*. In his account of the astronomical love-affair between Mars and Venus, Chaucer describes how the two planet-gods were 'knyt and regnen as in hevene / Be lokyng moost', where the word 'lokyng' cleverly combines references to both astrological aspect and amorous glances.[53] This is 'le message des ialz' of which Chrétien speaks in his *Erec et Enide* (l. 2041). In Thomas Usk's *Testament of Love*, Love advises the narrator 'to wete by a loke evermore what she meneth'.[54] Only Charles d'Orléans – surprisingly enough – expresses doubts about the reliability of such knowledge. In one of his balades, which takes the form of a dialogue between himself and his love for a lady, Charles responds with scepticism to love's optimistic reading of a recent 'praty look'. It

---

[50] See G. Simon, *Le regard, l'être et l'apparence dans l'optique de l'antiquité* (Paris, 1988). Euclidean optics were still current in the sixteenth century, proving that 'l'interprétation fondée sur l'émission de rayons visuels continuait à représenter une alternative crédible' (p. 59). The encyclopaedic poem *Sidrak and Bokkus* speaks of 'beemes of þe sight / þat upon þat þing shal alight / þat be seen shal': ed. T. L. Burton, EETS, 311, 312 (1998–9), Lansdowne Ms, ll. 8395–7. For further examples, see *MED*, *bem* n. 10(b) and *sight(e* n. 1 (e).

[51] See Habicht, *Gebärde*, pp. 105–13, for further discussion of love-behaviours in Middle English texts.

[52] B II 90. Later, Hawkin's coat is soiled with 'likynge of lecherie as by lokynge of his ei3e. / For ech a maide þat he mette he made hire a signe / Semynge to synneward', B XIII 343–5. For other examples, see *MED loking(e* ger., in senses 1 a(a) and (b). In Isaiah 3.16, the dissolute daughters of Sion 'walked with stretched out necks and wanton glances of their eyes [*nutibus oculorum*]'.

[53] *Romaunt of the Rose*, l. 920 ('Douz Regart' in the French, l. 906); *Complaint of Mars*, ll. 50–1.

[54] Ed. W. W. Skeat in *Chaucerian and other Pieces* (Oxford, 1897), Book III, Chapter vii, ll. 63–4. The lover in Machaut's *Jugement du Roy de Behaigne* reads his lady's sweet parting look: 'ses regars me disoit vraiement: / "Amis, je t'aim tres amoureusement"': *Le Jugement du Roy de Behaigne and Remede de Fortune*, ed. and transl. J. I. Wimsatt and W. W. Kibler (Athens, Georgia, 1988), ll. 558–9.

Looks

is folly, he objects, to trust the evidence of looks or expressions: 'For countenaunce or lookis of hir face / Knowist thou hir thouȝt?'[55]

It is when they are communicating by looks that lovers in romance show themselves most wincingly sensitive. Men anxiously read their ladies' faces. In the fifteenth-century poem *The Isle of Ladies*, a lover takes comfort from the silent smile of his beloved, 'For as I thowght that smylinge sygne / Was token that the hart inclyne / Wold to request reasnable'. Yet he cannot help worrying, because 'wordeles answere in no toune / Was tane for obligacyon, / Ne cauled sewertye, in no wyse', evidently recalling the disputes of lawyers about the binding force of wordless signs.[56] Since the meaning of looks can always be disavowed, lovers may on occasion resort to them for fear of the rebuff which outright speech might provoke. So it is with the hero and heroine of *Cligés*, at a stage in their relationship when each fears to be rejected by the other:

> Des ialz parolent par esgart,
> Mes des boches sont si coart
> Que de l'amor qui les justise
> N'osent parler an nule guise.
>
> ['They speak with looks of their eyes, but they are so nervous about their mouths that they dare not speak at all of the love which has them in thrall', ll. 3789–92.]

When in the Prose *Lancelot* Lancelot first sees Guinevere, he hardly dare return her gaze, let alone speak: 'La reine regarde lo vallet mout durement, et il li, totes les foiz qu'il puet vers li ses iauz mener covertement' ['The queen looked very hard at the young man, and he at her, whenever he could turn his eyes unobtrusively in her direction', 157.23–4]. When on the same occasion he takes his leave of her, his gaze wavers most expressively: 'il s'agenoille devant li, si la regarde mout debonairement tant com il ose. Et qant vergoigne lo sorvaint, si fiche vers terre ses iauz, toz esbahiz' ['he kneels before her and looks at her with a very good grace, so far as he dares. But when shame overcomes him, he fixes his eyes on the ground, quite overwhelmed', 164.28–30]. It is not only Guinevere's

---

[55] Ed. Arn, ll. 366–71.
[56] *The Isle of Ladies, or The Ile of Pleasaunce*, ed. A. Jenkins (New York, 1980), ll. 883–5, 889–91. For the lawyers' disputes, see Screech in his *Rabelais*, cited in n. 195 to Chapter 2 above.

beauty that Lancelot has to fear. Much later in their relationship, when he has offended her by a momentary reluctance to come to her rescue riding in an unknightly 'charrete' or cart, Chrétien describes how she punishes him by withholding both her greeting and her gaze: 'fet sanblant de correciee, / Si s'anbruncha et ne dist mot' ['she gave an angry look, lowered her head, and said nothing', *Chevalier de la Charrete*, ll. 3940–1]. Later, the queen reproaches herself for the 'two blows' that she struck on that occasion: 'Quant mon esgart et ma parole / Li veai, ne fis je que fole?' ['when I denied him my look and my word, did I not act foolishly?', ll. 4201–2]. 'Esgart' ranks with 'parole' here; and when the lovers again meet, Guinevere is pointedly said not to have refused her look: 'Lors ne lessa mie cheoir / La reine ses ialz vers terre' ['On that occasion the queen by no means let her eyes turn towards the ground', ll. 4460–1]. Withholding a look was a serious signal. Dante gives a very highly strung account of such an occasion in Chapters X–XII of his *Vita Nuova*. Beatrice denies him her 'most sweet salutation', and he is plunged into terrible grief.[57] In the *Remede de Fortune* of Guillaume de Machaut, similarly, the lover says that he almost died when his lady turned her eyes away from him:

> Car de semblant et de maniere,
> De cuer, de regart, et de chiere
> Qu'amis doit recevoir d'amie,
> Me fu vis qu'elle estoit changie.

> ['for I thought that the appearance and demeanour, the affection, look and expression that a lover deserves from his lady had changed'.][58]

In Malory's *Morte Darthur* it is Gareth and Lyones who are most often shown to communicate by the language of the eyes. When Gareth first arrives to relieve the besieged Lyones, he is struck by her beauty as she sits at her castle window: 'And ever he loked up to the wyndow with glad countenaunce, and this lady dame Lyones made curtesy to hym downe to the erth, holdynge up both her hondys' (321.30–2). Her appearance and her gestures are enough for him to fall instantly in love; and they exchange speaking looks shortly after, during a break in the

[57] *Le opere di Dante*, ed. M. Barbi et al., 2nd edn (Florence, 1960). Chapter XI makes it clear that the salutation was by eye alone.
[58] Ed. Wimsatt and Kibler, ll. 4151–4. Cf. ll. 721–30.

battle between Gareth (Bewmaynes) and the lady's besieger: 'And than sir Bewmaynes, whan his helme was off, he loked up to the wyndowe, and there he sawe the fayre lady dame Lyones, and she made hym suche countenaunce that his herte waxed lyght and joly' (323.31–5). Later, when they meet face to face, 'they had goodly langage and lovely countenaunce' (331.18–19); and they are finally reunited with 'many a goodly loke and goodly wordys, that all men of worshyp had joy to beholde them' (359.21–2).

Gareth and Lyones have nothing to hide, and their goodly looks are there for all to admire. It is, however, most often for fear of discovery by others that lovers resort to looks. No doubt this is what Boncampagno da Signa had in mind when he included 'amatores qui loqui non audent' among those who employ signs rather than words.[59] Even whispered words may be overheard; but gazes, and better still glances, can more easily be exchanged in secrecy. A courtly poem in the fifteenth-century Fairfax Manuscript, 'The Ten Commandments of Love', devotes the fifth of its commandments to secrecy:

> Secretly behave you in your werkes,
>   In shewing countenance or meving of yur iye;
> Though soche behavor to some folke be darke,
>   He that hath loved woll it sone aspie.[60]

The most common purpose of such significant face- and eye-movement is to escape the attentions of malicious gossip. An Anglo-Norman prose text says that love, having originated in the heart, is 'conveyed by the eye, without evil-speakers knowing'.[61] Gower describes a jealous husband who has a spy, a 'janglere, an evel mouthed oon', to keep watch on his wife, so that she can neither 'speke a word, ne ones loke' without being maligned (*Confessio* v 519–23). Elsewhere in the *Confessio*, Danger guards a lady so strictly that 'The leste lokynge of hire yhe / Mai noght be stole, if he it syhe' (v 6625–6). The 'least looking of an eye' represents

---

[59] See above, p. 64.
[60] Ed. Robbins in *Secular Lyrics of the XIVth and XVth Centuries*, no. 177, ll. 43–6.
[61] 'Conveyee de l'oiel santz savoir de medisantz': cited from C. B. West, *Courtoisie in Anglo-Norman Literature* (Oxford, 1938), p. 141. In his *Siege of Thebes*, Lydgate describes festivities at which 'The touches stole and the amerous lookes / By sotyl craft leyd oute lyne and hokes, / The Ialous folk to trayssshen and begyle / In their awayt with many sondry wile': ed. A. Erdmann, EETS, E.S. 108 (1911), ll. 1669–72.

communication near an absolute minimum – yet even this, evidently, a hostile observer may be able to spot.

Among the occasions where such looks might be cast, according to Gower's Confessor, was a church service. Genius condemns this behaviour as a sacrilege of lovers (v 7032ff.). A poem by Humfrey Newton (d. 1536) describes how his true love, sitting in church with an older woman, often stole him some looks under pretence of smiling at her companion, and also how, kneeling in prayer, 'yet ones or twyes at the lest, / Sho did on me her ee kest.'[62] A more common context was the dance or the feast. It is on such social occasions that Gower's jealous husband keeps a sharp eye out for any furtive signalling:

> Wher that sche singe or that sche dance,
> He seth the leste contienance,
> If sche loke on a man aside
> Or with him roune at eny tyde,
> Or that sche lawghe, or that sche loure,
> His yhe is ther at every houre.
> (v 475–80)

Sidelong glances, along with whispers, laughs and frowns, here make up the expressive behaviour or 'contienance' of a flirtatious wife. The occasion is similar to the dance at the court of King Cambyuskan described by Chaucer's Squire:

> Who koude telle yow the forme of daunces
> So unkouthe, and swiche fresshe contenaunces,
> Swich subtil lookyng and dissymulynges
> For drede of jalouse mennes aperceyvynges?
> No man but Launcelot, and he is deed.
> (*Canterbury Tales* v 283–7)

Such dissimulation by 'fresshe contenaunces' and 'subtil lookyng' calls to mind Lancelot's conduct of his affair with Guinevere. Somewhat similar again is Chaucer's description in the *Legend of Good Women* of the feast at which Dido entertains Aeneas, an occasion marked by 'many an amorous lokyng and devys'.[63]

---

[62] Robbins, *Secular Lyrics*, no. 194, ll. 9–10, 17–18.
[63] *Legend of Good Woman*, l. 1102. In the early sixteenth-century romance *Clariodus*, a banquet is accompanied with 'secreit blenkis and inwart beholding, / With smyllyng

Amorous looking at dinner parties was a sufficiently familiar motif for the author of *Sir Gawain and the Green Knight* to make it the subject of a quick and amusing allusion (below, p. 149). A full-scale treatment may be found in the Anglo-Norman romance *Ipomedon*, composed by Hue de Rotelande in the twelfth century, and in the Middle English version known as *Ipomadon A*.[64] Hue devotes as many as 10,580 lines to the adventures of young Ipomedon in his love for La Fiere (the Proud One), ending with their marriage; and the early fifteenth-century English version follows at almost equal length. It is at a dinner that the two principals first exchange significant looks:

> La damaisele cele part,
> Coment qe seit, feit meint regard;
> Mes qe folie ne pensast,
> Bien li fust qe la regardast.
> A une foiz issi ala
> Qe la Fiere mult l'avisa,
> E li meschin regarda li
> Si qe nul d'eus le oil ne flechi,
> Mult se entregardent longement.
> Li vallet veit qe doucement
> L'ad regardé e de bon oil.

['However, the lady gave many a look in that direction, for, although she had nothing foolish in mind, she would have been pleased if he had looked at her. So it happened one time, when she was gazing attentively at him, that the young man looked at her, and neither of them turned their eyes away but went on exchanging looks for a long time. The youth saw that she had been looking at him affectionately and with a friendly eye', ll. 769–79.]

The English version renders these lines in a twelve-line stanza.[65] It follows the French quite closely, but spells out the amorous nature of the glances more explicitly ('love lokynge', 'lovely loke') and makes it clear that both parties understood the message: Ipomadon 'ful wele understode', and the lady 'ful well undertoke'. The English poet also

---

loukis full of cherising': ed. D. Irving, Maitland Club, 9 (Edinburgh, 1830), Book II, ll. 1863–4 (kindly pointed out to me by Dr Purdie).
[64] For the French, see *Ipomedon: Poème de Hue de Rotelande*, ed. Holden; the English *Ipomadon* (known as *Ipomadon A*), ed. Purdie.
[65] Lines 809–20 in the EETS edition.

completes his tail-rhyme stanza by adding the customary explanation for such behaviour: fear of slanderous talk.

Hue goes on to describe further looks on the same occasion, citing the common proverb that 'the eye goes quickly to what one loves, and the finger to a painful place' (ll. 799–800); but the translator has had enough and misses this whole section out. By the end of the dinner La Fiere is in love, yet she is also mortified that Ipomedon, a mere 'vallet', should see her so affected. She conveys her anger obliquely, employing a trick or device – what the French calls a 'qeintise' and the English a 'wyle'. She looks indignantly, not at Ipomedon, but at her nephew Jason, accusing the latter of presuming to make eyes at her damsel Ismeine: 'La Fiere garde de mal oil / Son neveu par mult grant orgoil, / Par mult fiere regardeüre' ['The Proud One gave her nephew a black look, in a very haughty fashion and with a very severe gaze', ll. 861–3]. Her look is deliberately misdirected by this very artful lady; but the hero, understanding that it is meant for him, responds by lowering the head and withdrawing his offending gaze: 'on hur durste he loke no more' (l. 879). The whole scene, in the French especially, registers very fully the part played by looks, direct and indirect, in exchanges between lovers committed, like these, to the conventions of what the English poem calls 'derne love', secret love (l. 797).

It is not only lovers, however, who employ 'the language of the eyes'. People under a variety of other circumstances may express anger, scorn and the like by averting their eyes or looking askance. In the Prose *Lancelot*, Arthur in his anger at Guinevere greets all the knights of her company, 'mais il ne regarda onques la reine' ['but he never looked at the queen at all', 598.4–5]. In the English stanzaic *Morte Arthur*, again, where Guinevere stands accused of poisoning a knight, she appeals for support to Sir Bors, but he angrily refuses to meet her gaze: 'Bors de Gawnes stille stode / And wrothe away hys yȝen wente'.[66] To look at someone askance – 'en travers', or 'aside' – has similar hostile significance. The Latin *invidere* has the sense 'to look askance at', hence 'to regard with ill will or envy'; and this etymological association with obliquity of gaze survives in medieval treatments of envy. So in the

---

[66] *Le Morte Arthur*, ed. Bruce, ll. 1348–9. Gower's Cupid 'with yhen wrothe / His chiere aweiward fro me caste' (*Confessio* I 140–1).

Romaunt of the Rose, Envy 'hadde a wonderful lokyng, / For she ne lokide but awry / Or overthwart, all baggyngly'.[67] In the Prose *Lancelot*, when Lancelot is greeted by an enemy, 'cil lo regarde an travers, si li a randu son salu a mout grant paine' ['he looked at him askance, and returned his greeting with very great reluctance', 320.24–5]; and later in the same work, Hector responds to an unwelcome approach in the same way: 'li chevaliers lo regarde an travers et mout li anuie' ['the knight looked at him askance, much annoyed', 369.8].[68] A milder form of snub is conveyed by the Black Knight in Chaucer's *Book of the Duchess*, responding to the dreamer's request to learn about his sorrows: 'With that he loked on me asyde, / As who sayth, "Nay, that wol not be"' (ll. 558–9). Here a verbal gloss confirms the negative force of the knight's sidelong look.

Gaze plays its part, along with other non-verbal signals, in the tense exchanges between the men of Ghent and their angry overlord, as described by Froissart in an episode already referred to (above, pp. 18–19). The count of Flanders has been at war with certain Flemish cities, and especially with Ghent; but an uneasy peace has been agreed, and the count reluctantly consents to pay Ghent a visit of reconciliation. Early in his journey he is met by a welcoming party of citizens, bowing to him deeply; but the count responds coldly: 'Li contes chevaucha tout droit oultre, sans euls regarder, et mist un petit sa main à son cappel, ne onques sus tout le chemin il ne fist samblant de parler à eulx' ['The count rode straight on through without looking at them, touching his hat just a little and giving no sign of wanting to speak to them throughout the whole journey'].[69] The very slight acknowledgement of their presence, raising his hand 'a little' to his hat, is quite outweighed by the count's prolonged silence and by his pointed refusal to look at his welcomers. The next day, as he enters the town's market-place for a public meeting, the count singles out his particular enemies, the radical 'White Hats', with his gaze: 'Li contes, en fendant le marchiet, jettoit communement

---

[67] Lines 290–2. In the French: 'avoit trop laide esgardeure; / Ele ne regardast neant / Fors en travers, em bornant' (ll. 280–82). See *MED asquint* adv., and *askoin*.

[68] Elsewhere in the Prose *Lancelot*, Lanbegues, surrendering to his enemy King Claudas, 'ne mot ne dist, n'onques lo roi ne regarda de droit enmi lo vis, mais del travers' ['said not a word, nor looked the king straight in the face, but askance', 127.35–6].

[69] *Chroniques*, Vol. IX, ed. G. Raynaud (Paris, 1894), p. 212 (Book II, Section 127).

Gestures and looks in medieval narrative

ses ieulx sus ces blans capprons qui se mettoient en sa presence' ['The count, as he crossed the market-place, kept shooting looks at those of the White Hats who appeared before him'].[70] When he leaves at the end of the meeting, the White Hats respond by refusing to bow and by glaring at him: 'Quant li contes passa parmi iaulx, il s'ouvrirent, mais fellement le regardèrent, che li sambla, et ne le daignèrent onques encliner, dont il fu mout merancolieus' ['When the count passed among them, they made way for him; but they looked fiercely at him, as it seemed to him, and did not deign ever to bow to him, at which he was very angry'].[71] No wonder the count was angry. The challenging looks, coupled with the refusal to bow, presented a wordless public affront to his authority.

The White Hats' stare illustrates another function of gaze; for it can, in certain circumstances, be rude and provocative to fix one's eyes too long or too hard on someone else's face. Malory describes how Balyn, when he encounters Garlon, 'avised hym longe', whereupon 'thys Garlon aspyed that Balyn vysaged hym, and so he com and slapped hym on the face with the backe of hys honde and seyde, "Knyght, why beholdist thou me so?"'[72] The backhand slap is a violent response to an offence, here called 'visaging', which would still be recognised today. As a social psychologist observes: 'Sometimes people stare at strangers in a hostile or threatening way. The "hate stare" once used by whites towards blacks in the southern states is an example... Prolonged staring in public places, between strangers, is found threatening'.[73] In primates, we are told, 'gaze is related to dominance'.[74] So protracted staring, where no dominance can be admitted, gives offence. The case is somewhat different, however, where the starer has a valid claim to the upper hand: gods and personifications have every right to stare down at people. In Skelton's *Bowge of Courte*, the narrator describes how he was treated by the stand-offish Daunger:

---

[70] Ibid., p. 216.
[71] Ibid., p. 217. In *Guy of Warwick*, the hostile Duke Berard 'Stared on Gij as he wer wode, / And egrelich seyd his þou3t': Auchinleck Ms, stanza 178, ll. 2–3.
[72] *Works*, 84.9–12. See *MED visagen* v. (a) and (b).
[73] Argyle, *Bodily Communication*, p. 165. See also Argyle and Cook, *Gaze and Mutual Gaze*, pp. 74–5, 92–3.
[74] Argyle and Cook, *Gaze*, p. 75. See also Argyle, *Bodily Communication*, p. 164.

Looks

> And with that worde, on me she gave a glome
> With browes bente, and gan on me to stare
> Full daynnously, and fro me she dyde fare.[75]

Daunger here behaves like a lady of the court, haughtily visaging a timorous outsider. Another great lady, the goddess Venus, treats a narrator more subtly, but with equal condescension. Reappearing at the end of *Confessio Amantis* after Amans has completed his confession, Venus finds him on his knees, praying for her favour. She responds by gazing into his face:

> Sche caste hire chiere upon mi face,
> And as it were halvinge a game
> Sche axeth me what is mi name.
> (VIII 2318–20)

'Halvinge a game' ('half in jest') marks both the look and the words as equivocal; and there is a similar characterisation later when Venus gives Amans a long look before explaining that he is too old for love: 'For whan sche hath me wel beholde, / Halvynge of scorn, sche seide thus ...' (VIII 2396–7). Finally, after Amans has been cured of his love-sickness, the goddess looks at him with a laugh and asks one more teasing question:

> Venus behield me than and lowh,
> And axeth, as it were in game,
> What love was.
> (VIII 2870–2)

Amans no longer knows the answer. There is a somewhat similar moment in the passage from *Piers Plowman* referred to earlier, where Lewty both laughs at Will and 'looks on him hard' (above, p. 73); but such playfulness is not generally to be looked for in Langland's allegorical powers. Dame Study responds angrily to her husband with a dark stare, 'al starynge dame Studie sterneliche seide' (B X 4); and Piers Plowman checks Will's curiosity about the Trinity with a severe look: 'And egreliche he loked on me and þerfore I spared / To asken hym any more þerof.'[76]

---

[75] Ed. Scattergood, ll. 80–2.
[76] B XVI 64–5. See *MED egreli* adv. for the sense 'sharply' or 'severely'.

Gestures and looks in medieval narrative

There are also eye-gestures (*Blickgebärden* in German) which serve, like pointing with the finger, to single something out for the attention of another. Langland's Wit does this, in an amusing passage, once his wife Study has come to the end of an angry speech:

> And whan þat Wit was ywar how his wif tolde
> He bicom so confus he kouþe noȝt mele,
> And as doumb as a dore drouȝ hym aside.
> Ac for no carpyng I kouþe, ne knelyng to þe grounde,
> I myȝte gete no greyn of his grete wittes,
> But al lauȝynge he louted and loked upon Studie
> In signe þat I sholde bisechen hire of grace.
> (B X 140–6)

With some ironical deference to his wife, Wit conveys his withdrawal from the discussion entirely by dumbshow. He steps back, laughs, bows, and directs Will's further enquiries to Study with a look. Will reads this last 'sign', and transfers his attention accordingly to her. French writers use the expression *mostrer a l'uel* ('show with the eye') of this kind of deictic look. In the Prose *Lancelot*, when Guinevere singles out the Dame de Malohaut for the attention of Galehot, she points her out with a glance ('la li mostre a l'uel', 353.22); and in Chrétien's *Chevalier de la Charrete*, she uses her eyes to identify the particular window at which she and Lancelot may later talk: 'Et la reine une fenestre / Li mostre, a l'uel, non mie au doi' ['And the queen indicated a window to him, with her eye not her finger', ll. 4506–7]. As the poem here implies, to look is more polite, and certainly more discreet, than to point.[77] Such looks can also prompt action more directly. In the twelfth-century chanson de geste *Le Moniage Guillaume*, the hero, wishing to repay the hospitality of a townsman who has entertained him to dinner, directs a look at his servant, who is carrying their purse: 'Li quens Guillaumes a son fame esgardé; / Cil sot tantost que il ot en pensé' ['Count William looked towards his man, and he knew immediately what he had in mind'].[78] In

---

[77] For rulings against pointing in the courtesy books, see above, p. 60. In Metham's *Amoryus and Cleopes*, a less discreet heroine draws the hero's attention to a significant picture in a book 'with chere and fynger' (l. 834): 'sche a-purpose made with her fynger demonstracion / Askauns, Constrwe now, for off my menyng this ys the entencion': ed. H. Craig in *The Works of John Metham*, EETS, 132 (1916), ll. 826–7.

[78] Ed. W. Cloetta, 2 vols. (Paris, 1906, 1911), Second Version, ll. 1078–9.

the dinner scene in *Piers Plowman*, again, the host Conscience invites Will to contribute to the conversation by shooting a look down the hall towards him and his companion Patience: 'toward us he loked' (B XIII 102). Will's intemperate response to this invitation, launching an attack on the friar who sits at the high table, prompts his host to another look, this time somewhat anxiously directed at Patience, asking him to exercise some control over his unruly companion:

> Than Conscience curteisly a contenaunce made,
> And preynte upon Patience to preie me be stille.
> (XIII 112–13)

The word 'preynte', used by Langland in the line last quoted, is the past-tense form of a Middle English verb, *prinken*. This word belongs, along with two others, *winken* and *twink(l)en*, to a group of verbs which I want to consider in more detail in the remainder of this chapter. They are interesting in themselves, and they also provide illustrations of difficulties that can arise with such NVC terms. What did Conscience actually do, physically, when he 'preynte upon Patience to preie me be stille'? We will find that the lexical evidence for the word itself offers no firm answer to this question; nor can the form of the action be safely inferred from the message which it so clearly conveys ('Keep that man quiet!'). The difficulty arises here from that structure of 'double signification' already noticed as a feature of NVC words: from the reporting word to the reported action and from that action to the meaning it carries. The problem with *prinken*, as with *winken* and *twink(l)en*, is that it denotes an act whose form can be determined with certainty neither by reading forward, as it were, from the word nor by reading back from what the act signifies.

Prinken is a quite uncommon word in Middle English. On the evidence of its few occurrences, it clearly refers to some meaningful movement of the eye.[79] Apart from the example just quoted, *Piers Plowman* manuscripts show one other instance. Confronted with his mysterious Palm Sunday vision, Will asks Faith for an explanation: '"Is Piers in þis place?" quod I, and he preynte on me' (B XVIII 21). Remaining examples of the verb (with a single exception, referred to later) all occur in the

---

[79] See *MED prinken* v. and *OED Prink* v.¹.

Gestures and looks in medieval narrative

Charlemagne romance *Sir Ferumbras*, and all concern orders swiftly and secretly given by the eye. The Saracen heroine Floripas, intent on rescuing some prisoners, signals that she needs a staff: 'sche preynte with hur eȝe oppon hur chamberere þar sche stod. / þat mayde was boþe wys and sleȝe and knew ful wel hur mod.' A little later, she prompts a male attendant to throw an old lady out of a window: 'Florippe stod up and preynte þenne toward hure chamberlayn'. On another occasion, a knight signals to his companions that they should advance on a bridge: 'With þat Richard preynte ys eȝe / Oppon ys feleschip þat was him neȝe, / Hure purpos to bygynne.'[80]

What does the word mean? *OED* gives 'To wink, to give a wink'; but *MED* shows some uncertainty, offering 'To signal with the eye, wink.' The more specific gloss 'wink' presumably rests on connecting the verb with an Old English noun *princ*, which occurs in the phrase 'on prince eages' rendering the Latin *in ictu oculi*.[81] This phrase refers to the batting of an eyelid ('the twinkling of an eye'), understood to represent the shortest conceivable length of time – a sense still present in the sole Middle English instance of the noun *prink*.[82] It is easy to see how a verb related to this noun might carry the sense of the modern *wink*, that is, to flick one eyelid down rapidly in a meaningful *ictus oculi*. This supposition gains some support from variants in two *Piers* manuscripts, where 'preynte' is replaced by 'twynclid'.[83] In fact the word evidently caused difficulty to *Piers* scribes, as other variants show, perhaps because it belonged to Langland's west-country dialect (*Ferumbras* originated somewhere near Exeter). Indeed, if Kane and Donaldson are to be believed, scribal tradition lost the word altogether in another line, B XIII 86. Here the text of the archetype evidently had Patience, again in the dinner

---

[80] *Sir Ferumbras*, ed. S. J. H. Herrtage, EETS, E.S. 34 (1879), ll. 1238–9, 1365, and 4507–8. The French original, *Fierabras*, ed. A. Kroeber and G. Servois (Paris, 1860), has no corresponding expressions at ll. 2083 ('Son canberlenc apiele coiement, à celer'), 2195, or 4800.

[81] Cited from *Defensoris Liber Scintillarum* in the *Supplement* to *An Anglo-Saxon Dictionary*, ed. T. N. Toller (Oxford, 1921), under *princ*. See also the original dictionary, ed. J. Bosworth and T. N. Toller (Oxford, 1898), under *princ*: 'on prince *in ictu, in puncto*'.

[82] *MED prink(e* n. cites only an instance from Charles d'Orléans.

[83] At B XVIII 21, one copy has 'twynclid'. At C XV 120 (= B XIII 113), one copy has 'twynkeled': *Piers Plowman: The C Version*, ed. G. Russell and G. Kane (London, 1997), p. 497.

scene, 'winking' at Will to keep him quiet; but the editors restore the alliteration of the line with a conjectural 'preynte': 'Pacience parceyved what I þoughte and [preynte] on me to be stille.'[84]

All these prinkers, with the exception of Faith, have occasion to convey their messages secretly or discreetly, just as modern winkers do. Yet one can understand why some scholars have found themselves unable to render *prinken* simply as 'wink'. A wink nowadays carries messages distinctly less serious than those in *Ferumbras* or *Piers*: commands to be silent, to advance, and even to kill. These occasions seem to call for something a little less light and friendly than a modern wink. It is no doubt for this reason that *MED* offers 'To signal with the eye' as its leading definition. In his edition of the C text of *Piers*, similarly, Derek Pearsall glosses 'preynte' as 'looked significantly'.[85] The alternative solution, which I prefer, is to suppose that Conscience and the rest did indeed flick one eyelid, in the way of a modern wink; and that our difficulty in seeing this as an action appropriate to the circumstances arises from the fact that the act itself has undergone changes in its range of uses and applications since the fourteenth century. If that is the case, to gloss *prinken* with 'wink' would be true to the physical act denoted by the medieval verb – but also unavoidably misleading, for a modern reader, about the tone and meaning of the act. The word, in fact, presents glossators with an insoluble problem.

The more common medieval word *winken* raises similar problems.[86] Like *prinken*, it is commonly applied to acts of command or invitation. In a scene at the king's court in *Piers Plowman*, Lady Mede summons lawyers to her side with a 'wink': 'For I seiȝ Mede in þe moot halle on men of lawe wynke' (B IV 152). In the romance *Gamelyn*, Adam arranges to give a secret signal for action to the hero in the presence of

---

[84] See Kane and Donaldson's edition of the B version, p. 195, on substitution of unalliterating synonyms in the archetype, listing XIII 86 as an example of a 'lexically or contextually easier reading'. All B MSS read 'wynked' there, except RF which have different words again.

[85] *Piers Plowman: An Edition of the C-Text*, ed. D. Pearsall (London, 1978).

[86] 'Winken' has a number of senses not involving NVC, notably 'to close one's eyes', as in sleep. My examples are confined to the relevant senses: *OED* Wink sb.¹ sense 2, *Wink* v.¹ senses 7 and 8, *Winking* vbl. sb.¹ sense 2; *MED winken* v. sense 1(d), *winking(e* ger. sense (a). I am grateful to Professor Lewis for letting me see drafts of the *MED* entries before publication.

his enemies: 'Whan I wynke on thee, loke for to goon.'[87] Chaucer in the Squire's Tale plays on two senses of the verb, 'to signal with the eye' and 'to close the eyes in sleep', when he has Sleep in person urge revellers to rest:

> The norice of digestioun, the sleep,
> Gan on hem wynke and bad hem taken keep
> That muchel drynke and labour wolde han reste.[88]

More in accordance with modern usage, winks also serve to mark private understandings. Lovers wink at each other. To know about love, according to the *Roman d'Eneas*, one must understand 'les engins, et les trestors, / Et les reguarz et les cligniers' ['the devices, the tricks, the looks and the winks'].[89] Courtiers exchange winks. In the nightmare world of Skelton's *Bowge of Courte*, the courtman Deceit ingratiates himself with the poem's narrator thus:

> 'Parde, remembre whan ye were there,
> There I wynked on you – wote ye not where?
> In A *loco*, I mene *juxta* B.'
> (ll. 515–17)

Even Jesus may 'wink', for one poet uses that word (admittedly in rhyme) in his version of the poignant moment in the Passion story where 'the Lord turning looked on Peter. And Peter remembered the word of the Lord, as he had said: Before the cock crow, thou shalt deny me thrice' (Luke 22.61): 'Ihesu stod stille as any stone / And lokid on

---

[87] *The Tale of Gamelyn*, ed. W. W. Skeat, in Vol. IV of *The Complete Works of Geoffrey Chaucer*, 6 vols. (Oxford, 1894–7), l. 453. Three of the seven manuscripts read 'twinke', which Skeat adopts. French *cligner* can denote similar conspiratorial winks, as in the fabliau *Du prestre qui ot mere mal gré sien*: 'Lors regarde, sa mere voit / Qui li cligne c'outre passat, / De nule riens l'arainast' ['Then he looks and sees his mother, who winks at him that he should pass by and not speak to her']: ed. T. B. W. Reid, *Twelve Fabliaux* (Manchester, 1958), ll. 154–6.

[88] *Canterbury Tales* v 347–9. Shakespeare has a similar play on words in *Henry V*. Joking with the Duke of Burgundy about the virgin modesty of Katherine, Henry asks him to 'teach your cousin to consent winking' (that is, with her eyes shut), to which Burgundy replies, 'I will wink on her to consent': *Works*, ed. P. Alexander (London, 1951), Act 5, Scene 2, lines 299–300.

[89] Cited by Tobler–Lommatzsch under *cluignier*, glossed 'blinzeln, jem. zublinzeln'. See also their entry, with the same definition, of *guignier* (etymologically related to *winken*).

Looks

Petir sone anone; / Petir saw Ihesu on him winke / And þan began he sone to þinke'.[90]

The *OED* made a bold and interesting attempt to handle the difficulties presented by the historical record of significant 'winks'. It registered two distinct senses of the verb. Its sense 7 is: 'To give a significant glance, as of command, direction, or invitation: usually constructed with *on, upon*, later *to, at. Obsolete*'. This is distinguished from sense 8: 'To close one eye momentarily, in a flippant or frivolous manner, especially to convey intimate information or to express good-humoured interest.' The passages cited show these two senses in complementary distribution over time. Sense 7 is the earlier, illustrated by citations from Middle English (including some of those just given here) and from later writers, ending with Dickens in 1835. For the modern sense 8, the earliest quotation is from Dickens, again, and the latest from Shaw's *Pygmalion* ('He winks at Higgins'). There is certainly something to be said for these definitions. Medieval 'winks' do indeed often carry messages of command and the like; and they can rarely be described as 'good-humoured', let alone 'flippant or frivolous'. One notices, however, that the lexicographers appear to have assumed that, if the action's significance was different in the past, then its physical form must also have been different. For they suppose that older 'winks' must have taken the form of 'significant glances' rather than the familiar modern 'momentary closing of the eye'. But there is nothing intrinsically or naturally flippant or frivolous about the latter action: it is just as much a creature of convention as the word 'wink' itself. In the absence of evidence to the contrary, therefore, one is perfectly free to suppose that pre-Dickensian winks were just like modern ones – in their physical form, that is, however they may have been used.

This supposition gains some support, in fact, from the evidence of medieval glosses. *OED* itself cites as the earliest of its examples under sense 7 the Old English glossary entry '*Annicto vel annuto*, ic wincie'. Latin dictionaries define *annictare* as 'to wink (at)'.[91] The

---

[90] *The Northern Passion*, ed. F. A. Foster, EETS, 145 (1913), ll. 735–8. Other MSS read 'blenke' or 'blenche' ('glance').

[91] So the *Dictionary of Medieval Latin from British Sources*, ed. R. E. Latham and D. R. Howlett, Vol. 1 (Oxford, 1997). The Classical form is *adnictare*.

Gestures and looks in medieval narrative

other verb, *annutare*, belongs to an important group of NVC words in Medieval Latin, including also *nutare* and the noun *nutus*. These are said to refer primarily to headnods in Classical Latin; but in medieval use they evidently extended their meaning, for *nutus* can there refer quite generally to bodily signs. So when words of this group are applied to particular actions, one cannot easily determine what is intended. It is sometimes a nod, but sometimes also a *nutus oculorum*.[92] A much later glossary, the fifteenth-century *Promptorium Parvulorum*, has a more elaborate entry. For 'Wynkkyng with the ey' it gives 'Nicitacio...Conquinicio...Connivencia...Nictus'.[93] *Nictus* is a wink, and *nicitacio* derives from a verb *nic(i)tare*, defined by one medieval dictionary as 'palpebras movere' ('to move the eyelids').[94] *Connivencia* denotes a shutting of the eye or eyes.[95] *Conquinicio* is less straightforward, for it derives from a verb *conquiniscere*, which meant 'crouch' or 'stoop' in antiquity and commonly had the sense 'bow down' in Medieval Latin. In another *Promptorium* gloss, however, the noun *conquinicio* is given as the Latin equivalent for 'noddynge wythe the heed'.[96] That is what it probably means in the 'Wynkkyng' gloss also, but I do not take this as a challenge to what the other three Latin words there clearly suggest. I suppose rather that it provides early evidence for a form of behaviour still to be observed today, where the message of a wink will often be supported by a quick simultaneous nod of the head.

There remains one other common word in the same semantic field, *twinken* or *twinklen*. The *Promptorium* has an entry, 'Wynkyn, *idem quod* Twynkelyn', and it gives very similar Latin equivalents for the two words.[97] *Twinken* and its frequentative form *twinklen* are in fact quite as well attested in the relevant sense as *winken* itself, and with a similar

---

[92] There is a full and valuable entry for *nutus* in *Novum Glossarium Mediae Latinitatis*, ed. F. Blatt *et al.*, fascicule 'Norma–Nisus' (Copenhagen, 1969). See there sense 1, 'geste, signe'; and sense 1 C 1 (for *nutus oculorum*), 'clin d'oeil exprimant une connivence, un ordre muet'.

[93] *Promptorium Parvulorum*, ed. Mayhew, col. 530.

[94] Hugutio of Pisa, cited by Blatt, *Novum Glossarium*, 'Ne–Norma' (Copenhagen, 1967) under *nicto*, sense 1, 'cligner des yeux'.

[95] See the *Dictionary of Medieval Latin from British Sources*, under *coniventia*, 'wink (visible expression of approval)'. See also *conivere* there.

[96] Cited by *OED* under *Nod* v., sense 1, together with a similar gloss from *Catholicon Anglicum*.

[97] From the version of the *Promptorium* edited by A. Way, Camden Society, 25, 55, 89 (1843–65), under 'Wynkyn'.

range of applications.[98] There is no sign of the genial or Pickwickian sense of the modern *twinkle* (rather obscure, in truth, so far as any action of the eye is concerned). People give orders with twinkles. A schoolmaster prompts his subordinate to flog their pupils with 'twinkelinges of his eye';[99] and *MED* quotes from the romance *Bone Florence of Rome*, ll. 1748–9: 'And he twynkylde wyth hys eye, / As who seyth "Hold the stylle." ' Elsewhere twinkles, like winks, carry amorous messages. One girl reports that Jolly Jankyn communicated with her silently in church when 'he twynkelid, but sayd nowt, and on myn fot he trede'; and another parish clerk does the same at a dance: 'he trippede on my to, and made a twynkelyng.'[100] Not surprisingly, moralists disapproved of such suggestive winks, as in a sermon quoted by *MED*: 'Liþir lok and tuingling... arin toknes of horeling' ['sinful looking and winking are signs of a fornicator'].

Other writers reflects a more general suspicion of winks as a form of covert communication. Such 'twinkling' could, for one thing, be impolite and even vulgar. One late medieval courtesy book, John Russell's *Boke of Nurture*, lists it among 'symple condicyons of a persone þat is not taught', along with such things as scratching one's head, sniffing, and picking one's nose.[101] More seriously, several passages in the Old Testament associate winking with wickedness – the relevant Latin expression *annuere oculo* being rendered in each case as 'twinkle with the eye' by English translators. Of a deceitful man, Ecclesiasticus has 'annuens oculo fabricat iniqua', Englished as 'þe twinclere with þe eʒe forgeþ wicke thingis'.[102] The Psalmist complains of unscrupulous enemies 'qui oderunt me gratis, et annuunt oculis'; in Middle English, 'þat hateden me wiþoute cause and twynclen with eʒen'.[103] In Proverbs,

---

[98] *OED Twink* v.[1] sense 1, *Twinkle* v.[1] sense 2, *Twinkling* vbl. sb.[1] sense 2; *MED twinken* v., *twinklen* v. sense (a), *twinkling(e* ger. sense 1 (a).

[99] *The Oxford Book of Medieval English Verse*, ed. C. and K. Sisam (Oxford, 1970), no. 229, l. 20.

[100] *Secular Lyrics*, ed. Robbins, no. 27, l. 17, and no. 28, l.8. In his Introduction, p. xl, Robbins quotes a Middle English fragment: 'Ne saltow never, levedi, / Twynklen wyt thin eyen.'

[101] *Babees Book*, ed. Furnivall, p. 134, l. 281: 'twynkelynge with youre yʒe'.

[102] Ecclesiasticus 27.25, with Middle English from the Wycliffite Bible: *MS. Bodley 959... The Earlier Version of the Wycliffite Bible*, ed. C. Lindberg, Vol. IV (Stockholm, 1965), p. 340.

[103] Psalm 34.19 (A.V. 35.19), ed. Lindberg, p. 185.

Gestures and looks in medieval narrative

Solomon warns that 'qui annuit oculo dabit dolorem', rendered as 'who twyncleþ with eȝe shal ȝyven sorewe'.[104] But much the most widely cited passage occurs elsewhere in Proverbs, in Chapter 6: 'Homo apostata vir inutilis, graditur ore perverso; annuit oculis, terit pede, digito loquitur.' The translation has: 'A man apostata, a man ful of strengþe unprofitable, goþ with pervertid mouþ; he twyncleþ with þe eȝen, he trampleþ wiþ þe foot, with þe fynger he spekeþ.'[105]

This last passage is quoted no less than three times in what may have been the best known of all discussions of gesture in the Middle Ages, to wit, the twelfth chapter of the treatise *De Institutione Novitiorum* by Hugh of St. Victor. The chapter is entitled 'De disciplina servanda in gestu'.[106] Addressing novices in his order of Victorine canons, Hugh instructs them to exercise control over 'motus et figuratio membrorum corporis' ['the movement and positioning of your bodily members', col. 938A]. They must avoid 'inordinati motus corporis' ['unregulated movements of the body', col. 938B]. Such 'vitia gesticulationum' are signs of inner, moral weaknesses, he argues, citing Proverbs 6 for the first time here to prove the point (ibid.). Later, in the course of a more detailed analysis, he invokes the same passage to illustrate 'inconstantiae et levitatis signa' ['signs of instability and lightmindedness', 940C]; and he returns to it once more to enforce his main point, that such 'confusio actionis' has its source in moral disorder (942C–D).[107] The latter part of the same chapter announces two general principles which, according to Hugh, ought to govern *gestus*. Each bodily member should be called on to perform only its own proper function and should not usurp the function of another (941C–943B); and all parts should conduct themselves with propriety and moderation (943B–C). In stating the first of these principles, Hugh writes:

---

[104] Proverbs 10.10, ed. Lindberg, p. 255.
[105] Proverbs 6.12–13, ed. Lindberg, p. 251.
[106] *Patrologia Latina*, Vol. CLXXVI, cols. 938–43. The work survives in 172 manuscripts according to Schmitt, *La raison des gestes*, p. 174. I am indebted to Schmitt's extensive discussion in his Chapter V.
[107] Hugh has quoted the same passage in an earlier chapter, to illustrate how 'de inconstantia mentis nascitur inordinata motio corporis' (col. 935B). St Bernard had also cited it, as representing the 'insolens corporis motus' of the proud: *De Gradibus Humilitatis et Superbiae*, x 28, in *Opera*, ed. J. Leclercq and H. M. Rochais, Vol. III (Rome, 1963), p. 38.

> Discretio actionum in membris conservanda est, ut scilicet id agat unumquodque membrum ad quod factum est, ut neque loquatur manus, neque os audiat, nec oculus linguae officium assumat.
>
> ['One must respect distinctions between what the parts of the body do, so that every part performs the function for which it was created: the hand should not speak, nor the mouth listen, nor the eye usurp the function of the tongue', 941 c.]

'Nec oculus linguae officium assumat.' The function of the eye is to see, not to speak; so when it does duty for the tongue, by 'twinkling' or otherwise, it contravenes the natural, God-given order of what Hugh calls the 'respublica' of the body. This amounts to a very far-reaching clerical rejection, not only of speaking looks, but also of speaking hands, along with all other forms of behaviour where parts of the body are put to 'unnatural' purposes.

Hugh of St Victor was concerned more generally with 'the movement and positioning of bodily members', not only with their use for acts of communication. For the purposes of this study, however, the criterion of *voluntas significandi* is critical; and no less a philosopher than Gilbert Ryle can be found applying that criterion to winks, in his discussion of what he was the first to call 'thick description'. The passages merits citation here:

> Two boys fairly swiftly contract the eyelids of their right eyes. In the first boy this is only an involuntary twitch; but the other is winking conspiratorially to an accomplice. At the lowest or thinnest level of description the two contractions of the eyelids may be exactly alike. Yet there remains the immense but unphotographable difference between a twitch and a wink. For to wink is to try to signal to someone in particular, without the cognisance of others, a definite message according to an already understood code. It has very complex success-*versus*-failure conditions. A wink is a failure if its intended recipient does not see it; or sees it but does not know or forgets the code; or misconstrues it; or disobeys or disbelieves it; or if anyone else spots it. A mere twitch, on the other hand, is neither a failure nor a success; it has no intended recipient; it is not meant to be witnessed by anybody; it carries no message. It may be a symptom but it is not a signal.[108]

---

[108] Gilbert Ryle, *Collected Papers*, Vol. II (London, 1971), p. 480. This is the essay from which Clifford Geertz took up and popularised the idea of 'thick description'.

I conclude my discussion of winks with a curious medieval anecdote which turns on exactly this distinction between speaking and non-speaking eye-shuts. It also involves all three of the verbs I have been considering. The story occurs in a fourteenth-century rhyming chronicle. It concerns an encounter between Bad King John and a fletcher, that is, an arrow-maker. The king is entering a gate:

> He come ride in at bischopes ʒat,
> He seye a flecher sitt þerat.
> He biheld and underʒat
> Hou he gan to prie
> And tvincle wiþ þat oþir eye.
> King Jon seyd þo,
> 'Flecher, whi lokestow so?'
> þe flecher answerd oʒain,
> 'Sir, for soþe ichil ʒou seyn:
> So help me God and Seyn Miʒhel,
> For it schuld be even and wel.
> So help me God and Seyn Austin,
> Y no dede it for non oþer gin.'[109]

In fact, the fletcher is simply checking that his latest arrow shaft is straight and true ('even and wel'). He sights along the shaft with one eye, momentarily shutting the other for the purpose. As he innocently protests, he has no other intention. But what King John 'sees and understands' is a stare ('prie') from one eye and an even more impertinent wink ('tvincle') from the other. He is outraged: 'Flecher, whi lokestow so?' How dare such a man eyeball or wink at a king? True to his evil nature, accordingly, John orders that one of the man's eyes should be put out:

> King Jon dede as a schrewe:
> Hede put out his on eyʒe,
> For he no schuld no more prinke
> No wiþ that oþer eyʒe winke.
> (ll. 2210–13)

---

[109] I quote from the Auchinleck text of the *Anonymous Short Metrical Chronicle*, ed. M. C. Carroll and R. Tuve, *PMLA*, 46 (1931), 115–54, ll. 2197–2209, correcting their 'tvincke' to 'tvincle' from the facsimile.

Looks

The last two lines quoted both evidently refer to the same eye, the eye which John saw as winking or prinking at him.[110] Being a 'schrewe', he misreads a purely practical act as an impertinent signal. The story provides a drastic illustration of Ryle's distinction. It also, incidentally, evokes a strange but powerful image of gaze as an active and potentially threatening thing, in its picture of a man with an arrow held to point straight out from his eye.

---

[110] *MED* cites this use of *prinke*, along with the *Piers* and *Ferumbras* examples, under their sense, 'To signal with the eye, wink.' The other two copies are clearer than Auchinleck at this point: 'Kyng Jon dude for envye / Let putte out his ouþer eie / For he ne scholde nomore swynke / Ne nomore with þat eie wynke': *Anonymous Short Metrical Chronicle*, ed. E. Zettl, EETS, 196 (1935), ll. 942–5.

CHAPTER 4

Two Middle English narratives

At a moment in *Troilus and Criseyde* when Chaucer is passing, as he says, 'shortly' over a period in the relationship between the two lovers, he offers readers an apology for such summary treatment:

> But now, paraunter, som man wayten wolde
> That every word, or soonde, or look, or cheere
> Of Troilus that I rehercen sholde,
> In al this while unto his lady deere –
> I trowe it were a long thyng for to here –
> Or of what wight that stant in swich disjoynte,
> His wordes alle, or every look, to poynte.
>
> For sothe, I have naught herd it don er this
> In story non, ne no man here, I wene;
> And though I wolde, I koude nought, ywys;
> For ther was som epistel hem bitwene,
> That wolde, as seyth myn autour, wel contene
> Neigh half this book, of which hym liste nought write.
> How sholde I thanne a lyne of it endite?[1]

Concerned here with exchanges between Troilus and Criseyde, Chaucer for a moment plays with the idea of total narrative, in which every kind of communication, verbal and non-verbal alike, would be registered: all their spoken words, messages, and letters, and also all their looks and facial expressions. He says that he has not found this done in any past narrative, and could not himself do it now, even if he wanted to. The apology is, of course, quite unserious; but it draws attention

---

[1] III 491–504. All quotations are from *The Riverside Chaucer*, 3rd edn, ed. Benson.

Two Middle English narratives

to the matter of narrative scale – scale in the cartographers' sense – and its bearing on the registration of non-verbal messages such as the 'look' or the 'cheere'. Total narrative could no more exist than could a Borgesian map on a scale of one inch to an inch, and even the most circumstantial of modern novels falls far short of such totality. Readers learn a great deal, but not everything, about the breakfasts of Leopold Bloom and his cat in Joyce's *Ulysses*. Nor is there any simple measure of comparison, since narrative texts, unlike maps, conform to no single set scale. Each one will vary in the amount of detail recorded, to a greater or lesser extent, according to the importance or interest of what is being recorded. Nevertheless, one can readily see that some narratives, broadly speaking, treat their stories on a larger scale than others; and since texts of this kind are particularly hospitable, as Chaucer evidently noticed, to the recording of little acts of non-verbal communication, among other such details, they are of special value to the present enquiry. Accordingly, I devote the present chapter to two of the most conspicuous examples of larger-scale narrative in medieval English: Chaucer's *Troilus* itself, and then the anonymous *Sir Gawain and the Green Knight*. Both these long poems confine their attention quite strictly to a single and not very extended sequence of events – the 'double sorrow' of Troilus in one, the Adventure of the Green Chapel in the other – and both treat their events according to what Henry James was to call the 'scenic method'. They select key scenes for large-scale treatment, while passing in summary fashion over the rest.[2] Even these scenes, needless to say, fall very far short of recording 'wordes alle or every look', and readers of James Joyce, Henry James, or Proust may even find them disappointing; yet they offer much richer representations of looks, gestures and the like than one finds in most medieval writings.

The main source and inspiration of Chaucer's *Troilus and Criseyde* was *Il Filostrato* by Giovanni Boccaccio. The *Filostrato* is a very early poem, written about 1335, when Boccaccio was in his early twenties; and Italian critics have no very high opinion of it – one speaks of 'la tenuità culturale

---

[2] See G. Genette on 'the contrast of tempo between detailed scene and summary', in the chapter 'Duration' in his *Narrative Discourse: an Essay in Method*, transl. J. E. Lewin (Ithaca, N.Y., 1980), pp. 86–112.

e la debolezza stilistica del poemetto'.[3] Chaucer was no doubt attracted by the story, which Boccaccio was the first to tell consecutively and at length; but he may well also have been struck by the sheer 'scale' of the narration, devoting all of 5704 lines to a quite simple love-story. Indeed, it is hard to think what Chaucer elsewhere might have read that matched the *Filostrato* in this particular respect; and it may have been this very poem that prompted his thoughts about total narrative. Certainly, Boccaccio devotes an exceptional amount of space to what his characters say and what they write in letters; and he also pays more attention to their looks and gestures than medieval writers can commonly afford.

Chaucer's poem is half as long again as Boccaccio's, and it makes significantly more of non-verbal messages between its characters, as I hope to show. At the same time, the two poems, considered together, also suggest some cross-cultural observations about the customary behaviours of English and Italian societies in the fourteenth century – or, more precisely, of London in the 1380s and Naples in the 1330s. For the social worlds portrayed by both poets are essentially those of their own time and place, not that of ancient Troy. In many ways these worlds are very similar, which is not surprising given that Chaucer and Boccaccio both had connections with court circles – those of Richard II and Robert I of Naples, respectively – and were familiar with the same courtly French writers.[4] So, much the same international code of manners governs the behaviour of their characters. This is evident, for example, on those gesture-rich occasions when people meet or part. Since there is never any question in either poem of marking social inferiority, gestures of greeting and farewell in both take the common form appropriate to polite behaviour between equals. Thus, when Pandarus comes to visit his niece, Criseyde and he take (not shake) each other by the hand (*Troilus* II 88–9 and *Filostrato* II stanzas 34, 108); and Troilus and Criseyde take their final, public leave of each other with a handclasp (*Troilus* V 81,

---

[3] Vittore Branca, p. 5 in the Introduction to his edition of the poem, from which I quote throughout: *Tutte le opere di Giovanni Boccaccio*, Vol. II (Milan, 1964).

[4] See N. R. Havely, *Chaucer's Boccaccio: Sources for 'Troilus' and the 'Knight's' and 'Franklin's Tales' (Cambridge, 1980)*, Introduction, pp. 1–9. I take most of my translations from Havely. On Boccaccio's acquaintance with the Neapolitan court and with French verse, see also B. Nolan, *Chaucer and the Tradition of the 'Roman Antique'* (Cambridge, 1992).

Fil. v st. 12). In private, the lovers mark both meetings and partings with embraces and kisses (*Troilus* IV 1131, 1689, *Fil.* III st. 30, IV st. 167). But in the English poem it is not only lovers who meet or part in this way. Chaucer's Pandarus embraces Criseyde on her arrival at his house (III 606); Eleyne kisses Troilus when she leaves his sick-room (III 225); and the English Troilus greets Antenor on his release by the Greeks with a kiss (V 77), where the Italian Troiolo merely 'welcomed him with a cheerful expression [con buon viso]' (*Fil.* V st. 11). Why does Chaucer's Troilus but not Boccaccio's kiss his fellow Trojan? Perhaps Chaucer had in mind, here as elsewhere, the irony of welcoming back to Troy one who is later to betray the city. Or perhaps the kiss reflects a distinctively English custom, noted by Erasmus later: 'When you arrive anywhere, you are received with kisses on all sides' (pp. 32–3 above).

Chaucer's addition of these formal kisses of greeting and parting contrasts significantly with his omission of those kisses that a grateful Troiolo bestows on Pandaro in Boccaccio's version of their scenes together. The English poet was apparently not happy, as one critic remarks, with such 'Italianate clasping and kissing of the friend'.[5] Where Troiolo 'embraced Pandaro a thousand times and kissed him as often' (*Fil.* II 81), Chaucer's hero 'held up both his hands' in gratitude (II 974); where Troiolo 'embraced and kissed' his friend (*Fil.* II 33), Troilus knelt and embraced him (I 1044–5); and where Troiolo hugged Pandaro and 'kissed him tenderly on the forehead' (*Fil.* III 56, also 57), Chaucer's Troilus

> with al th'affeccioun
> Of frendes love that herte may devyse,
> To Pandarus on knowes fil adown,
> And er that he wolde of that place arise
> He gan hym thonken in his beste wise.
> (III 1590–4)

Barry Windeatt, in his essay 'Gesture in Chaucer', commenting on these and other passages, observes that 'Chaucer suggests the less relaxed approach and greater formality with which the English characters treat

---

[5] S. B. Meech, *Design in Chaucer's 'Troilus'* (Syracuse, N.Y., 1959), p. 186, in the chapter 'Expressive Actions'. There is a chapter on *Troilus* in Benson, *Medieval Body Language*, pp. 82–100.

their expressions of feeling.'[6] Speaking more generally, Windeatt remarks on 'an almost ceremonial deliberateness about the order and the pace with which the gestures of the emotional life are expressed' in Chaucer's writings (ibid., p. 154).

Windeatt rightly instances the gesture of kneeling as strong evidence of the greater formality that Chaucer introduces into the manners of his poem. The only example of kneeling in the *Filostrato* occurs towards the beginning, when Criseida 'throws herself on her knees at Hector's feet', appealing to his clemency (I 12). Chaucer takes over this classic bit of petitionary behaviour (*Troilus* I 110); but he also has eight other references to kneeling, none of them in the Italian. His Pandarus kneels twice in the presence of Criseyde, marking the gesture on each occasion with that arch self-mockery with which he throughout plays the part of a servant of the servants of love ('he gan at hymself to jape faste', II 1164). Having delivered Troilus' first letter to his niece, he begs her to write a reply:

> 'Aquite hym wel, for Goddes love,' quod he;
> 'Myself to medes wol the lettre sowe.'
> And held his hondes up, and sat on knowe;
> 'Now, goode nece, be it nevere so lite,
> Yif me the labour it to sowe and plite.'
> (II 1200–4)

Although Pandarus is bent on encouraging Criseyde to show Troilus her first sign of favour – and although, on this occasion, he goes down on only one knee – his petitionary gestures, being directed ostensibly only to the folding and sewing of a letter, are comically extravagant.[7] So too are his same gestures when later, at Deiphebus' house, Criseyde kisses Troilus for the first time, and Pandarus thanks Cupid and Venus for that miracle of love: 'Fil Pandare on knees, and up his eyen / To heven threw, and held his hondes highe' (III 183–4). Given that Pandarus can on occasion take familiar liberties with his niece, the formalities with which he marks the progress of her affair strike equivocal notes, as between deference, burlesque, and an unspoken element of mutual

---

[6] Barry Windeatt, 'Gesture in Chaucer', *Medievalia et Humanistica*, n.s. 9 (1979), 143–61 (pp. 158–9). See also Windeatt's notes in his edition of *Troilus*, where the poem and *Il Filostrato* are printed in parallel.

[7] Windeatt, 'Gesture in Chaucer', speaks of 'a gesture excessive in the context of his visit' (p. 158).

understanding. Somewhat similar in effect, though more muted, is the parting gesture with which Pandarus leaves Criseyde to spend what turns out to be a night of love in his guest-room:

> Tho Pandarus, hire em, right as hym oughte,
> With wommen swiche as were hire most aboute,
> Ful glad unto hire beddes syde hire broughte,
> And took his leve, and gan ful lowe loute.
> (III 680–3)

A bow such as this – the only bow in the poem – might appropriately be given by a host to a lady guest; but its greater depth speaks for further meanings, at least on the part of Pandarus himself.

Intentions are much simpler and more wholehearted when Troilus kneels – in gratitude to Pandarus, as already noticed, and especially in submission to his mistress. When Criseyde in tears reproaches him for his jealousy, he hangs his head and falls to his knees before her (III 1079–80). The two other occasions, both also in bedrooms, are more interesting, for each involves some play with conflicting social rules. In the first of them, Troilus is in bed in the house of Deiphebus, pretending to be ill. When Pandarus leads Criseyde in to talk with him, Troilus greets her with an apology: 'Allas, I may nought rise, / To knele and do yow honour in som wyse' (III 69–70). Any gentleman would want to rise on such an occasion, and a lover might want to kneel; but Troilus can do neither, because he has to keep up the pretence of illness. His distress at his inability to do her honour is further compounded, however; for, as he raises himself in his bed, Criseyde gently pushes him down again. Do not rise to me, she says, for I am myself indebted to you for your 'lordship' – patronage, that is, and protection – and am seeking your favour in future. The implication must be that it is she, as both beneficiary and petitioner, who ought to be kneeling to him, and not the other way round. The thought that his enforced incapacity to do Criseyde honour as her servant in love might be condemning him to behave as if he were her lord incapacitates Troilus with shame:

> This Troilus, that herde his lady preye
> Of lordshipe hym, wax neither quyk ne ded,
> Ne myghte o word for shame to it seye,

> Although men sholde smyten of his hed.
> But Lord, so he wex sodeynliche red.
> (III 78–82)

As we saw in an earlier chapter (above, p. 24), knights feel shame and 'honte' when they are honoured by one to whom they should properly kneel: Malory's Sir Bors says to the kneeling Guinevere, 'Madam, ye do me grete dishonoure.'

In a later scene, in the bedchamber of Pandarus' house, the roles are reversed, but the conflict in social rules is somewhat similar. This time it is Criseyde who is in bed, and the social dilemma is hers. On entering the bedchamber, Troilus instantly falls to his knees by the bed, rather as Chrétien's Lancelot bows before Guinevere in bed (above, p. 23):

> This Troilus ful soone on knees hym sette
> Ful sobrely, right be hyre beddes hed,
> And in his beste wyse his lady grette.
> But Lord, so she wex sodeynliche red!
> Ne though men sholde smyten of hire hed,
> She kouthe nought a word aright out brynge
> So sodeynly, for his sodeyn comynge.
> (III 953–9)

Criseyde's dumbfounded blush is described in the same words as that of Troilus earlier (III 82). The reaction here – or so we are invited to believe – is simply one of surprise at a sudden event; but the situation also again brings a social awkwardness. Pandarus implies this by his observation to Criseyde: 'Nece, se how this lord kan knele! / Now for youre trouthe, se this gentil man!' It is no small thing for such a great lord, a king's son, to kneel to Pandarus' niece; so he goes to fetch a cushion.[8] Criseyde for her part, of course, ought to respond by telling Troilus to rise; but this she fails to do. For this omission in the rituals of courtesy, Chaucer feels bound to offer two alternative explanations: either she was so distressed and distracted by Troilus' supposed jealousy, 'Or elles that she took it in the wise / Of dewete, as for his observaunce' (III 969–70).

---

[8] Windeatt, p. 158, suggests that Pandarus is 'mocking' Troilus here; but the way Chaucer introduces his words to Criseyde suggests otherwise: 'But Pandarus, that so wel koude feele / In every thyng, to pleye anon bigan' (960–1). What chiefly motivates his 'playing' is 'feeling' – here, a sympathetic wish to break the deadlock in which the lovers appear to be caught.

Two Middle English narratives

Of the other significant formal 'observaunces', apart from kneeling, the most frequent in *Troilus* are gestures of bonding: hand in hand, or arm in arm. Characters may, as we have seen, clasp hands when they meet or part; but it is not only on those occasions that they link up physically as a sign of familiarity. Indeed, this behaviour is much more common than in modern Western societies. The expression 'arm in arm' is recorded by the dictionaries first in this poem (with no Boccaccian origins).[9] When Criseyde walks arm in arm in her garden with her nieces (II 823) and with Pandarus (II 1116), the descriptions suggest no more than domestic intimacy; but when she enters the room where Troilus lies 'sick' at Deiphebus' house arm in arm with her uncle (II 1725), the action carries further meanings. The occasion is one on which Criseyde is looking for the favour and support of great ones; so Pandarus is making a public display of his backing and sympathy, just as Eleyne did a little earlier by holding Criseyde's hand (II 1604). Yet the entry also calls for ceremony because, as both of them privately know, Pandarus is introducing his niece for the first time into the presence of her would-be lover. Distinctly more alien to general modern Western manners is the holding of hands between men, as when Troilus goes hand in hand with Pandarus into the garden to talk of his love (III 1737–8).[10] There is also one other handclasp which carries a quite different significance. Diomede attempts to extract an early expression of interest from Criseyde, as they ride together across no man's land to her father's tent:

> 'And nere it that we ben so neigh the tente
> Of Calcas, which that sen us bothe may,
> I wolde of this yow telle al myn entente –
> But this enseled til another day.
> Yeve me youre hond; I am, and shal ben ay,
> God helpe me so, while that my lyf may dure,
> Youre owene aboven every creature.'
> (V 148–54)

---

[9] *MED arm* n. 1 b(b) records only the two *Troilus* examples, together with one other of a quite different kind. Tobler–Lommatzsch, under *brace* s.f., records one medieval French example of 'brace a brace', as a sign of love.

[10] Chaucer here follows Boccaccio: 'He would sometimes take Pandaro by the hand and go off into a garden with him' (*Fil.* III st. 73). Elsewhere in Boccaccio (not in Chaucer), Troiolo takes Pandaro by the hand to visit Criseida's empty house (V st. 51).

Gestures and looks in medieval narrative

I quote the whole stanza because the reference to sealing also deserves comment. Diomede seeks to pledge himself to Criseyde as her man with her hand held in his, that is, with the traditional gesture of trothplight. 'Enseled' in the previous line refers back to 'al myn entente' – Diomede is not yet ready to reveal, or open, everything that he has in mind. Yet his use of the sealing metaphor also suggests that his commitment has all the force of a formal document. We may see here a passing reminder of the fact that Chaucer lived at a time when, as Richard Green puts it, 'a dramatic growth in lay literacy was leading to an increasing reliance on written evidence in the common processes of verification and authentification', at the expense of oral and gestural trothplight, among other things.[11]

Chaucer follows Boccaccio more closely in describing gestures expressive of distress and sorrow – a highly conventional repertoire of actions, very well represented in the French narratives with which both authors were familiar. In both poems, hero and heroine alike give quite similar operatic performances as their final separation approaches. Boccaccio employs the word 'sign' in this connection, speaking of 'vero segno degli aspri martiri' ('true sign of bitter sufferings', *Fil.* IV st. 96, cf. also st. 84); and Chaucer's rendering preserves the technical term: 'verray signal of martire / Of deth' (IV 818–19, cf. also IV 710). When Troilus first returns to his room from the meeting at which the exchange of prisoners was agreed, he rushes about roaring:

> Smytyng his brest ay with his fistes smerte;
> His hed to the wal, his body to the grounde
> Ful ofte he swapte, hymselven to confounde.
> (IV 243–5)

Chaucer here follows Boccaccio, whose Troiolo inflicts pain upon his body in much the same way: 'He unrestrainedly battered his head against the wall, beat his face with his hands, and his breast and his wretched arms with his fists' (*Fil.* IV st. 27). In both poems, too, the heroine beats her breast (*Troilus* IV 752, *Fil.* IV st. 87) and falls to the ground (*Troilus* IV 911–12, *Fil.* IV st. 106). But the distinctively female 'signal of martire' was to tear the hair and let it hang wildly loose. Boccaccio's Criseida 'pulling,

---

[11] Green, *A Crisis of Truth*, p. 40. Diomede would benefit from the fact that lovers' hearts are spoken of as sealed by love, as at *Troilus* IV 293.

tore her golden hair' (IV st. 87), an action which Chaucer beautifies further: 'Hire ownded heer, that sonnyssh was of hewe / She rente' (IV 736–7). Later, when Pandaro calls upon Criseida in the Italian, he finds her 'scapigliata', that is, dishevelled (IV st. 96), a distracted condition which Chaucer again beautifies:

> The myghty tresses of hire sonnysshe heeris
> Unbroiden hangen al aboute hire eeris,
> Which yaf hym verray signal of martire
> Of deth, which that hire herte gan desire.
> (IV 816–19)

In the one gesture of grief which he adds to his Italian original, the wringing of hands, Chaucer distinguishes between male and female performance, preserving the elegance of the latter by specifying long, slender fingers. Criseyde wrings 'hire fyngeres longe and smale', where Troilus simply wrings 'his hondes' (IV 737, 1171).[12]

One can observe a much more informal register of gestural behaviour – rarely represented in medieval narratives and not at all in *Il Filostrato* – among the private exchanges between Criseyde and her uncle, most notably in the long and elaborate scene where Pandarus first reveals Troilus' love to her. Progress of the revelation here is marked by a series of small behaviours which punctuate the conversation. When Pandarus first declines to tell her his interesting bit of news, she submits with lowered eyes and a sigh (II 141–5); but later, after a further appeal from her, he relents and embarks on his revelation:

> And with that word hire uncle anoon hire kiste,
> And seyde, 'Gladly, leve nece dere!
> Tak it for good, that I shal sey yow here.'
>
> With that she gan hire eighen down to caste,
> And Pandarus to coghe gan a lite,
> And seyde...
> (II 250–5)

The kiss marks Pandarus' affectionate intentions at this critical moment, like his taking of her hand during the speech which follows (293); and

---

[12] The gestures discussed in this paragraph are among those treated and illustrated as 'dramatic gestures of self-injury' in Barasch, *Gestures of Despair*. See page 88 there, on Florentine rituals of mourning.

Criseyde's lowered eyes express docility again, but also here a polite avoidance of staring curiosity. Pandarus then 'coughs a little' before embarking. The word 'coughen' had a wider range of meanings in Middle than in Modern English, and one may suppose that Pandarus just clears his throat – 'ahem!'.[13] As a non-verbal prologue to speech, such a 'cough' portends some matter of moment, as when the pompous friar doctor in *Piers Plowman* 'coughed and carped' (B XIII 101). Windeatt observes that Pandarus 'is Chaucer's only character to cough outside the characters of the fabliaux',[14] referring to the meaning coughs with which Absolon twice draws attention to his presence outside the window in the Miller's Tale (*Canterbury Tales* I 3697, 3788), and the cough directed at Damyan by May in the Merchant's Tale (IV 2208). Chaucer perhaps thought this other kind of significant coughing rather vulgar, and he evidently had no time for the cough by which Boccaccio's Criseida secretly communicates with Troiolo when he is hiding in her house (*Fil.* III st. 26).[15] Having begun his speech with a prelusive cough, Pandarus concludes it by himself 'casting down his head', as if to await Criseyde's response (II 407). She is in fact angry; but when he gets up to leave, ostensibly in despair, 'she agayn hym by the lappe kaughte' (448).

Later in Book II, Criseyde returns from a private reading of the letter from Troilus which Pandarus has just brought her and, finding him deep in thought, 'took him by the hood' to go in to dinner (II 1181). She can take liberties with her uncle, but when he asks, after dinner, whether she approved of the letter, she responds less robustly: 'Therwith al rosy hewed tho wex she, / And gan to homme, and seyde, "So I trowe"' (1198–9). Her indistinct verbal reply ('I suppose so') is accompanied by a non-committal paralinguistic sound: 'hm...', as it would be rendered in modern times.[16] Here as elsewhere, it is the uncertain balance of power, responsibility, and knowledge between uncle and niece that

---

[13] Neither expression is recorded in Middle English: see *OED Clear* v. 7, *Ahem* int. Cp. *MED coughen* v., sense (b): 'to clear one's throat or cough (to attract attention or announce one's presence)'.

[14] 'Gesture in Chaucer', p. 152. Cp. Benson, *Medieval Body Language*, p. 89.

[15] In the *Tale of Beryn*, a barmaid objects to being taken by surprise by the Pardoner: 'Yee shuld have couȝid when ye com. Wher lern ye curtesye?' ed.: Furnivall and Stone, line 323. For examples of courteous signal-coughs, see below, pp. 165–8.

[16] *OED Hum* v.¹ 2c: 'To make an inarticulate murmur in a pause of speaking, from hesitation, embarrassment, etc.'

makes their exchanges, verbal and non-verbal alike, so intriguing. Thus, when Criseyde first confronts the bedridden Troilus at Deiphebus' house, Pandarus takes the liberties of the upper hand: he 'poked evere his nece new and newe' (III 116).[17] By that gesture he is urging her to speak, but when she does, she pointedly declines to give Troilus the encouragement Pandarus wants. He takes an even greater liberty, notoriously, when he visits Criseyde in bed at his house after her first night there with Troilus. He asks how she is, and she in reply reproaches him for his double-dealing:

> With that she gan hire face for to wrye
> With the shete, and wax for shame al reed;
> And Pandarus gan under for to prie,
> And seyde, 'Nece, if that I shal be ded,
> Have here a swerd and smyteth of myn hed!'
> With that his arm al sodeynly he thriste
> Under hire nekke, and at the laste hire kyste.
> (III 1569–75)

Hiding the face for shame or sorrow is a distinctively feminine gesture, as at III 1056 and IV 820–1 (the latter from *Fil.* IV st. 96). Meanwhile, Pandarus responds to Criseyde's reproaches ('Fox that ye ben!') by offering her, not very seriously, first vengeance and then reconciliation: a sword, and then an embrace and a kiss. In the circumstances, this embrace and kiss can hardly be quite untouched by suggestions of avuncular or vicarious eroticism; but they are offered as *signa reconciliationis*, and it is as such that Criseyde happily accepts them. She forgives him:

> I passe al that which chargeth nought to seye.
> What! God foryaf his deth, and she al so
> Foryaf, and with here uncle gan to pleye,
> For other cause was ther noon than so.
> (III 1576–9).

I turn now from gestures to looks and expressions in the poem. Chaucer could not, as he confesses in his mock apology, represent every single

---

[17] Again, poking is a gesture found elsewhere in Chaucer only in fabliau: Aleyn pokes John in the Reeve's Tale to get his attention (I 4169). See *MED poken* v. (1) (a).

Gestures and looks in medieval narrative

'look' or 'chere' that passed between his characters; but there are some scenes, mainly in the first three books, where such representations cluster very thickly. The richest of these scenes happens to be the first in the poem, partly because, being set in a temple, it has little occasion for those conversations which bulk so large later.

In the temple of Pallas, Troilus is first seen expressing his scorn of love. His short speech to a companion suspected of such weakness is flanked by bodily signs of superior wisdom. First, a smile: 'he wolde smyle and holden it folye' (I 194). As noticed in an earlier chapter (above, p. 75), varieties of such knowing smiles occur frequently in medieval narrative, and Windeatt observes that in *Troilus* too 'smiling is often associated with the superiority of unshared knowledge' – as when the prophetess Cassandra smiles before telling Troilus what his dream of the boar portends (V 1457).[18] Boccaccio's Troiolo also expresses his superiority to lovers 'ridendo' (*Fil.* I st. 21); but there is no source in the Italian for that further sign of self-satisfaction with which the hero concludes his speech:

> And with that word he gan caste up the browe,
> Ascaunces, 'Loo! is this naught wisely spoken?'
> (I 204–5)

Troilus shoots his eyebrows up and tosses his head. These actions contrast with those downward movements of the eyes or head which more frequently, elsewhere in the poem, signify modesty or humility, in Troilus himself (II 648, III 96) and in Criseyde (II 142, 253, V 1005). Casting up the brow occurs quite commonly in Middle English and elsewhere as an expression of pride or scorn;[19] but Chaucer offers a verbal equivalent to make the meaning more precise. The rather obscure word *ascaunces*, here to be glossed 'as if to say', occurs again at line 292 in this book, where Criseyde's look is in question; and it evidently struck some Chaucerian imitators as a neat way of supplementing a non-verbal sign with

---

[18] 'Gesture in Chaucer', p. 161, n. 12. Of a similar, but much graver, significance is Troilus' laugh from the eighth sphere at the very end of the poem: V 1821.

[19] *MED broue* n. 2, citing *Piers* A text XII 12. When Dante refers to the rebellion of Satan, it is enough for him to say only that he 'contra'l suo fattore alzò le ciglia' ('lifted up his brows against his Maker', *Inferno* XXXIV 35). Quintilian observed that 'humility is shown by a lowered head and arrogance by the head thrown back': *Institutio Oratoria*, XI iii 69.

the greater precision of words.[20] Certainly, 'Loo! is this naught wisely spoken?' are words which catch exactly the quality of Troilus' pride in his own wisdom; and the very fact that he does not utter them himself adds to the effect of complacency. It is enough for him to cast up the brow.

After reflections on the folly of such pride in Troilus, Chaucer proceeds to his humbling. 'Yet with a look his herte wex a-fere' (I 229). The fatal look is described a little later:

> And upon cas bifel that thorugh a route
> His eye percede, and so depe it wente,
> Til on Criseyde it smot, and ther it stente.
> (I 271–3)

The nouns 'look' and 'looking' occur frequently in *Troilus* (eighteen and eight times, respectively), and they show three of the senses distinguished by *OED*. The single look which first inflames the hero at line 229 is evidently his own 'act of looking' (*OED* sense 1). *OED* sense 1 b has the word again applied to that act, but 'with epithet denoting the feelings expressed by the look', as in an angry look and the like. *OED* sense 2 is more general and less ocular: 'appearance of the countenance (sometimes, of the whole person); visual or facial expression; personal aspect'. It is often difficult, as the dictionary observes, to distinguish in particular instances between senses 1 b and 2, and indeed for present purposes they belong together. Speaking looks and facial expressions both, with varying degrees of *voluntas significandi*, offer meanings to be read by an observer. These are, indeed, just the 'look' and 'chere' which Chaucer coupled as means of communication with words and messages.

The Criseyde that Troilus falls in love with at first sight is described in two stanzas, Book I lines 281–94. One critic has objected that Troilus succumbs to nothing more than simple physical attraction: 'he has never talked to Criseyde, knows nothing of her character and manners...'.[21] On the contrary, the passage strikes me as remarkable for its overriding concern precisely with character and manners, as these are manifested

---

[20] See the examples cited by *MED, ascaunce* adv. & conj., 2(a). *OED* gives examples also from Sidney and Gascoigne.

[21] D. W. Robertson, *A Preface to Chaucer: Studies in Medieval Perspectives* (Princeton, N.J., 1963), p. 479. See also p. 477 there: 'Instead of approaching her to discover what she is like... Troilus is overcome by the fact that Criseyde is "fair to the eyes and delightful to behold".'

and expressed by Criseyde's body, and as they are read by the observing Troilus. In the two stanzas of *Il Filostrato* to which Chaucer here owes much (I sts. 27–8), Boccaccio speaks of Criseida's 'bellezza celestiale', 'occhi lucenti', and 'angelico viso'; but the English omits these physical particulars, and confines itself to a rather abstract account of her womanly proportions (281–4). Chaucer's stanza is then completed by three lines only loosely based on the Italian. Boccaccio writes, 'nelli suoi sembianti / quivi mostrava una donnesca altezza' ['in her looks she there displayed a womanly dignity'], where Chaucer has:

> And ek the pure wise of hire mevynge
> Shewed wel that men myght in hire gesse
> Honour, estat, and wommanly noblesse.
> (I 285–7)

To what degree, if at all, does Criseyde set out to create such a favourable impression? Chaucer does not ask. Nor, despite his use of the word 'gesse', does he raise the still more delicate question of whether that impression is to be borne out by subsequent events. Her 'mevynge' does not betray her inadvertently, like modern 'body language'; but neither is it to be considered calculated. It was believed that gentlewomen naturally conducted themselves with dignity and restraint, avoiding extravagant *gesticulatio* and hasty or abrupt movements. In such ways, their bodies spontaneously spoke their status.

Chaucer was evidently much struck by what follows after Boccaccio's reference to 'donnesca altezza':

> e col braccio il mantel tolto davanti
> s'avea dal viso, largo a sé faccendo,
> ed alquanto la calca rimovendo.
>
> Piacque quell'atto a Troiolo e 'l tornare
> ch'ella fé 'n sé alquanto sdegnosetto,
> quasi dicesse: 'E' non ci si può stare.'
> (*Fil.* I sts. 27–8)

Havely translates these lines (which present some difficulties) as follows:

> With one arm she had drawn her mantle away from her face, thus making room for herself and keeping the crowd at some distance.

Two Middle English narratives

> This action appealed to Troiolo, and so did the way she had wrapped herself up again disdainfully, as if to say: 'They shall not stand here.'

Chaucer, I guess, found the act of drawing away a mantle (or is it a veil, as Windeatt suggests in his note?) an odd way of making space for oneself, and he probably considered the unspoken message of the gesture a little too aggressive to be ladylike; but he clearly also saw the potentialities in such minute notation of non-verbal behaviour:

> To Troilus right wonder wel with alle
> Gan for to like hire mevynge and hire chere,
> Which somdel deignous was, for she let falle
> Hire look a lite aside in swich manere,
> Ascaunces, 'What, may I nat stonden here?'
> And after that hir lokynge gan she lighte,
> That nevere thoughte hym seen so good a syghte.
> (I 288–94)

The demeanour of both heroines is described as rather haughty, but Criseyde makes her claim upon personal space more delicately than Criseida.[22] She employs not a gesture but a look, and indeed a quite subtle look. She was previously (before Troilus saw her) said to be taking up only a small amount of temple floor-space, 'in litel brede', standing near the door 'ay undre shames drede' (I 178–80); and the downward direction of her present look matches that description, conforming to familiar conventions of female 'shame'. But the look also serves to appropriate some of her small standing-area insofar as it is directed 'a lite aside' from the vertical; for gaze is one way of defining and indeed defending personal territory. Speaking looks, according to *OED*, are characterised by 'epithets denoting the feelings expressed'; but no epithet could match the precision of Chaucer's verbal gloss: 'Ascaunces, "What, may I nat stonden here?"'. This imagined utterance, introduced like that of Troilus earlier by 'ascaunces' (a word prompted here by 'quasi dicesse' in the Italian), hovers somewhere between timidity and self-assurance, with just enough of the 'somdel deignous' about it for its message to call for the corrective look that follows: 'And after that hir lokynge gan she lighte.'

---

[22] See Argyle, *Bodily Communication*, Chapter 11, 'Spatial Behaviour'. The authority on what he called 'proxemics' is E. T. Hall.

These very active looks prompt one to recall again that, in the classical and medieval theory of optics, sight was held to depend on visual rays emitted by the eye itself (see above, pp. 91–2). Hence, when Chaucer goes on to say of Criseyde's look that 'Love hadde his dwellynge / Withinne the subtile stremes of hir yen' (I 304–5), his word 'stremes' (like Boccaccio's 'raggio' at the same point) is more than a metaphor. So it was, too, in the earlier account of how Troilus first set eyes on her:

> And upon cas bifel that thorugh a route
> His eye percede, and so depe it wente,
> Til on Criseyde it smot, and ther it stente.
> (I 271–3)

Like the 'acer intuitus' by which Petrarch's Walter judged Griselda, Troilus' deep-piercing eye reads off the qualities of Criseyde from 'hire mevynge and hire chere'; and it is above all 'hire loke' – not 'her looks', in the modern, physical sense – that carries the message to his heart (lines 295, 307, 325, 364). He has indeed never talked to Criseyde, but he does not need to: the sight of her conveys all he needs to know.[23]

Criseyde does not herself set eyes on Troilus in the temple; but she later has two sightings, in each case looking down from a window in her house to the street below (II 610–65, 1247–74). The first of these corresponds in position to the one such sighting in *Filostrato* (II sts. 81–3), for each occurs in the aftermath of the visit at which Pandarus first tells her of Troilus' love; but the two accounts differ greatly in character. In Boccaccio, Troiolo sets off with Pandaro to see what effect his friend's revelation may have had; and Criseida, standing at a window, coquettishly returns his gaze: 'She did not behave cruelly or harshly towards Troiolo as he looked at her, but turning around gazed modestly at him over her right shoulder' (II st. 82). Chaucer recasts this episode in the mould of those episodes in romance where a lady looks down from a window upon a knight who fights on her behalf, as the besieged Lady Lyones looked down from her castle at Sir Gareth of Orkney in Malory.[24] Criseyde, in this domesticated version, looks down from the

---

[23] In his discussion of looking, the sociologist Georg Simmel remarks that 'it is remarkable how much we know about a person from the first look at them': *Simmel on Culture: Selected Writings*, ed. D. Frisby and M. Featherstone (London, 1997), p. 113.

[24] Malory, *Works*, 321.30–2, 323.31–5. See above, pp. 94–5.

window of her private room to see Troilus riding back from battle with the Greeks – 'a knyghtly sighte trewely'. He passes on, quite unconscious of her gaze; but Criseyde has been struck, most especially by what she sees of his mute responses to the plaudits of the bystanders in the street:

> For which he wex a litel reed for shame
> When he the peple upon hym herde cryen,
> That to byholde it was a noble game
> How sobrelich he caste down his yen.
> Criseyda gan al his chere aspien,
> And leet it so softe in hire herte synke,
> That to hireself she seyde, 'Who yaf me drynke?'
> (II 645–51)

Here, as in the temple scene, it is looks and expressions that most strike home. Troilus' blush and his sober lowering of the eyes express to the bystanders his becoming 'shame' or embarrassment at being compared by them to Hector; but they also convey to Criseyde something of the noble nature of that stranger who, she has just been told, is in love with her. His 'chere' speaks for him, just as Criseyde's did before.

The second episode, without a parallel in Boccaccio, brings the first two-way exchange of looking between the lovers. Pandarus organises it, telling Troilus in advance that he should ride past Criseyde's house at a time when he will make sure to be sitting at a window with his niece: "'And if the list, than maystow us salue; / And upon me make thow thi countenaunce'" (II 1016–17). Accordingly, having manoeuvred Criseyde into a bay window overlooking the street, he draws her attention to the approach of Troilus:

> 'O fle naught in (he seeth us, I suppose),
> Lest he may thynken that ye hym eschuwe.'
> 'Nay, nay,' quod she, and wex as red as rose.
> With that he gan hire humbly to saluwe
> With dredful chere, and oft his hewes muwe;
> And up his look debonairly he caste,
> And bekked on Pandare, and forth he paste.
> (II 1254–60)

Pandarus suggested that Troilus might salute both his niece and him, but in the event his salutation is directed at Criseyde alone. Riding past on his courser, he may be supposed to bow his head in the equestrian equivalent of a bow, expressing his feelings at the same time with apprehensive 'chere' and (like Criseyde) blushes.[25] But he, like Criseyde, is capable of 'lightening' his look – here by raising his head and looking up at the window 'debonairly'. He then singles out Pandarus with a 'beck', just as Pandarus had advised him to do: 'upon me make thow thi countenaunce'. These two difficult words, 'beck' and 'countenaunce', evidently refer here to some gesture of recognition, perhaps in this context a nod of the head. Such an act – more rapid and casual than his near-bow to Criseyde – would serve to acknowledge the acquaintance of the two men without betraying their actual complicity. Troilus then rides on, leaving Criseyde once more to reflect on what she has seen:

> To telle in short, hire liked al in-fere,
> His persoun, his aray, his look, his chere,
> His goodly manere, and his gentilesse.
> (II 1266–8)

It is a comprehensive and characteristic list, in which 'look' and 'chere' take their rightful place, between 'persoun' and 'aray' on the one side and 'goodly manere' and 'gentilesse' on the other.

Eyes and faces, however, do not always tell the truth. Indeed, the most intensive performance of love-looking in the poem comes, not from Troilus, but from the 'sudden' Diomede. Visiting Criseyde in Calkas' tent on the tenth day after her arrival in the Greek camp, Diomede embarks on a set speech, in the course of which he offers himself as her servant in love. When he comes to this offer, he breaks off, as if overcome with emotion:

> And with that word he gan to waxen red,
> And in his speche a litel wight he quok,
> And caste asyde a litel wight his hed,
> And stynte a while; and afterward he wok,

---

[25] Windeatt, in the note to lines 1257–8 in his edition (*Troilus and Criseyde*, Harlow, 1984), cites the advice given by Love in the English *Romaunt of the Rose* on haunting a lady's house: 'And if so be it happe thee / That thou thi love there maist see, / In siker wise thou hir salewe, / Wherewith thi colour wole transmewe, / And eke thy blod shal al toquake, / Thyn hewe eke chaungen for hir sake' (2523–8).

Two Middle English narratives

And sobreliche on hire he threw his lok,
And seyde...
(v 925–30)

Chaucer follows Boccaccio closely here (*Fil.* vi st. 23), tracing much the same sequence of expressions and looks, from agitation to a recovered composure.[26] Even the repetition of 'a litel wight' in successive lines matches the repetition of 'alquanto' in the Italian: 'His voice trembling somewhat, he lowered his gaze, somewhat turning his eyes away from her.' That repetition (Diomede is not overdoing his effects) may have suggested Chaucer's bolder repetitions, whereby all his six lines begin with 'And', creating an impression of NVC at its most calculated and mechanical. For Diomede belongs to that class of hypocritical lovers, described by Gower, who 'feignen hem an humble port' and employ 'fals pitous lokynge' to ensnare women (above, p. 90).

Nowhere else in the poem are speeches interrupted by such set pieces. In long scenes of conversation or complaint, looks and expressions occur dispersedly, expressing the feelings of speakers and the relationships between them. I conclude with a couple of examples from the scenes in Book II between Criseyde and her uncle. In the first of these, as we have seen, Pandarus approaches his revelation of Troilus' love with a circumspect 'cough'. Following this with a promise of going straight to the point, he nevertheless breaks off:

And with that word he gan right inwardly
Byholden hire and loken on hire face,
And seyde, 'On swich a mirour goode grace!'

Than thought he thus: 'If I my tale endite
Aught harde, or make a proces any whyle,
She shal no savour have therin but lite,
And trowe I wolde hire in my wil bigyle;
For tendre wittes wenen al be wyle
Theras thei kan nought pleynly understonde;
Forthi hire wit to serven wol I fonde' –

---

[26] Chaucer adds the sober look. After lowering his eyes, Boccaccio's Diomede 'soon regained his composure, becoming more confident than he had been before, and continued smoothly...'.

> And loked on hire in a bysi wyse,
> And she was war that he byheld hire so,
> And seyde, 'Lord! so faste ye m'avise!
> Sey ye me nevere er now? What sey ye, no?'
> 'Yis, yys,' quod he, 'and bet wole er I go'.
> (II 264–78)

Such a long, slow look – 'inward' and 'busy' – invites interpretation of its meaning, just as it does at the corresponding moment in the *Filostrato*, where Pandaro gazes fixedly ('fiso') at Criseida's face (II st. 35). So in both poems, the heroine expresses her curiosity (in Boccaccio with a smile, st. 36) by a bantering question – 'Have you never seen me before, or what?' – to which her uncle responds that he is simply admiring her beauty. This is one of the moments in Boccaccio's poem which evidently intrigued Chaucer, showing the subtle uses to which looks can be put; for he strengthens the effect by intercalating a stanza of his own (II 267–73). By setting this stanza where he does, between two statements of the look (one of them added by him), Chaucer lengthens Pandarus' gaze to accommodate a period of reflection, in which he considers how his 'wil' or intention can be adjusted to his niece's 'tendre wittes'.

When, later in the same book, Pandarus pays her another visit, to deliver Troilus' letter, Criseyde is no longer in the dark. She knows what is going on, and the production of the letter shocks her into an indignant response:

> Ful dredfully tho gan she stonden stylle,
> And took it naught, but al hire humble chere
> Gan for to chaunge, and seyde...
> (II 1128–30)

Criseyde's expression and demeanour here, like her ensuing words of refusal, are more uncompromising than in the Italian;[27] and Pandarus takes offence:

> This Pandarus gan on hire for to stare,
> And seyde, 'Now is this the grettest wondre
> That evere I seigh! Lat be this nyce fare!'
> (II 1142–4)

---

[27] In Boccaccio, Criseida alters her meek expression only slightly ('un poco') and goes on to speak quietly ('pianamente'): *Fil.* II st. 110.

It is an incredulous stare: how could she suppose that he would do anything improper? The stare is Chaucer's, for Boccaccio's Pandaro is simply 'alquanto di questo turbato' (II st. 112). Pandaro has, in fact, less cause to be disturbed than Pandarus; for, after he has told Criseida that she has no call to be bashful, she just smiles, takes the letter, and puts it in her bosom. Chaucer's Pandarus needs to take more drastic measures. After his own speech of reassurance, he takes hold of his niece 'and in hire bosom the lettre down he thraste'. Here, as on that other occasion when Pandarus 'thrust' his arm under Criseyde's neck, his gesture is more delicate than it might appear, for it allows Criseyde to accept the letter without loss of face. She may still talk of throwing it away; but when she declares that she will send no reply, it is with a smile; and when Pandarus offers to do the writing himself, she laughs (line 1163). The letter is accepted, the answer will be written, and Pandarus is forgiven. From Criseyde's indignant 'chere', through Pandarus' incredulous stare, to those smiles and laughs, expressions and looks trace the trajectory of an episode which, like that in Criseyde's bedroom later, begins in tension and ends in playful reconciliation, with no dishonour to either party.

It will, I hope, have been evident from the present discussion that the same code of manners, broadly speaking, governs social exchanges in the Troys of Boccaccio and Chaucer. Greetings and partings, for instance, take similar forms in both. This is not surprising, given the polite circles in which both poets moved, and the polite French writings with which both were familiar. Yet one may also see some evidence of cross-cultural differences, in changes made by the English poet: his omission of 'Italianate clasping and kissing of the friend', and especially his addition of occasions when men fall on their knees. These kneeling gestures reflect Chaucer's greater concern with honour, the giving and receiving of honour (especially that of Criseyde). They also contribute to that greater overall formality of manners noted by Windeatt. Perhaps Chaucer's London was, in such respects, more old-fashioned than Boccaccio's Naples. Not all occasions call for formality, however; and Chaucer was evidently impressed by Boccaccio's notation of those small behaviours, especially looks, by which characters communicate their thoughts and feelings. When he finds them in the Italian, he takes them up and develops them: such things as, in the temple scene, the head-toss of Troilus and the downward gaze of Criseyde. He also introduces significant looks, expressions, and little movements of his own invention, especially in his extended scenes between Pandarus and Criseyde. Hence *Troilus* becomes one of the richest of all medieval narrative sources for an understanding of the part played by non-verbal communication in familiar private exchanges.

Sir Gawain and the Green Knight belongs to that type of Arthurian text which focusses on a single adventure. It confines itself strictly to its chosen story, the Adventure of the Green Chapel, leaving aside all 'collateral' matter just as Chaucer does in *Troilus*. Although much shorter than Chaucer's poem (2,530 lines as against 8,239), *Sir Gawain* employs, on a more modest scale, the same scenic method of narrative, and so finds room, in telling its not very extended story, for a comparable wealth of gestural detail. Indeed, the poem furnished Werner Habicht with a last and culminating set of examples in his study of gesture in Middle English poetry.[28] For present purposes, its action may be treated as a series of encounters, marked off by formalities of greeting and farewell (or by the equally significant absence of such formalities). I shall take these in turn: first, the encounter at Camelot with the Green Knight; then, the hero's encounters in the castle of Hautdesert; and finally, his second encounter with the Green Knight at the Green Chapel. In most of these scenes, looks and gestures play a significant part, along with words, in expressing or concealing the feelings of characters and articulating their relationships.

Immediately after the Green Knight has ridden into Arthur's hall, and before he has spoken a word, there occurs a long description of his appearance and of the impression he creates, including the remark: 'He ferde as freke were fade' (line 149). If this means, as it probably does, 'he behaved like a man who was an enemy', then it provides the key to his subsequent behaviour.[29] For a man to ride straight in to a lord's hall may itself act as a sign of hostile intention (unless, like the young

---

[28] *Gebärde*, pp. 148–56. Although I consider that Habicht makes too much of the distinctively realistic and 'individualising' nature of the gestures in *Gawain*, I am indebted to his discussion. Valuable also are the studies of manners and etiquette in the poem by Jonathan Nicholls in *The Matter of Courtesy*, Chapter 8, and by Ad Putter, *'Sir Gawain and the Green Knight' and French Arthurian Romance* (Oxford, 1995), Chapter 2.

[29] All quotations are taken from the edition of the poem by Tolkien and Gordon, revised Davis. *MED fad(e)* pred. adj. distinguishes two meanings: '(a) Having the character of

Perceval, he simply does not know the rules); and that significance finds confirmation in what the Green Knight then does:

> Þis haþel heldez hym in and þe halle entres,
> Drivande to þe heȝe dece, dut he no woþe,
> Haylsed he never one, bot heȝe he over loked.
> (221–3)

To ride straight up to the place of honour, to offer no greeting, and (in what follows) to address the lord of the hall with an unceremonious singular pronoun 'thou' – these are all, as several writers have noticed, conventional marks of the challenger or hostile messenger in romances.[30] The Green Knight is playing his part by the book, employing those signs by which newcomers customarily first communicate their unfriendly intentions.

The Green Knight has, of course, even more reason than ordinary Arthurian challengers to be playing a part; for Morgan le Fay has despatched him in transfigured form to test the pride of the Round Table and frighten Guinevere to death, as we later learn. Hence, throughout the scene in Fitt 1 he enriches his performance with an exceptional range of looks and actions, all provocatively expressive of scornful superiority. 'Accordant to his wordes was his cheere', as Chaucer's Squire says of a very different emissary. His 'looks' are there to be read from the first:

> He loked as layt so lyȝt,
> So sayd al þat hym syȝe;
> Hit semed as no mon myȝt
> Under his dynttez dryȝe.
> (199–202)

In their edition of the poem, Andrew and Waldron have a note on line 199 here: '"His glance was as swift as lightning (*layt*)"; *loked* means

---

a foe, an intruder, or a transgressor: inimical, hostile, troublesome...'; and '(b) having the spirit of a warrior: eager for battle, bold, fierce.' Like *OED*, which makes a similar distinction, *MED* places the *Gawain* use under (b); but sense (a) has more point in the context.

[30] See J. A. Burrow, *A Reading of 'Sir Gawain and the Green Knight'* (London, 1965); Nicholls, *Matter of Courtesy*, p. 119; Putter, *SGGK and French Arthurian Romance*, pp. 86–9, citing from Chrétien's *Chevalier de la Charrete* and *Perceval*, the Vulgate prose romances, *Guy of Warwick*, and *Sir Degrevant*.

"glanced a look" rather than "appeared".³¹ This is right: the Green Knight directs what Habicht calls an 'übliche wilde Heldenblick' at the company, causing them to recognise him as a man of strength and prowess.³² A little later (in the passage already quoted), instead of offering a courteous salute, 'heȝe he over loked' (223). Editors take this to mean that he directed his gaze high over the heads of the company, which sounds suitably haughty; but an alternative interpretation is suggested by two obsolete senses of the verb 'overlook' recorded in Middle English: *OED* sense 4, 'To look down upon; to survey from above', and sense 5, *figurative*, To "look down upon" as from a higher social or intellectual position; to despise; to treat with contempt, to slight.' So perhaps, from his high position still on horseback, the Green Knight both looks down upon the company and 'looks down upon them', as he contemptuously withholds the customary words of greeting: '"Wher is", he sayd, "þe governour of þis gyng?"' Following this not very polite question, he again uses his eyes:

> To knyȝtez he kest his yȝe
> And reled hym up and doun;
> He stemmed, and con studie
> Quo walt þer most renoun.
> (228–31).

The pronoun 'hym' is plural here, referring to the eyes; and 'reled', to judge by other occurrences in the poem, denotes some kind of abrupt and spasmodic movement. As the Green Knight looks 'up and down' to identify the governor, he evidently moves his eyes with a calculated discourteous freedom. The courtesy books disapprove:

> When thou shalt speake to any man,
>   Role not to fast thyne eye,
> Gase thou not to and fro as one
>   Thats voyd of curtesye.³³

---

[31] *The Poems of the Pearl Manuscript*, ed. Andrew and Waldron, p. 215. Sarah Stanbury's chapter 'The Framing of Gaze in *Sir Gawain and the Green Knight*', in her *Seeing the 'Gawain'-Poet: Description and the Act of Perception* (Philadelphia, Pa., 1991), concerns 'shifting perceptual frames', not expressive looks.
[32] 'Customary fierce hero's glance', *Gebärde*, p. 152.
[33] Hugh Rhodes, *Boke of Nurture*, lines 173–6, p. 76 in Furnivall, *Babees Book*, cited in this connection by Nicholls, p. 119, n. 25.

Two Middle English narratives

Faced with these provocations, Arthur responds with studied correctness. He greets the stranger with a bow ('rekenly hym reverenced', 251), inviting him to dismount and join them. The Green Knight, however, goes on to announce his mission, the Beheading Game; and when this announcement is greeted with stunned silence, reacts with a series of most expressive actions:

> Þe renk on his rouncé hym ruched in his sadel,
> And runischly his rede y3en he reled aboute,
> Bende his bresed bro3ez, blycande grene,
> Wayved his berde for to wayte quo-so wolde ryse.
> When non wolde kepe hym with carp he co3ed ful hy3e,
> And rimed hym ful richely, and ry3t hym to speke:
> 'What, is þis Arþures hous...?'
> (303–9)

In a doctor's waiting-room, or outside an occupied telephone kiosk, the simple act of looking at one's watch will serve as a sign of impatience; and so it is here.[34] The Green Knight needs to watch the whole hall for a response to his challenge; so turning in his saddle, like darting his eyes about and waving his beard, has a practical purpose, 'to wayte quo-so wolde ryse'. But all three gestures also speak, as if to say, 'I am waiting.' The eyes and beard further communicate anger and menace, along with the contraction of the bristling green eyebrows in a frown. Red eyes were held to be signs of manly courage and strength, and the adverb 'runischly', though its precise meaning is uncertain, evidently marks the looks as alarming.[35] The line about the beard means that the Green Knight turned his head from side to side, 'to see if anyone would get up'; but the rather strange synecdoche whereby the beard stands for the whole head adds another intention. Beards stand for masculine power, and the stranger is asserting his superior machismo by flaunting his big

---

[34] Remarking that the category 'gesture' has no sharp boundaries, Adam Kendon observes that 'almost any action can be performed in such a way that it is seen as having a gestural component added to it', instancing the waiter who removes a cork from a wine bottle with a flourish: 'Geography of Gesture', p. 135.

[35] 'Runischly' has been variously glossed as 'fiercely', roughly', 'violently', or 'rudely': see the note *ad loc.* in the Tolkien–Gordon–Davis edition. On the eyes, see R. B. White, 'A Note on the Green Knight's Red Eyes', in *English Language Notes*, 2 (1962), 250–2, and *MED red* adj. 1 c(d).

bushy one in the faces of those whom he calls 'berdlez chylder' (280).[36] When none of the beardless children respond to his provocations, he prepares to speak, first with a loud 'cough'. Pandarus prefixed his important announcement to Criseyde with a 'cough'; and here, as there, the word may be understood as referring either to a cough proper or to a significant clearing of the throat ('ahem!').[37] But, whereas Pandarus makes his prelusive noise only 'a lite', the Green Knight trumpets his out 'ful hyȝe', suggesting not only his intention to speak publicly but also the scorn that he is about to express. His remaining gesture, too, occurs elsewhere as a sign of an intention to speak. In the alliterative *Wars of Alexander*, Alexander enters the Temple of the Sun and, finding the god in bed, kneels to greet him. Whereupon,

> Þe renke within þe redell þan raxsils his armes,
> Rymed him full renyschly & rekind þire wordis:
> 'Haile, Alexsandire...'[38]

The collocation with 'raxsils' ('stretches') supports a meaning such as 'drew himself up' for 'rimed hym' in both poems; and in both, the gesture – performed 'ful richely' in *Gawain* – expresses a lordly, or godly, self-possession.[39] It concludes what has been a notable piece of dumbshow, as the Green Knight plays out the part determined for him by Morgan. What confronts the court is not, as Arthur later suggests to reassure Guinevere, a mere Christmas 'laykyng of enterludez'; but the stranger's actions, like his words, are all directed, theatrically, at a watching audience, and are governed by a consistent *voluntas significandi*.

The Green Knight's ensuing speech ends with a scornful laugh, and prompts Arthur to his one uncontrolled, indeed uncontrollable, response: 'þe blod schot for scham into his schyre face.' Blushing is an

---

[36] In *Purgatorio* XXXI, when Dante hangs his head before Beatrice, she tells him to 'lift up your beard' (line 68); and he comments: 'when by the beard she asked for my face, well I knew the venom of the argument' (74–5). He is to behave like a male adult, not an ashamed child.
[37] Andrew and Waldron gloss with 'coughed, cleared his throat' (and see their note to l. 307). Tolkien–Gordon–Davis glosses 'cried out, shouted', but I cannot accept the arguments for this in the note to l. 307.
[38] Ed. Duggan and Turville-Petre, ll. 5057–9.
[39] Most editors agree on 'drew himself up' (from Anglo-Saxon *ryman*, to make room); but Andrew and Waldron suggest, as an alternative, 'cleared his throat (?)'.

involuntary symptom, not a sign; but, in what follows, the king and Sir Gawain between them reassert the dignity of the court by the deliberation of their gestures. Gawain seeks Arthur's permission to leave his seat beside Guinevere at the high table with a bow (340), and, having received his command to rise, comes and kneels before him to take over the Green Knight's axe:

> Kneled doun bifore þe kyng, and cachez þat weppen;
> And he luflyly hit hym laft, and lyfte up his honde,
> And gef hym Goddez blessyng...
> (368–70)

This little scene has something of the quality of a formal investiture. Gawain is invested with the adventure, on behalf of the whole Round Table, by the symbolic act of handing over the axe.[40] In the process, he also publicly takes possession of the weapon: it is now his own to keep, as the Green Knight earlier promised (293, cf. 477). Arthur adds a further touch of liturgical solemnity when he blesses the knight, raising his hand and making the sign of the cross.[41] These are performative gestures, producing an immediate and significant effect. Henceforth, Gawain has possession of the adventure, the axe, and no doubt God's blessing too. They are all his by virtue of Arthur's gestures. Yet here, as elsewhere in the scene, one has to reckon also with a second intention. By acting and speaking as they do, Arthur and Gawain signify that they are not so easily shaken – 'overwalt wyth a worde of on wyȝes speche' – as the Green Knight had claimed. There is, to that extent, a supplement of 'laykyng' in their ceremonious behaviour.

The Augustinian criterion of *voluntas significandi* encounters in this poem a writer capable of considerable subtlety. When Gawain kneels before Arthur he has, as it were, one eye on the king and the other on the Green Knight. He signifies both deference to the one and defiance to the other. Even actions which may appear purely practical, like looking

---

[40] On the part played by such symbolic objects in various ceremonies of *traditio* or handing over, see R. F. Green, *A Crisis of Truth: Literature and Law in Ricardian England* (Philadelphia, Pa., 1999), pp. 50–7 ('Tokens').

[41] T. Silverstein, in a note to ll. 366–71 in his edition of the poem (Chicago, 1984), observes that such formal blessing 'does not generally appear in Arthurian romance at the beginning of quest or adventure'. He notes, however, *Lybeaus Desconus*, ed. Mills, Cotton Ms, ll. 247–9.

round for a response, can manifest a second intention. The same can be said of the moment when the Green Knight 'draws down his coat' as he prepares to receive a blow. He needs to expose his neck for the purpose, but the action, as it is described, takes its place also among speaking gestures of self-possession:

> Wyth sturne schere þer he stod he stroked his berde,
> And wyth a countenaunce dryȝe he droȝ doun his cote,
> No more mate ne dismayd for hys mayn dintez
> Þen any burne upon bench hade broȝt hym to drynk
>   Of wyne.
> (334–8)

He is indeed not dismayed by Arthur's practice strokes. Habicht says that stroking one's beard is a 'typical anger-gesture' (p. 153); but anger does not seem quite the point here, despite the 'sturne schere' ('severe expression'). The Green Knight is rather preparing himself to submit his neck to the axe with ostentatious dignity and coolness. Hence also the 'countenaunce dryȝe', the impassive expression, with which he pulls down the collar of his coat.

At the end of this first encounter, the adversary rides away without any ceremony of leavetaking, just as he had ridden in with no greeting, leaving Camelot to make what it can of the affair. Arthur, with Gawain, takes the lead in reducing the shock of what they have seen:

> Þe kyng and Gawen þare
> At þat grene þay laȝe and grenne,
> Ȝet breved watȝ hit ful bare
> A mervayl among þo menne.
> (463–6)

To 'grin' here is probably to bare the teeth in a scornful smile – a facial expression which serves, along with the laugh, to dismiss the marvel as merely ridiculous. Yet this behaviour conceals Arthur's true feelings, as the next lines make plain:

> Þaȝ Arþer the hende kyng at hert hade wonder,
> He let no semblaunt be sene, bot sayde ful hyȝe
> To þe comlych quene wyth cortays speche...
> (467–9)

Two Middle English narratives

This is the first of several occasions when the poet remarks on a lack of fit between 'semblaunt' and 'hert'. For a variety of reasons, gestures and looks may be used, like words, to express feelings which people do not have, or to conceal feelings which they do have. On the present occasion, Arthur's 'wonder' is suppressed by two display rules: it is both unknightly and, in company, discourteous to show that one has been shaken.[42] The latter consideration motivates the 'cortays speche' that Arthur goes on to make to Guinevere, comparing what they have just seen to a mere 'laykyng of enterludez'.

In the baldest of summaries of the poem's plot, the second fitt would contribute only a departure, a journey, and an arrival, ending with the host's proposal of the Exchange of Winnings. Both the departure and the arrival are described with some elaboration, especially the latter. Unlike the Green Knight, Sir Gawain leaves Camelot at the beginning of the fitt with all due ceremony. The first of the poem's many kisses occurs here, as he takes his leave of the lords and ladies of Arthur's court: 'And þay hym kyst and conveyed, bikende hym to Kryst' (596). As a gesture of leavetaking, this conforms to English (and French) custom as observed by Erasmus in the letter already quoted: 'when you take your leave they speed you on your way with kisses' (above, p. 33). In the account of the arming of Gawain, as he prepares to go to meet his death making 'ay god chere' in the best heroic fashion (562), there is a second and more unexpected kiss. He receives his helmet from an attendant and, before putting it on, 'hastily hit kysses' – a symbolic gesture of bonding with the equipment upon which he is to depend in his journey. During that journey, the helmet figures again, in the gesture with which Gawain signifies his gratitude to God and St Julian for answering his prayer for lodging on Christmas Eve: 'Þenne hatz he hendly of his helme, and heȝly he þonkez / Jesus and sayn Gilyan' (773–4). Doffing headgear is a familiar sign of deferential greeting, and the examples given in an earlier chapter (above, p. 30) included some where knights doffed their helms on such occasions; but it is unusual for the gesture to be employed as a sign of gratitude to God – a notable expression of that

---

[42] See above, pp. 84–5. There is a somewhat similar point of courtesy in the behaviour of ladies competing for New Year's gifts earlier in the scene: 'Ladies laȝed ful loude, þoȝ þay lost haden' (69).

knightly piety, or pious knightliness, attributed by the poet to his hero throughout.

Gawain's reception and entertainment at Hautdesert on Christmas Eve are narrated at length (lines 807–994). Both Nicholls and Putter, drawing on evidence from French romances and the courtesy books, have shown how everyone concerned here acts according to the highest standards of polite behaviour.[43] On occasions such as this, stranger guests and their hosts will be reading each other for information about status and intentions, conveyed by gestures and looks, as well as by words. The first such exchange occurs when members of the castle household come out across the drawbridge to welcome the newcomer:

> Þay let doun þe grete draȝt and derely out ȝeden,
> And kneled doun on her knes upon þe colde erþe
> To welcum þis ilk wyȝ as worþy hom þoȝt.
> (817–19)

To this act of deferential greeting Gawain responds in exemplary fashion, by 'raising' them, that is, bidding them arise (821). Then, having entered the castle, he is met by the lord, who has courteously come down from his chamber to the hall. They exchange civilities and embrace: 'As frekez þat semed fayn / Ayþer oþer in armez con felde' (840–1). 'Semed' implies no falseness here. Both men are really glad; but when they embrace, they are making their gladness show in the expressive gestures prescribed when equals meet and greet.

The closely-observed scene in the castle chapel that evening has a number of significant small behaviours. As Gawain first enters the chapel, 'Þe lorde laches hym by þe lappe and ledez hym to sytte', after which the two men renew their speeches of welcome and thanks, and again embrace (936–9). Leading a guest to a suitable seat, as the host does also at lines 1029–30 and 1083, is in itself no more than a common gesture of hospitality; but the poet's verbs in these three places, 'laches... lachchez... sesed', represent actions more vigorous and insistent than the customary leadings by hand. In particular, the host's gripping on Gawain's 'lappe' (some loose-hanging piece of his clothing such as a sleeve) may recall another active and dominating character,

---

[43] Nicholls, *Matter of Courtesy*, pp. 124–9; Putter, *SGGK*, pp. 53–9, 69–70.

Two Middle English narratives

Chaucer's Pandarus; for Pandarus also leads Criseyde into Troilus' sickroom 'by the lappe' (III 59), and it is by the lap again that he brings Troilus into her room later (III 742). I do not think that Werner Habicht is right in his claim that *Gawain* can be clearly distinguished from other Middle English writings by its particular cultivation of 'individuelle Gebärden', individualising gestures.[44] Can this be said of the hero himself? Yet Bertilak, like Pandarus, does certainly have his own distinctive ways of behaving. So again, when the party has withdrawn from the chapel to a chamber, he hangs his hood up on a spear and laughingly offers it as a prize to whoever will make the greatest contribution to their Christmas entertainment. It has always been a special obligation upon hosts to uphold the party spirit; but this host puts his message across with a zest that is almost alarming.

Meantime, Gawain has already met his host's wife in the chapel, accompanied there by an old lady:

> An oþer lady hir lad bi þe lyft honde,
> Þat watz alder þen ho, an auncian hit semed,
> And heʒly honowred with haþelez aboute.
> (947–9)

These lines send out signals of a puzzling kind. The unidentified 'auncian' is highly honoured by everyone; and indeed, at the Christmas feast on the following day, it is she, not Sir Gawain, that takes the place of honour on the host's right-hand side (1001). But who is she, that she can 'lead' the lady of the house? If the left hand in question belongs to the younger lady, as seems probable, then the old one is leading her on the honorific right side.[45] Yet to give honour in this way is the privilege of a hostess, not a guest, as Nicholls observes: 'This line shows that Morgan is not a guest at the castle. If she were a guest, then the position of the two ladies would be reversed ... As it is, Morgan shows herself to be in the dominant role, and possibly of greater rank in the castle, because she is able to give an honoured position, rather than take

---

[44] The discussion of *Gawain* by Habicht in his book is headed: '*Sir Gawain and the Green Knight*: Die individuellen Gebärden'. (Habicht excludes Chaucer from his study.)

[45] For 'by' in such expressions, see *OED By* prep., adv. 28. In the Prose *Lancelot*, an officer at Arthur's court, honouring a newcomer, 'lou prist par la main senestre, si lou mena devant lou roi' (ed. Kennedy, 55.31–4). For discussion of leading on the right side, see above, p. 49.

it.'⁴⁶ It is a subtle bit of 'lateral symbolism', creating an enigma which is only resolved when the Green Knight finally identifies the old lady as 'Morgne la Faye, þat in my hous lenges' (2446).

After exchanging glances with the younger woman and receiving the host's permission, Gawain approaches the pair:

> Þe alder he haylses, heldande ful lowe,
> Þe loveloker he lappez a lyttel in armez,
> He kysses hir comlyly, and kny3tly he melez.
> (972–4)

The gestural distinction that Gawain makes here turns, not on sexual attractiveness, but on perceived status. To quote again the cultural anthropologist Raymond Firth: 'A basic function of greeting and parting rituals is in creating occasion for establishment of relative status positions, or in providing a code (a "vocabulary") in which status relations can be expressed.'⁴⁷ An embrace and a kiss are perfectly normal forms of polite greeting when a man meets a lady of similar status to himself. Perhaps it is the outstanding attractiveness of his host's wife that prompts a discreet Gawain to underperform his embrace ('lappez a lyttel'); but, if he fails to embrace the older lady altogether, this is emphatically not because she is so ugly. His verbal greeting and his deep bow to her (overperformed, in this case) belong rather to the gestural vocabulary of deference, offered here in recognition of the visible fact that she is (for whatever reason) top lady in the castle.⁴⁸ Certainly no offence is given, for the ladies 'take him between them' and lead him into the chamber, where the rest of the evening passes merrily.

The last scene of the second fitt, in a chamber on the evening of 28 December, shows Bertilak exerting his authority as host. Since Gawain can stay for another three days, the Green Chapel being so near, he first proposes that he should go hunting while his guest rests in bed. Gawain responds with a bow:

---

⁴⁶ *Matter of Courtesy*, p. 131, n. 48. I have also benefitted from an unpublished note by Dr Nicholls.
⁴⁷ Above, p. 27. See pp. 28–38 there for discussion of deferential and non-deferential types of greeting ritual.
⁴⁸ Nicholls draws a similar conclusion: 'He can kiss his hostess, but does not feel of sufficient status to kiss the mysterious person of high power' (*Matter of Courtesy*, pp. 132–3).

> Gavayn grantez alle þyse,
> Hym heldande, as þe hende.
> (1103–4)

Hosts have power, including the power to hurt; and guests who are courteous ('hende') will submit to their will with appropriate ceremony. Later in the same scene, a more momentous gesture is referred to by Bertilak, when he first proposes the Exchange of Winnings:

> 'Swete, swap we so, sware with trawþe,
> Queþer, leude, so lymp, lere oþer better.'
> (1108–9)

Editors who gloss 'swap' here as 'exchange', or 'swap' in the modern sense, are certainly wrong.[49] *OED* gives the sense correctly: 'to "strike hands" in token of an agreement or bargain'.[50] Bertilak refers, not to future acts of exchange, but to the present agreement to do so and the act of striking hands together by which that agreement is to be performed. Like the clasping of hands, this gesture belongs to the ritual of formal contract. Gawain is to commit himself and his 'trawþe', on this and the two subsequent occasions, more deeply than a modern reader may appreciate. The ceremony, as Richard Green observes, takes the form of 'ancient trothplight': 'Their *couenauntez* are made in front of witnesses, confirmed with a handslap and an oath – "Swete, swap we so, sware with trawþe" (line 1108) – and sealed with a drink – "Who bryngez vus þis beuerage, þis bargayn is maked" (1112)'.[51] After the drink is summoned, Gawain and Bertilak both laugh (1113) and the company shortly breaks up with parting kisses (1118).

In the third fitt, on the second of the three days of the Exchange of Winnings, Bertilak has killed a boar, and he presents the company with its remains, including the head: 'Þenne hondeled þay þe hoge hed, þe hende mon hit praysed, / And let lodly þerat þe lorde for to here' (1633–4). The same general principle of courtesy which earlier

---

[49] So Tolkien–Gordon–Davis and Silverstein. 'Swap' (originally, to strike) is first recorded by *OED* as meaning 'exchange' in 1594.
[50] *OED Swap, swop* v. 7a; so *MED swappen* v. 4. See also *OED Strike* v. 69, and *MED striken* v. 12 (a) and (b).
[51] *A Crisis of Truth*, p. 317. For a lawyer's view, see H. K. Lucke, 'Striking a Bargain', *Adelaide Law Review*, 1 (1962), 293–311, noting that the 'clapping noise marked the moment when the bargain was clinched' (p. 296).

required Arthur and Gawain to betray no sign of their 'wonder' at the decapitated Green Knight this time requires the hero, as a 'hende mon', to praise ('here') or flatter his host with a show of horror at another huge head – grimacing, perhaps, or throwing up his hands. This moment is characteristic of a fitt in which gestures and looks cannot safely be taken at face value, especially in the bedroom scenes between Gawain and the lady. People behave as if something were the case where it is not; and more than once, the poet represents such behaviour by use of the verb *leten* ('behave'), as in 'let lodly' in the lines just quoted.[52] At the beginning of the first bedroom scene, Gawain, hearing the lady's quiet entrance, 'layde hym doun lystyly and let as he slepte' (1190). After pretending to sleep for a time, he pretends to wake up: 'And unlouked his yȝe-lyddez, and let as hym wondered' (1201). The same verb is then used of the lady, whom he sees smiling at him: 'Ful lufly con ho lete / Wyth lyppez smal laȝande' (1206–7); and again, later in the same scene:

> And ay þe lady let lyk as hym loved mych;
> Þe freke ferde with defence, and feted ful fayre.
> (1281–2)

Perhaps 'feted' also here suggests, if not pretence, at least behaviour calculated to produce a desired effect.[53] The underlying intentions are 'defence' on Gawain's side, and attack on the side of the lady. Like her husband, the latter is playing a part, supporting her words with appropriate looks and actions.[54] As she prepares to leave on the first morning, she flashes him a laughing glance (1290), and on the second morning she softens her teasing reproaches with laughter and 'a luflych loke' (1480). If there are not more such love-looks in the bedroom

---

[52] See *OED Let* v.¹, sense 15: 'To behave, comport oneself; to have (a particular) behaviour or appearance; to make *as though*, to pretend'. *MED leten* v. 16 and 17(b). See Putter, *SGGK*, p. 79.

[53] *MED feten* v. 2. The verb is related etymologically to, though distinct from, *MED faiten* v.(1), 'To act or speak falsely; to dissemble'.

[54] The illustrator of the Cotton manuscript adds a bold gesture not in the text: the lady touches the beard of the sleeping Gawain with the index finger of her left hand (fol. 129). On 'chin-chucking' as an amorous gesture, see Stanbury, *Seeing the 'Gawain'-Poet*, pp. 28–30.

scenes, that is because this form of communication belongs chiefly – in romances, at least – to occasions where the presence of others imposes a requirement of secrecy (above, pp. 95–8). The *Gawain*-poet gives a brief but expert sketch of such an occasion, when Gawain and the lady are sitting together at dinner in hall on the evening of the second day:

> Such semblaunt to þat segge semly ho made
> Wyth stille stollen countenaunce, þat stalworth to plese,
> Þat al forwondered watz þe wyȝe, and wroth with hymselven.
> (1658–60)

More common in the bedroom scenes themselves is laughter. This is associated at line 1212 with 'bourdez', or jests; but more often in these scenes the word 'laugh' has been taken to denote smiling, as when the lady approaches Gawain 'wyth lyppez smal laȝande', or 'laȝande swete' on the second morning (1757).[55] In the latter scene, however, the word 'smile' itself does occur twice (for the only time in the four poems in the manuscript). Once greetings have been exchanged, 'With smoþe smylyng and smolt þay smeten into merþe' (1763), and again a little later, the lady, pressing Gawain hard, asks whether he has another mistress:

> Þe knyȝt sayde, 'Be sayn Jon,'
> And smeþely con he smyle,
> 'In fayth I welde riȝt non,
> Ne no wil welde þe quile.'
> (1788–91)

Editors commonly gloss the adjective 'smoþe' at line 1763 with 'gentle, courteous', or 'pleasant, friendly', and take the related adverb 'smeþely' in the same way; but the second case, at least, surely calls for other implications of smoothness to be taken into account. Smooth things may be pleasant, but they can also elude one's grasp – an ambiguity noticed by *OED*, *Smooth* a., sense 6: 'Of looks, words, etc.: Pleasant, affable, polite; seemingly amiable or friendly; having a show of sincerity or

---

[55] The distinction between audible laughing and inaudible smiling is unclear in Middle English, as in Old French: see above, pp. 76–8. Davis's glossary entry for *laȝe* has 'smile 1207, etc.'.

friendliness'; also sense 6b: 'Of the tongue, or of persons: speaking fair or smoothly; using specious or attractive language; plausible, bland, insinuating, flattering.'[56] When Gawain smiles 'smoothly' in responding to the lady's embarrassing question, he is behaving pleasantly enough; but he is also – blandly, one might say – evading her challenge. The poet attributes this same defensive purpose more explicitly elsewhere to what he calls Gawain's 'love-laughing':

> With luf-laȝyng a lyt he layd hym bysyde
> Alle þe spechez of specialté þat sprange of her mouthe.
> (1777–8)

The metaphor of 'laying aside' is from sword-play: Gawain evades the lady's thrusts with his amorous-seeming laughter (or smiles?). Non-verbal behaviour is here conveying a negative message with every show of friendliness, and the lady has to admit defeat.

But it is, of course, the kisses which carry most of the weight of meaning in the third fitt; and their significance, like that of other gestures and looks, is by no means simple. For one thing, as a modern reader may not understand, the lady can claim, if pressed, that all those private kisses were no more than customary gestures of greeting and farewell.[57] It is immediately before leaving Gawain on the first morning that she embraces and kisses him (1305–8). On the second visit, she kisses him shortly after her arrival (1505), though not until she has invoked social convention ('þe costez of compaynye', 1483) to persuade him; and she kisses him again on leaving (1555–7). When she arrives on the third morning, she greets him immediately with a kiss (1758); but on this occasion there are two farewell kisses: the first, 'at þis departyng', once she has admitted defeat (1794–6), and the second once she has, as an apparent afterthought, persuaded Gawain to accept the belt (1868–70). Yet, whatever their timing, kisses offered by a lady in a private chamber to a man lying (naked) in bed can hardly fail to be

---

[56] For *Smeethly* adv., *OED* offers only 'smoothly', citing another occurrence in Trevisa's Higden: 'þe kyng excused hym self smeþeliche', where the king is excusing himself ('blande' in Higden's Latin) from lending support to an accused churchman. The adverb collocates with a verb of smiling in the alliterative prose *Seinte Katerine*, where the saint rebuts her pagan adversary 'smirkinde smetheliche': ed. S. R. T. O. d'Ardenne and E. J. Dobson, EETS, S.S. 7 (1981), lines 129–30.

[57] This is observed by Nicholls, *Matter of Courtesy*, pp. 133–4.

Two Middle English narratives

compromising. This is presumably why the lady has to use arguments to persuade Gawain to accept the first, parting, kiss, and again on the second morning (1291–1301, 1481–97); and why Gawain on those two occasions protests that he allows her kisses only because he feels bound to do so 'at her commandment' (1303, 1501).

When it comes to the exchanging of winnings with the host, the question about the kisses becomes one of value, for Bertilak treats the exchange as a kind of competition: Who has done best during the day? In the roundel by Charles d'Orléans noticed in an earlier chapter, Charles dismisses formal, public kisses as worthless: they are given, he says, 'for a countenaunce' and lots of them can be bought for nothing. It is the 'prive cossis of pleasaunce' that he values. So, Bertilak will try to discover what the kisses Gawain pays over to him are worth, once by asking where he got them (1393–4), and later, more enigmatically, by asking what price he paid for them (1938–9).[58] On both occasions, Gawain declines to do more than their agreement requires of him ('þat watz not forward'). It is enough, evidently, that his embraces and kisses should match those that he has received – match them, that is, simply as physical acts, as if that is all they were. The poet has himself characterised the performance of the lady's kisses rather discreetly, with the adverbs 'comlyly', 'fetly', and 'semly' (1505, 1758, 1796); and these rather noncommittal words are matched on the first two evenings of exchange, when Gawain is said to kiss the host as 'comlyly' as he can (1389) and 'hendely' (1639). But perhaps the truth of the matter emerges more fully on the third evening, when he delivers his three kisses 'as saverly and sadly as he hem sette couþe' (1937) – an extra energy and relish upon which Bertilak remarks, in the course of apologising for his own meagre contribution.[59] Like many gestures, embraces and kisses vary a great deal in their significance according as they are over- or underperformed, and Gawain is evidently determined to play fair with his host. So far as the kisses are concerned, at least, he has behaved with

---

[58] See Jill Mann, 'Price and Value in *Sir Gawain and the Green Knight*', *Essays in Criticism*, 36 (1986), 294–318.

[59] Carolyn Dinshaw considers the homosexual possibilities suggested by these episodes, and argues that they are closed down because the poem is committed to the promotion of normative heterosexuality: 'The narrative... produces the possibility of homosexual relations only to – in order to – preclude it': 'A Kiss is Just a Kiss: Heterosexuality and its Consolation in *Sir Gawain and the Green Knight*', *diacritics*, 24.2–3 (1994), 205–26.

perfect good faith – as indeed the Green Knight acknowledges when they later meet.

The third fitt ends with Gawain's late-night farewells, since he is due to set out early next morning for the Green Chapel: he takes hold of his host and kisses the ladies (1961, 1979), thanking them all for their hospitality. The pattern of ceremonious arrivals and departures, observed here at Hautdesert, is broken, however, when the hero encounters the Green Knight at the Green Chapel in the fourth fitt. This encounter repeats in little the pattern followed in the first fitt at Camelot. Acting now as 'host', the Green Knight welcomes Gawain to 'his place' with teasing civility, in terms almost identical with those used by Arthur earlier: 'Iwysse þou art welcom, wyȝe, to my place' (2240, compare 252); and this time it is Gawain who pointedly withholds customary ceremony: 'Sir Gawayn þe knyȝt con mete, / He ne lutte hym noþyng lowe.' An underperformed bow such as this commonly signifies reserve or even hostility. Or perhaps one is to understand that Gawain did not bow at all. Either way, the behaviour carries a strong message, especially as it comes from 'Gawain the hende', a knight whose very first act in the poem was a bow (line 340).

Behaviours in the ensuing encounter have something in common, as one might expect, with what was described in the first fitt. So far as Gawain himself is concerned, the occasion calls for a show of heroic impassivity:

> He lened with þe nek, and lutte,
> And schewed þat schyre al bare,
> And lette as he noȝt dutte;
> For drede he wolde not dare.
> (2255–8)

It is not that he feels no 'drede' – like Arthur and the rest at Camelot (246, 467), he is susceptible to common feelings – but he is determined not to show it; so he behaves (*leten* again) as if he were not afraid, giving himself away only when he 'schranke a lytel with þe schulderes' beneath the axe – an action entirely inadvertent and very far from any intention to communicate fear. By contrast, here as in the first fitt, the behaviour of the Green Knight in delivering his three strikes positively bristles with unspoken messages. Raising his axe for a second time, his expression is one of anger, even madness, 'waytez as wroþely as he wode were' (2289), and as he prepares to strike the third blow, he frowns and purses his lips: 'frounsez boþe lyppe and browe' (2306).

These facial expressions form part of a performance, a 'laykyng', which comes to an abrupt halt once the blow has been delivered and the adventure terminated; and the behaviour of the Green Knight thereafter, though equally expressive, carries quite different meanings:

> The haþel heldet hym fro, and on his ax rested,
> Sette þe schaft upon schore, and to þe scharp lened,
> And loked to þe leude þat on þe launde 3ede,
> How þat do3ty, dredles, dervely þer stondez
> Armed, ful a3lez: in hert hit hym lykez.
> Þenn he melez muryly wyth a much steven...
> (2331-6)

The Green Knight is resting when he leans on his axe, but the action also – chiefly – constitutes a reply to Gawain's excited talk of possible further conflict, as if he were to say that the young man can now relax. The shaft of the axe now serves only as a leaning post, with one insouciant arm resting on the once-terrifying blade. Here as elsewhere the poet shows his awareness of how actions other than prescribed 'gestures' can serve the purposes of NVC. The Green Knight is no longer Gawain's enemy. Indeed, the look that he directs to Gawain ('to' being a somewhat unusual preposition here), representing his response to what he sees, expresses positive admiration. It is authenticated by a glimpse, for the first and only time in the poem, into what Bertilak is really feeling: 'in hert hit hym lykez'. So he goes on to speak 'muryly'. Gawain cannot be spared the revelations which follow, causing him to blush and shrink for shame; but Bertilak responds to his confession of fault with a laugh and a gracious speech of forgiveness (2389), coupled with an invitation to return to Hautdesert for the rest of the New Year feast. Courteous relations being now restored, Gawain declines with due formality:

> 'Nay, for soþe,' quoþ þe segge, and sesed hys helme,
> And hatz hit of hendely, and þe haþel þonkkes.
> (2407-8)

Gestures and looks in medieval narrative

Having earlier taken his helmet off to receive the blow, Gawain had put it on again once the blow was struck (2317), marking his restored freedom to fight; but now he again disarms himself, so to speak, softening his negative response with a gesture of deferential gratitude for the invitation. It is therefore not surprising that, when the two men finally part, they should do so with full brotherly ceremony, the *acoler* and *baiser* of French romance:

> Þay acolen and kyssen, and kennen ayþer oþer
> To þe prynce of paradise, and parten ryȝt þere
>   on coolde.
> (2472–4)

The poem's sequence of greetings and farewells ends with Gawain's return to Camelot. The moment is marked with kisses and embraces: 'Þe kyng kyssez þe knyȝt, and þe whene alce, / And syþen mony syker knyȝt þat soȝt hym to haylce' (2492–3). The customary gestures draw extra meaning from the occasion, a welcome back to one who was thought to have very probably died. Even Barbour's *Bruce* finds time for a little ceremony when Robert Bruce and his men, having given up hope of ever seeing the Earl of Lennox again, 'welcummyt him mar hartfully' when he turns up: 'And all þe lordis þat war þar / Rycht ioyfull off þar meting war, / And kyssyt him in gret daynte'.[60] After his reception, Gawain is quick to confess his failing in the Exchange; but this confession prompts the last of the poem's many laughs:

> Þe kyng comfortez þe knyȝt, and alle þe court als
> Laȝen loude þerat, and luflyly acorden
> Þat lordes and ladis þat longed to þe Table,
> Uche burne of þe broþerhede, a bauderyk schulde have...
> (2513–16)

The court's reaction to Gawain's shame is very like that of his adversary at the Green Chapel: 'Thenn loȝe þat oþer leude and luflyly sayde ...' (2389). In both passages the same adverb, 'luflyly', defines the mood,

---

[60] Book III, ll. 503–5, ed. McDiarmid and Stevenson, replacing editorial *y* with þ. The warriors also weep 'for ioy and pite gret', prompting Barbour to some interesting reflections on varieties of weeping: see above, pp. 78–9.

as friendly or affectionate (*MED lovelili* adv. (a)). Amusement at the intensity of the hero's self-reproaches is also to be reckoned with, certainly in the Green Knight's laugh (though hardly at Gawain's expense). At Camelot, the laughter of king and court contributes to the 'comforting' of a discomfited hero; but it also expresses their delight that, contrary to all expectation, he has managed to uphold the honour of the Round Table without losing his life in the process. It is a richly expressive act, marking without words whatever in the end of the poem may be called happy.

5

Dante's *Commedia*

Dante's great poem may seem an unlikely subject for the present study. His encounters in hell, purgatory, and paradise are too numerous to allow leisurely or large-scale treatment in the manner of *Troilus* or *Sir Gawain*; and the persons he encounters have no ordinary bodies with which to express themselves, for they are all awaiting the general resurrection. In fact, however, the poem proves to be exceptionally rich in non-verbal acts of communication. Dante himself is the only person who has his own real body, capable of casting a shadow or weighing down a boat; yet the visible presence of the shades he meets is most vividly imagined, everywhere except in parts of the *Paradiso*.[1] Thus, one critic has observed the poet's remarkably 'corporeal' representations of the other world, attending to bodies 'in the finest detail of movement and response'.[2] Dante's ferocious economy and concentration of expression allows him to find room for such details, sometimes even in the briefest of encounters; and it is often through small bodily movements that his characters communicate their thoughts and feelings – by gestures, glances, and the like, as well as by what they say.[3]

---

[1] The nature of the shades (*ombre*) is explained by Statius: 'By this we speak and by this we laugh, by this we make the tears and sighs which you may have heard about the mountain. According as the desires and the other affections prick us, the shade takes its form' (*Purg.* XXV 103–7).

[2] R. Kirkpatrick, 'Dante and the Body', in S. Kay and M. Rubin, eds., *Framing Medieval Bodies* (Manchester, 1994), pp. 236–53 (p. 245). Also M. Shapiro, *Dante and the Knot of Body and Soul* (Basingstoke, 1998).

[3] See A. Franz, 'Seelische und körperliche Bewegung in Dantes Divina Commedia', in *Estudios eruditos in memoriam Adolfo Bonilla y San Martín* (Madrid, 1927), Vol. I, pp. 415–30. Franz considers bodily movements generally as expressive of mental states, with extensive discussion of the scene with Statius in *Purgatorio* XXI.

Dante's Commedia

Unlike most, perhaps all, of the medieval writers considered elsewhere in this book, Dante can be shown to have been acquainted with learned thinking about *signa*, as found in Augustine's *De Doctrina* and in scholastic writings on the subject.[4] From such authorities he would have learned to take a broad view of human communication, as involving non-verbal as well as verbal signs. So, the scholastic treatise *De Modis Significandi* by Martin of Dacia, which the poet perhaps knew, explains that the category *signum* includes not only words but also other bodily signals (*nutus corporei*).[5] Arguments such as this lie behind Dante's rather curious apology, in the *Convivio*, for his inability to comprehend or express the full truth about his love:

> è posto fine al nostro ingegno, a ciascuna sua operazione, non da noi ma da l'universale natura; e però è da sapere che più ampi sono li termini de lo 'ngegno a pensare che a parlare, e più ampi a parlare che ad accennare.
>
> [a limit is set for our intelligence in all its operations, not by us but by the universal nature of things; and so one can see that limitations of intelligence are set more widely for thought than for speech, and more widely for speech than for signs.][6]

The verb *accennare*, like its related noun *cenno*, denotes the communication of meanings by non-verbal bodily signs. The *Enciclopedia Dantesca* defines *cenno* as 'segno fatto con la mano, col capo, con gli occhi, a fare intendere qualcosa senza parlare' ['a sign made by the hand, the head, or the eyes to make something understood without speaking'].[7] The

---

[4] See most recently Z. G. Barański, 'Dante's Signs: An Introduction to Medieval Semiotics and Dante', in J. Barnes and C. Ó. Cuilleanáin, eds., *Dante and the Middle Ages* (Dublin, 1995), pp. 139–80. Note 28 there lists previous studies. M. Corti argues for the influence upon Dante's sign-theory of the modist semiotics of Boethius of Dacia and Martin of Dacia: 'La teoria del segno nei logici modisti e in Dante', in P. Lendinara and M. C. Ruta, eds., *Per una storia della semiotica* (Palermo, 1981), pp. 69–86.

[5] '"Sign" has a wider application than "word", for all words can be called signs, but not the other way round; for "sign" can refer to a bodily signal [*nutu corporeo*], a vocal utterance, and other things, but "word" can refer only to vocal utterance': translated from H. Roos, ed., *Martini de Dacia Opera*, Corpus Philosophorum Danicorum Medii Aevi, II (Copenhagen, 1961), p. 9; cited by Corti, note 5.

[6] *Convivio*, III iv 11, *Le opere di Dante*, ed. Barbi *et al.* Cf. *Convivio* III vii 8–13.

[7] *Enciclopedia Dantesca* (Rome, 1970–78), *s.v.* The word derives from Late Latin *cinnus*, a wink or grimace.

Gestures and looks in medieval narrative

Convivio allows that such signs provide a more restricted method of communication than do words, which in turn cannot match the range of thought; but they have their own part to play alongside speech, here and in the *Commedia* itself. In what follows, I shall consider some of the *cenni* in that poem. I take examples involving, first, Dante with Virgil, then Dante with Beatrice, and finally the various shades of the judged.

> Les gestes révèlent les structures de pouvoir, les hiérarchies fondamentales de la société: car les gestes que les hommes font entre eux ou qu'ils adressent aux puissances invisibles manifestent, jusque dans les rituels d'inversion, la supériorité supposée de Dieu sur les hommes, des mâles sur les femmes, du roi sur ses sujets, des clercs sur les laïcs.[8]

In the relationship between the Dante *personaggio* and Virgil, the superior power enjoyed by the latter, as *maestro*, *guida*, and *patre*, finds expression in a variety of looks and gestures. Virgil himself notices the fact when, in *Purgatorio* XXVII, he takes his leave of Dante, releasing him into a new freedom: 'Non aspettar mio dir più né mio cenno' ['No longer expect word or sign from me', *Purg.* XXVII 139].[9] In Virgil's words, as in the *Convivio*, verbal and non-verbal communication are coupled together: in this case *dir* and *cenno*. Virgil will no longer be present to exert the kind of authority that he has up to now imposed upon Dante. Thus, when they encountered the venerable old Cato:

> Lo duca mio allor mi diè di piglio,
> e con parole e con mani e con cenni
> reverenti mi fé le gambe e 'l ciglio.
>
> ['My leader then laid hold on me, and with speech and hand and sign made reverent my legs and brow', *Purg.* I 49–51.]

This is largely dumbshow. Virgil seizes Dante and, speaking some unspecified words, urges him with 'hand and sign' to adopt a posture of reverence, kneeling and with bowed head. Head and knee respond to a message from face and hand. In the *Inferno*, the arrival of a messenger from heaven prompts a similar response to Dante's mute inquiry. Virgil

---

[8] Schmitt, *Raison des gestes*, p. 357.
[9] Quotations and translations are taken from Dante Alighieri, *The Divine Comedy*, ed. and transl. Charles S. Singleton, 6 vols. (Princeton, 1970–75).

Dante's Commedia

makes a sign (*segno*) that he should silently bow down – an act as uncommon in the *Commedia* as it is in *Il Filostrato*:

> Ben m'accorsi ch'elli era da ciel messo,
> e volsimi al maestro; e quei fé segno
> ch'i' stessi queto ed inchinassi ad esso.
>
> ['Well did I perceive that he was a messenger from Heaven; and I turned to the master, who signed to me that I should stand quiet and bow down to him', *Inf.* IX 85–7.][10]

Immediately after losing him in the *Purgatorio*, Dante describes Virgil as 'dolcissimo patre' (*Purg.* XXX 50), and Virgil is indeed as much *patre* as *maestro* in his looks and gestures. Dante's reaction to the naming of Beatrice, in face of the purgatorial wall of flame, prompts Virgil to a shake of the head and a smile:

> Ond' ei crollò la fronte e disse: 'Come!
> volenci star di qua?'; indi sorrise
> come al fanciul si fa ch'è vinto al pome.
>
> ['at which he shook his head and said, "What? Do we desire to stay on this side?" then smiled as one does to a child that is won with an apple', *Purg.* XXVII 43–5].

This headshake and smile, taken with the spoken words and the simile, evidently express the sympathetic amusement of a spirit contemplating the power of those human desires to which he himself – perhaps even sadly – is no longer subject. Dante had been afraid to enter the wall of flame, but he no longer hesitates once he learns that Beatrice is to be found on the other side. Headshakes can signify scorn or sorrow, as we saw earlier (pp. 43–62); but here those significances are softened and subtilised.[11] Elsewhere, Virgil smiles in something more like simple fatherly approval, when Dante is honoured with a 'salutevol cenno' by

---

[10] Elsewhere, exceptionally, Dante makes a silencing gesture at his master: 'in order that my leader might remain attentive, I placed my finger upwards from my chin to my nose', *Inf.* XXV 44–5. De Jorio notes this as a common sign in his contemporary Naples and also in antiquity: *Gesture in Naples*, p. 372.

[11] On 'crollò la fronte', Singleton notes: 'The gesture expresses surprise or amazement, feigned, of course, in this instance, since Virgil knows that the mention of Beatrice has already had its calculated effect.' I prefer the note to the line in the Temple Classics *Purgatorio*, which speaks of 'a kind of half pathetic amusement on Virgil's part'.

the poets of antiquity (*Inf.* IV 98–9), and when he finds the mark of pride erased from his forehead (*Purg.* XII 136). At their first entry into hell, Virgil had taken the poet's hand and comforted him with a 'cheerful look' ('lieto volto', *Inf.* III 20); and much later he encourages him with a 'lieto cenno' to satisfy his unspoken desire to question Pope Adrian – a typical mute exchange:

> e volsi li occhi a li occhi al segnor mio:
> ond' elli m'assentì con lieto cenno
> ciò che chiedea la vista del disio.

['then I turned my eyes on the eyes of my lord: at which with a glad sign he gave assent to what the look of my desire was craving', *Purg.* XIX 85–7.]

Dante's violent display of righteous indignation at Filippo Argenti even prompts Virgil to put arms round his neck and kiss him (*Inf.* VIII 43–4). Elsewhere, in more schoolmasterly fashion, he singles out named souls with a pointing finger ('nominommi a dito', *Inf.* V 68), beckons Geryon to approach ('accennolle', *Inf.* XVII 5), raises a finger to command attention ('drizzò 'l dito', *Inf.* X 129), and urges Dante with a look to note the importance of what has just been said:

> Lo mio maestro allore in su la gota
> destra si volse in dietro e riguardommi;
> poi disse: 'Bene ascolta chi la nota.'

['Thereon my master turned round on his right and looked at me, then said, "He who notes it listens well"', *Inf.* XV 97–9.]

Virgil is also involved in one of the most subtle of all those scenes in the *Commedia* where *cenni* serve along with words to articulate attitudes and relationships. This occurs towards the end of *Purgatorio* XXI. The poet Statius, having just identified himself, has spoken of his debt to the *Aeneid* and of his intense desire to have met its author – the very Virgil to whom, all unknowing, he is now speaking. Virgil himself, delicately abstaining from the obvious response, turns to Dante with a look that is described, in a striking oxymoron, as silently speaking a command to be silent:

> Volser Virgilio a me queste parole
> con viso che, tacendo, disse 'Tace.'

['These words turned Virgil to me with a look that, silent, said "Be silent"', *Purg.* XXI 103–4.]

Dante does remain silent, but he cannot restrain a speaking look:

> ma non può tutto la virtù che vuole;
> ché riso e pianto son tanto seguaci
> a la passion di che ciascun si spicca,
> che men seguon voler ne' più veraci.
> Io pur sorrisi come l'uom ch'ammicca.

['But the power that wills cannot do everything; for smiles and tears are such close followers on the emotion from which each springs, that in the most truthful they least follow the will. I only smiled, like one who makes a sign', XXI 105–9.]

Dante smiles.[12] Franz, in his discussion of this passage, reads the smile as an ironical expression of superior knowledge – Dante, unlike Statius, knows who Virgil is.[13] I would prefer to understand the smile as gleeful, rejoicing in what Dante knows mainly because it allows him to relish a compliment paid to his master under those ideal circumstances where there can be no suspicion of flattery. The passage is especially interesting, however, for its subtle treatment of *voluntas significandi*. It might seem that Dante's smile was wholly involuntary, a symptom rather than a sign. Yet it appears also to be obscurely sanctioned by the 'virtù che vuole'.[14] For what does it mean to say that 'I only smiled, like one who makes a sign'? The comparison here barely keeps tenor and vehicle apart, as if it might as well be Dante himself who is the one who makes a sign.[15]

---

[12] Dante does not distinguish here between a smile and a *riso* (line 106, also 114). See above, p. 76, for the similar overlap between French *sourire* and *rire*.

[13] *Art. cit.*, pp. 423–4, comparing Dante's *riso* at the slothful Belacqua (*Purg.* IV 122) and Casella's smile when the poet tries to embrace him (*Purg.* II 83).

[14] Beatrice has a subtle analysis of how the *voluntà* may yield 'much or little' to forces working upon it: *Paradiso* IV 73–114.

[15] *Ammiccare* in modern Italian means 'wink' and is so understood here by Franz ('Seelische und körperliche Bewegung', p. 423). Singleton and others agree with the *Grande dizionario*: 'Guardare in segno di intesa, di intelligenza; far cenno di nascosto (con gli

Gestures and looks in medieval narrative

Certainly that is how Statius takes it. For him, Dante's smile is a message which he tries to read, first by silently gazing into the poet's eyes, there 'where the expression is most fixed' ('ne li occhi ove 'l sembiante più si ficca'). Not a word has been said so far; but at last Statius resorts to speech: '"Perché la tua faccia testeso / un lampeggiar di riso dimostrommi?"' ['"Why did your face just now show me the flash of a smile?"', XXI 113–14]. Statius has no way of guessing the reason for Dante's quite unexpected 'flash of a smile': he may even have thought it impertinent, as Dante's later explanation perhaps implies (127–8). His question leaves the poet's will divided between the spoken request of Statius and Virgil's silent command. So his only response is a sigh: 'ond' io sospiro, e sono inteso / dal mio maestro' ['so that I sigh and am understood by my master']. This frustrated sigh is almost the last of the *cenni* in the present scene, for Virgil, as one who 'knows what the dumb would say' (*Purg.* XIII 76), understands its meaning and releases Dante at last to speak freely. He reveals his master's identity, and this prompts Statius to bend as if to embrace Virgil's feet; but Virgil countermands that act of reverence and submission, in words of great beauty which perhaps reveal a deeper reason for his initial reluctance to respond:

> Già s'inchinava ad abbracciar li piedi
> al mio dottor, ma el li disse: 'Frate,
> non far, ché tu se' ombra e ombra vedi.'

> ['Already he was stooping to embrace my teacher's feet; but he said to him, "Brother, do not so, for you are a shade and a shade you see"', XXI 130–2.]

In the relationship between Dante and Beatrice, that 'supériorité supposée des mâles sur les femmes' of which Schmitt spoke finds itself decisively inverted. Beatrice's authority surpasses that of Virgil, and Dante bows the head to her, as he never did to his male master. In *Paradiso* VII he wishes to ask her a question, but cannot bring himself to speak:

occhi, con movimento del volto)', *s.v. ammiccare*. Singleton's rendering, 'make a sign', cannot, however, catch the word's apparent reference to a quick and elusive sign (Latin *micare*, to flash, gleam, etc.). C. S. Lewis, in his essay on Dante's similes, speaks of those similes in the *Commedia* where '*like*...is always tending to turn into *same*', *Studies in Medieval and Renaissance Literature* (Cambridge, 1966), p. 71.

> Ma quella reverenza che s'indonna
> di tutto me, pur per *Be* e per *ice*,
> mi richinava come l'uom ch'assonna.
>
> ['but that reverence which is wholly mistress of me, only by *Be* and by *ice*, bowed me like one who drowses', *Par.* VII 13–15.]

Here as elsewhere, the 'infallibile avviso' of *Beatrice* allows her to read Dante's unspoken thoughts (ll. 19–21); but that supernatural power is not clearly distinguished from the ordinary – or rather, extraordinary – human ability to interpret the meanings of silent looks or gestures. In *Paradiso* IV, the capacity of Beatrice to see into Dante's heart is compared to the prophetic insight of Daniel; yet the previous terzina has suggested that the poet's feelings were there to be read in his facial expression, communicated more vividly there than by any speech:

> Io mi tacea, ma 'l mio disir dipinto
> m'era nel viso, e 'l dimandar con ello,
> più caldo assai che per parlar distinto.
>
> ['I was silent, but my desire was depicted on my face, and my questioning with it, in warmer colours far than by distinct speech', *Par.* IV 10–12.]

Certainly Beatrice's powers do not make Dante's looks and gestures superfluous. On one occasion, for instance, he seeks further enlightenment from her 'con atto e con parola' (*Par.* III 94), and elsewhere he wins her permission to speak with a silent gaze (*Par.* VIII 40–2). She is like Matelda in the Earthly Paradise, who responds promptly when *voluntas* is conveyed by a *signum*:

> Come anima gentil, che non fa scusa,
> ma fa sua voglia de la voglia altrui
> tosto che è per segno fuor dischiusa.
>
> ['As a gentle spirit that makes no excuse, but makes its will of another's will, as soon as that is disclosed by outward sign', *Purg.* XXXIII 130–2.]

Beatrice herself is far from a disembodied voice, for she communicates with gesture and look, as well as speech. She has both the *atto* and the *voce* of a leader (*Par.* XXX 37), and Dante looks to her for guidance 'o per parlare o per atto segnato' (*Par.* XVIII 54). At the end of the

Purgatorio, she marshals Dante, with Matelda and Statius, to follow her 'solo accennando' ['merely beckoning', *Purg.* XXXIII 14], while in *Paradiso* she employs 'only a sign' to send Dante up Jacob's ladder ('un sol cenno', *Par.* XXII 101). In another silent exchange, the *cenno* is specified as a smile:

> Io mi volsi a Beatrice, e quella udio
> pria ch'io parlassi, e arrisemi un cenno
> che fece crescer l'ali al voler mio.
>
> ['I turned to Beatrice, and she heard before I spoke, and smiled to me a sign that made the wings of my desire increase', *Par.* XV 70–2.]

Having 'heard' Dante's unspoken message, Beatrice 'smiled to me a sign'. The smile of Beatrice is, of course, her most characteristic *cenno*. It is the nature of the human eye to be able to communicate joy – 'letizia per pupilla viva' ('gladness through a living pupil', *Par.* II 144) – but the smiling eyes of Beatrice express a joy and love beyond the human:

> Beatrice mi guardò con li occhi pieni
> di faville d'amor così divini,
> che, vinta, mia virtute diè le reni
> e quasi mi perdei con li occhi chini.
>
> ['Beatrice looked on me with eyes so full of the sparkling of love and so divine that my power, vanquished, took flight, and I almost lost myself with eyes downcast', *Par.* IV 139–42.]

There are several such transcendent smiles in the *Paradiso*; but on other occasions Beatrice's smile takes on a maternal character, expressing affectionate amusement at Dante's childlike failures to understand.[16] When he mistakes the faint outlines of spirit faces in the moon for reflections, he turns in bewilderment to find Beatrice smiling:

> 'Non ti maravigliar perch' io sorrida,'
> mi disse, 'appresso il tuo püeril coto,
> poi sopra 'l vero ancor lo piè non fida.'
>
> ['"Do not wonder," she said to me, "that I smile at your childish thought, since it does not yet trust itself upon the truth"', *Par.* III 25–7.]

---

[16] In *Paradiso* I 100–102, Dante's incomprehension prompts Beatrice to a pitying sigh, turning her eyes on him 'with the look that a mother casts on her delirious child'.

Smiles of a similar kind – more like what one finds in other texts – occur elsewhere, as when Beatrice smiles at Dante's failure to grasp the workings of Lethe, and at his question about spots on the moon (*Purg.* XXXIII 95, *Par.* II 52).

Yet another of Beatrice's smiles occurs in a context of particular interest for the present study. Canto XVI of the *Paradiso* opens with reflections on the folly of pride in inherited nobility; and this folly is promptly manifested by Dante himself, when he addresses his own ancestor, the crusader Cacciaguida, with the grand second-person plural pronoun *voi*. It is to this moment of family pride that Beatrice responds:

> onde Beatrice, ch'era un poco scevra,
>   ridendo, parve quella che tossio
>   al primo fallo scritto di Ginevra.

> ['at which Beatrice, who was a little withdrawn, smiled and seemed to me like her who coughed at the first fault that is written of Guinevere', *Par.* XVI 13–15.]

One cannot be sure whether the comparison here should be taken simply as a gloss to explain what Beatrice's smile meant, or whether she herself actually coughed as well as smiling. Given that Dante does not consistently keep tenor and vehicle apart in such comparisons, the latter possibility cannot be excluded; and it would make good sense for a smiling Beatrice to give a little cough here, or clear her throat, as a way of recalling Dante to himself.

Dante has called this cough to mind, by an extraordinary leap of the imagination, from an episode in the French prose romance *Lancelot*. There it is delivered by the Dame de Malohaut. She is sitting apart (like Beatrice) with others in a meadow at the moment when young Lancelot first declares his love for Guinevere there:

> 'Commant? fait ele, amez me vos tant?' 'Dame, fait il, ge n'ain tant ne moi ne autrui.' 'Et des qant, fait ele, m'amez vos tant?' 'Dame, fait il, des lo jor que ge sui apelez chevaliers et si ne l'estoie mie.' 'Et par la foi que vos me devez, d'ou vint cele amors que vos avez an moi mise?' A ces paroles que la reine disoit avint que la dame do Pui de Malohaut s'estosi tot a esciant et dreça la teste que avoit anbrunchiee.

['"What?" she said, "do you love me so much?" "Lady," he said, "I love no one more than you, not myself nor another." "And since when," she said, "have you loved me so much?" "Lady," he said, "ever since the day I was first called a knight and yet was not one." "And by the faith that you owe me, whence came that love which you have devoted to me?" At these words spoken by the queen, it happened that the Dame do Pui de Malohaut coughed quite deliberately and raised the head which she had kept bowed.']17

By coughing 'tot a esciant', the Dame de Malohaut evidently intends to convey a message to Lancelot. Hers is one of those 'tussiculae simulatae', little feigned coughs, by which people may communicate, according to the rhetorician Boncampagno da Signa.[18] The context in the *Paradiso* suggests that Dante remembered it as an action intended to recall Guinevere to herself at a moment of indiscretion, a little warning from a lady companion, just as his Beatrice is warning Dante not to get carried away.[19] Dante evidently understood the episode much as his early commentator Benvenuto da Imola described in his note on the lines. Taking the Arthurian allusion as an 'apt comparison' to Beatrice's smile, Benvenuto supposes that the 'fault' which prompted Malohaut's cough was that same first kiss between Lancelot and Guinevere to which Dante had so memorably alluded in the encounter with Paolo and Francesca in *Inferno* v. The commentator writes:

> For when Lancelot had, by the good offices of Prince Galehot, managed to talk with Queen Guinevere, and was too abashed to dare reveal the fire of his love, Prince Galehot intervened and brought them to the point of kissing. Then a certain lady companion of the queen named Damma, noticing that act, coughed and spat [!], as if to say,

---

[17] Cited from Kennedy's critical text, p. 345. The episode is printed at some length, from one manuscript, by Paget Toynbee, *A Dictionary of Proper Names and Notable Matters in the Works of Dante*, revised C. S. Singleton (Oxford, 1968), s.v. *Galeotto*.
[18] *Rhetorica Novissima*, ed. Gaudentius (p. 64 above), p. 284. The passage is translated by Schmitt, *Raison des gestes*, p. 287. De Jorio, noting that Neapolitans sometimes called attention to things with a little cough, cites Ovid, *Heroides*, xxi 24, where a nurse coughs or clears her throat to warn her mistress: 'Excreat, et ficta dat mihi signa nota' ('she clears her throat and thus gives me the sign agreed upon'): *Gesture in Naples*, p. 73.
[19] Malory's Guinevere directs a warning cough at Lancelot, under different circumstances: 805. 20.

Dante's Commedia

'I see you well.' So in the present passage, Beatrice smiled as if to say, 'I hear you well', or 'You are overheard, be careful what you say.'[20]

In supposing that Malohaut's cough was directed at Guinevere and her 'first fault' – evidently, as Benvenuto supposed, the kiss – Dante was misled by his memory. The kiss occurs a little later in the *Lancelot*, and Malohaut here has her eye on Lancelot, not Guinevere.[21] In fact, the scene in the French original offers a particularly subtle example of non-verbal signalling. The situation, when Lancelot and Guinevere are brought together by Galehot, is quite complex.[22] More than a year before, Lancelot killed the son of Malohaut's seneschal, and he has since been held by her as a prisoner. While holding him so, she has fallen in love with him. Knowing of his prowess, she guessed that he must be inspired by the love of some noble lady, but she could never discover who that lady was, or indeed who Lancelot himself was. On the day of the cough, Malohaut is staying with Guinevere and Arthur as an honoured guest, while Lancelot, released by her (still incognito) to fight in a battle, has joined Galehot in his tent. Galehot has divined his companion's passion, and arranges for Guinevere, accompanied by Malohaut, two other ladies, and himself, to walk out in the meadows one evening, while Lancelot is also brought there separately. When Malohaut sees Lancelot, not wishing to be recognised, she lowers her head. She already has suspicions, but it is only when she hears Lancelot and Guinevere, sitting apart, speak of his passion that she raises her head and coughs. Lancelot, hearing and recognising her, reacts with violent weeping to his realisation that she now knows the well-kept secret of his love. For that, evidently, is what Malohaut's cough meant: '*Now* I know.' She does not cough at any 'fault': indeed, very shortly after, she accepts Galehot as her lover and joins Lancelot and Guinevere in an amorous foursome. It is a delicate courtly moment, quite lacking that element

---

[20] The Latin translated here may be found in the Toynbee–Singleton Dante Dictionary, s.v. *Malehaut, Dama di*. For the whole note, consult the Dartmouth Dante Project, http://dciswww.dartmouth.edu.

[21] Kennedy's critical edition of the *Lancelot* gives no grounds for supposing that Dante might have read a variant version.

[22] The events summarised here extend over pp. 274–354 in Kennedy's edition. I am grateful to my colleagues Myra Stokes and Ad Putter for guidance and correction. See M. Stokes, 'The Contract of Love-Service: *Lancelot* and *Troilus*', *Litteraria Pragensia*, 9 (1999), 62–83.

of moral censure with which Dante's memory invested it. Yet his recall of this tiny detail, however imperfect, provides striking evidence of his sensitivity, as a reader as well as a writer, to little acts of non-verbal signing.

Because both Virgil and Beatrice act as Dante's leaders, there is a certain continuity in their gestural exchanges with him throughout the *Commedia*; but in the case of the souls he encounters, very different circumstances give rise to differing gestural registers, especially as between *Inferno* and *Paradiso*.

In medieval pictures, sculptures and writings, the evil and the damned are commonly characterised by a variety of grotesque gestures and distorted facial expressions. It is in this connection that Schmitt cites the passage from the Book of Proverbs referred to above (p. 110): 'Homo apostata vir inutilis, graditur ore perverso; annuit oculis, terit pede, digito loquitur, pravo corde machinatur malum'. ['A man that is an apostate, an unprofitable man, walketh with a perverse mouth, he winketh with the eyes, presseth with the foot, speaketh with the finger. With a wicked heart he deviseth evil'].[23] Schmitt illustrates the contrast between such inordinate *gesticulatio* and the measured gestures of virtue with pictures from a twelfth-century prayer book, in which the Beatitudes are represented by juxtaposed images of the blessed and their evil counterparts: 'ordre et mesure' on the one part, 'mouvements violents' on the other.[24] Representations of such 'gesticulation' in the *Inferno* exhibit a certain artistic restraint by Dante. Not all his damned souls, by any means, express themselves grotesquely. The heretic Farinata first rises from his burning tomb in an attitude of dignified pride, 'with chest and brow thrown back as if he had great scorn of Hell' (*Inf.* x 35–6). He responds to the news of Dante's identity with raised eyebrows ('ei levò le ciglia un poco in suso', x 45); and he exhibits the impassivity of a great soul when he 'changed not his aspect, nor moved his neck, nor bent his side' ('non mutò aspetto, / né mosse collo, né piegò sua costa', x 74–5). There is even one place where the dignity of a damned soul appears to inspire something like a gesture of respect from the poet. Crossing the burning

---

[23] Proverbs 6. 12–14; Schmitt, *Raison des gestes*, p. 153.
[24] Ibid., pp. 154–72.

Dante's Commedia

sand on a raised and sheltered bank in *Inferno* xv, Dante sees Brunetto Latini below him. They walk and talk together:

> Io non osava scender de la strada
> per andar par di lui; ma 'l capo chino
> tenea com' uom che reverente vada.
>
> ['I dared not descend from the path to go on a level with him, but I kept my head bowed like one who walks in reverence', *Inf.* xv 43–5.]

Dante could not, in the circumstances, have conversed with Brunetto without inclining his head, and the comparison with 'one who walks in reverence' ostensibly does no more than illustrate that physical necessity. Yet Brunetto has been Dante's dear master in life, as the poet later acknowledges; and his simile can hardly fail to suggest some intention of reverence in the bowing of his head – another case, as C. S. Lewis put it, of '*like* always tending to turn into *same* in Dante's similes'.[25]

Yet few of the damned souls are granted such dignity, and the poem does allow itself some quite striking representations of grotesque *gesticulatio*. The glutton Ciacco distorts or crosses his eyes ('annuit oculis'), and Geri del Bello violently threatens Dante with a finger ('digito loquitur').[26] Dante even imagines gesticulation by an unlikely part of the body when Pope Nicholas, upside down in his hole, expresses either rage or pangs of conscience by fiercely kicking his feet ('terit pede'): 'whether anger or conscience stung him, he kicked hard with both his feet' ('o ira o cosc̈ienza che 'l mordesse, / forte spingava con ambo le piote', *Inf.* xix 119–20). In the description of the flatterers, the word *muso* 'muzzle' suggests animality. They snort and slap themselves, in a distorted version of penitential breast-beating: 'col muso scuffa, / e sé medesma con le palme picchia' ['puffing with their muzzles and smiting themselves with their palms', *Inf.* xviii 104–5].[27] There is a more terrible 'bestial sign' in Canto xxxii, where Ugolino expresses his

---

[25] There is another hidden tribute to Brunetto – hidden, perhaps, even from the God who has condemned him – in the later comparison of him with a winner in the race for the green cloth (xv 121–4).

[26] 'Li diritti occhi torse allora in biechi' (*Inf.* vi 91, cf. the 'occhio bieco' of the hypocrites, *Inf.* xxiii 85); 'io vidi lui a piè del ponticello / mostrarti e minacciar forte col dito' (*Inf.* xxix 25–6).

[27] Among the panders and seducers in the same canto is Jason, who deceived Hypsipyle with *segni* and *parole ornate* (*Inf.* xviii 91).

Gestures and looks in medieval narrative

detestation of Ruggieri by gnawing at his neck, and a more disgusting one in Canto XVII, where a Paduan usurer distorts his mouth and sticks his tongue out 'like an ox that licks its nose' ('Qui distorse la bocca e di fuor trasse / la lingua, come bue che 'l naso lecchi', XVII 74–5).[28] Most remarkable of all, however, are the signs made by the sacrilegious thief 'Vanni Fucci bestia':

> Al fine de le sue parole il ladro
> le mani alzò con amendue le fiche,
> gridando: 'Togli, Dio, ch'a te le squadro!'
>
> ['At the end of his words the thief raised up his hands with both the figs, crying, "Take them, God, for I aim them at you!"', *Inf.* XXV 1–3.]

The *fica* or fig is an obscene gesture of contempt and insult, formed by the suggestive insertion of a thumb between the first and middle fingers. Already in antiquity Quintilian warned orators against doing this, and the gesture has survived into modern times – a clear instance of an emblem persisting in both form and meaning over millennia.[29] Medieval illustrators of the *Commedia* did not miss the opportunity to portray Vanni Fucci's two-handed *fica* at God – surely the ultimate in infernal gesticulation. 'Digito loquitur.'[30]

Dante is quite sparing with devils in his hell, by comparison with most medieval representations; but in one circle, that of the barrators in

---

[28] Singleton notes *ad loc.*: 'This grotesque gesture of derision and scorn is directed, not at the wayfarer, but at the Florentine usurers now in Hell and their "sovereign knight" who will one day join them. The gesture is known in Italian as *fare le boccacce*.' He compares Isaiah 57.4: 'Upon whom have you jested? Upon whom have you opened your mouth wide and put out your tongue?'

[29] Quintilian, *Institutio Oratoria*, ed. and transl. Butler, XI iii 98. On the history and modern European distribution of this gesture, see Morris *et al.*, *Gestures*, pp. 147–60. There is a discussion of the *fica* in de Jorio, *Gesture in Naples*, pp. 214–19, noting its use in early nineteenth-century Naples not only as an insult, but also to ward off evil. The use of both hands intensifies the message (as in the illustration on p. 126 of Morris, *Gestures*).

[30] 'Hardly any illustrator omits the blasphemy of Vanni Fucci, with his obscene gesture': P. Brieger, M. Meiss, and C. S. Singleton, *Illuminated Manuscripts of the Divine Comedy*, 2 vols. (London, 1969), Vol. I, p. 146, and Plates 260–7. Botticelli includes the double *fica* in his illustration to *Inf.* XXV: Sandro Botticelli, *The Drawings for Dante's Divine Comedy*, ed. H.-T. Schulze Altcappenberg (London, 2000), p. 105. In his edition, Singleton notes *ad loc.* the Statute of Prato against whoever 'has made the *fiche* [*ficas*] or has shown his buttocks towards heaven or the image of God'. Jews are portrayed employing the gesture against Christ: L. Réau, *Iconographie de l'art chrétien*, Vol. II, Part 2 (Paris, 1957), p. 459.

Dante's Commedia

Inferno XXI and XXII, they have a field-day. Devils are, of course, generally portrayed with grimaces and grotesque gestures. As Schmitt observes: 'Le mauvais exemple gestuel est donné par le diable et les démons, dont les gestes passent pour les plus orgueilleux, les plus indécents, les plus horribles qui se puissent imaginer.'[31] In the barrators' circle of boiling pitch, where the damned souls are reduced to communicating by whistles (*Inf.* XXII 104), the devils exhibit their customary fierce demeanour ('atto acerbo'), grinding their teeth with menacing frowns (XXI 32, 131–2). More singular are the *cenni* employed by the troop of devils when they set out on patrol:

> Per l'argine sinistro volta dienno;
>   ma prima avea ciascun la lingua stretta
>   coi denti, verso lor duca, per cenno;
> ed elli avea del cul fatto trombetta.
>
> ['They wheeled round by the bank on the left, but first each pressed his tongue between his teeth at their leader for a signal, and he had made a trumpet of his arse', XXI 136–9.]

Sticking the tongue out and farting are both, of course, rude non-verbal signs eminently appropriate for devils.[32] At the beginning of the next canto, nevertheless, they are treated with apparent seriousness as unfamiliar examples of the *segni* employed by fighting men on the move. The poet, speaking from his own experience on earth, remarks that he himself has witnessed many troop movements to the accompaniment of such things as trumpets, drums, bells and castle-signals ('cenni di castella').[33] But he has never seen anything like this:

---

[31] *Raison des gestes*, p. 140, with references in note 21. Grotesque and threatening diabolic gestures may be seen in *Illuminated Manuscripts of the Divine Comedy*, e.g. Plates 231a, 232c, 233b, 238a, 241a, 243a.

[32] Devils may be seen sticking their tongues out on p. 139 of F. Garnier, *Le Langage de l'image au moyen âge*, and a fart is represented by a trumpet in Illustration 86 of Camille, *Image on the Edge*. See also *Illuminated Manuscripts of the Divine Comedy*, Vol. I, p. 143, and Plate 243a; also Botticelli's illustration to *Inf.* XXI, pp. 93 and 95 in *The Drawings*. Benvenuto da Imola sees these shameful acts as figuring the scorn with which traffickers in public office often behave to each other. Observing such behaviour, he says, he has often been reminded of this scene of Dante's (Dartmouth Dante Project).

[33] In his note on 'cenni di castella', Singleton compares the use of flares as a *cenno* to communicate from the city of Dis in *Inferno* VIII 5. Benvenuto da Imola has an extensive discussion of the passage, understanding its general bearing: 'And he [Dante] says, in

> né già con sì diversa cennamella
> cavalier vidi muover né pedoni,
> né nave a segno di terra o di stella.

> ['but never to so strange a pipe have I seen horsemen or footmen set forth, or ship by sign of land or star', *Inf.* XXII 10–12.]

As this last line suggests, Dante here has in mind a general theory of signs, in which military signals were commonly included, as by Augustine: 'it is through the eyes that flags and standards convey the wishes of military commanders'.[34]

Unlike the damned – and the blessed – souls in purgatory are still *in via*, and they have a somewhat wider gestural range than either. They are able, unlike the damned, to see the folly and incomprehension of humanity from above. So Marco Lombardo is prompted to a deep sigh by Dante's failure to understand (*Purg.* XVI 64); and in the same spirit, Statius smiles a little when Dante makes a mistake (XXII 26), and Casella smiles when he flushes with surprise at their failure to embrace: 'Da maraviglia, credo, mi dipinsi; / per che l'ombra sorrise e si ritrasse' ['Wonder, I think, was painted in my looks, whereat the shade smiled and drew back', *Purg.* II 82–3]. Again, when Dante goes down on his knees before Pope Adrian, he is abruptly told by the pontiff to get up: such earthly reverence is no longer appropriate (XIX 127–35). At the same time, more often than shades in the other two *cantiche*, those in purgatory still employ gestures of common humanity, such as they might have used in life. When Statius hears Matelda say that the poets of antiquity may, in their portrayals of the Golden Ages, have been granted some inkling of the Earthly Paradise, the smile which he shares with Virgil expresses a very human gratification (*Purg.* XXVIII 146–7). One spirit points in amazement at Dante's shadow (V 3, and compare VIII 96, XXVI 116), and others indicate with a back-of-the-hand gesture

---

summary form, that he has seen at sea and on land, in peace and in war, various and diverse signs given for diverse affairs and diverse actions, but he has never seen any sign like that described above' (Dartmouth Dante Project). On military signs, see M. H. Keen, *The Laws of War in the Later Middle Ages* (London, 1965), Chapter VII.

[34] *De Doctrina*, II 5. Dante still has *signa* in mind when, a few lines later, he compares the way the barrators show their backs above the pitch with the way in which dolphins, by arching their backs, 'fanno segno' to warn mariners of an approaching storm: *Inf.* XXII 19–24.

that Dante and Virgil may go ahead of them (III 102). In Canto XXVI, shades exchange kisses of friendly greeting ('accoglienza amica'):

> Lì veggio d'ogne parte farsi presta
> ciascun' ombra e basciarsi una con una
> sanza restar, contente a brieve festa.
>
> ['There on every side I see all the shades making haste and kissing one another, without stopping, content with brief greeting', *Purg.* XXVI 31–3.]

Since this is the circle where lust is purged, the spirits' contentment with a short kiss of greeting marks their progress on the road to heaven. As Singleton puts it, they 'exchange in place of their former lascivious kisses the holy kiss as commended by the apostle Paul in Rom. 16:16: "Salutate invicem in osculo sancto" ("Greet one another with a holy kiss").'[35]

Most vivid of all is the gesture of Sapia, suffering with her eyelids wired together in the circle of envy. Hearing Dante speak of Italy, she responds:

> Tra l'altre vidi un'ombra ch'aspettava
> in vista; e se volesse alcun dir 'Come?'
> lo mento a guisa d'orbo in sù levava.
>
> ['Among the rest I saw a shade that looked expectant, and if any would ask how, it was lifting up its chin in the manner of the blind', *Purg.* XIII 100–2.]

Since the eyes are the most expressive organ of silent speech, Dante imagines a reader's objection: How could someone with eyes seeled communicate curiosity in his look? The answer appeals to the gestural behaviour of the blind on earth, who manifest attention by a lift of the head.[36] Here as elsewhere in purgatory, a soul undergoes terrible physical suffering, but there is no grotesque gesticulation as in hell. Together with

---

[35] Note to lines 32–3. This, the only kiss in *Purgatorio*, contrasts with that of Paolo and Francesca in *Inferno* V 136.
[36] On this scene, see Singleton, 'The Irreducible Vision', in *Illuminated Manuscripts of the Divine Comedy*, Vol. I, pp. 18–22. Later, Sapia recalls raising her head to different effect: 'I turned upwards my impudent face, crying out to God, "Now I fear Thee no more"' (XIII 121–2).

her fellow sufferers, Sapia weeps for her sins, and other souls beat their breasts (VII 106, X 120); but these are regular acts of penance, quite unlike the disorderly *atti* of the damned. Still more unlike are the prayerful actions of a soul in the beautiful evening scene of Canto VIII:

> Ella giunse e levò ambo le palme,
> ficcando li occhi verso l'oriente,
> come dicesse a Dio: 'D'altro non calme'.

> ['He joined and lifted both his palms, fixing his eyes on the East, as if he said to God, "For naught else do I care"', *Purg.* VIII 10–12.]

Turning to the *Paradiso*, one needs to make a distinction. There the blessed spirits appear in human form as 'shades' only in the two lowest spheres and then not again until Dante reaches the highest, the empyrean, where they are once more seen in their 'uncovered shape', as promised in *Paradiso* XXII 58–63. In the first sphere, of the moon, Piccarda responds to Dante's questions with joyful smiles (*Par.* III 42, 67); in the second, Mercury, the eyes of Justinian sparkle with joy (V 126); in the Primum Mobile, when Gregory first saw the order of angels there, we are told that he smiled at his old mistaken opinions ('di sé medesmo rise', XXVIII 135); and in the empyrean, St Bernard receives the poet with looks and gestures of paternal affection:

> Diffuso era per li occhi e per le gene
> di benigna letizia, in atto pio
> quale a tenero padre si convene.

> ['His eyes and cheeks were suffused with benign gladness, his mien kindly such as befits a tender father', *Par.* XXXI 61–3.]

Later, Bernard encourages Dante to look upon God himself, 'signing me with a smile to look upward' (XXXIII 49–50).

In the greater part of *Paradiso*, however, blessed spirits manifest themselves in displays of light, movement, and sound, with no face or body to be seen. These displays are all *segni* 'signs' – a term applied to the rose in the empyrean (XXXI 27), as well as to the letters shaped in the heaven of Jupiter and the Roman eagle there (XVIII 80, XIX 37, 101, XX 8). When that eagle of Jupiter, formed from just souls manifested as light, comes to speak, it is compared to a falcon in the way it moves its head and wings and so 'shows its will' ('voglia mostrando', XIX 36) – for, as Augustine observed, creatures also have signs by which they show their desires.[37] It might seem that these displays of *son et lumière* could bear little relation to ordinary human expression or gesture; but some of them are, in fact, represented as celestial surrogates for just such bodily acts. The poem itself suggests as much by its curious comparison purporting to explain how it could be that Adam, visible only as light, manifested his joy in approaching Dante:

> Talvolta un animal coverto broglia,
>   sì che l'affetto convien che si paia
>   per lo seguir che face a lui la 'nvoglia;
> e similmente l'anima primaia
>   mi facea trasparer per la coverta
>   quant' ella a compiacermi venìa gaia.
>
> ['Sometimes an animal that is covered so stirs that its impulse must needs be apparent, since what envelops it follows its movements: in like manner that first soul showed me, through its covering, how joyously it came to do me pleasure', *Par.* XXVI 97–102.]

The animal's feeling or impulse causes a bodily movement which, since the creature is 'covered' (in undergrowth? by a cloth?), can be seen only in the corresponding movement of its covering; so that movement is, as it were, a sign of a sign of the animal's feeling, at two removes from the original impulse, but still true to it. In this it resembles the light-displays of such as Adam.

Celestial signs conveying the *voluntas significandi* of blessed souls correspond most often to facial expression rather than bodily movement. When the bright light of St Peter changes from white to red, its 'transcolouration' expresses the anger he feels at the unworthiness of his papal successors, as if it were a flush of anger on his face (XXVII 11–27). The principle of correspondence is made explicit, with another slippery *come*, in an earlier passage concerning Cacciaguida:

> Come si vede qui alcuna volta
>   l'affetto ne la vista, s'elli è tanto
>   che da lui sia tutta l'anima tolta,

---

[37] *De Doctrina*, II 4.

> così nel fiammeggiar del folgór santo,
> a ch'io mi volsi, conobbi la voglia
> in lui di ragionarmi ancora alquanto.
>
> ['As sometimes here the affection is seen in the countenance if it be such that all the mind is taken up by it, so in the flaming of the holy glow to which I turned I recognized his wish to have some further speech with me', *Par.* XVIII 22–7.]

It is as if the image of an affectionate facial expression – such as Cacciaguida might have shown to his descendant on earth – is faintly superimposed on the featureless 'folgór santo'. Positive emotions such as love and joy are, of course, commonly associated with light. So, when the light of Peter Damian brightens before him, Dante can read its meaning: 'Io veggio ben l'amor che tu m'accenne' ['I clearly perceive the love which you are signalling to me', XXI 45]. The poet himself compares such effulgence to a smile: 'Per letiziar là sù fulgor s'acquista, / sì come riso qui' ['Through rejoicing, effulgence is gained there on high, even as a smile here', IX 70–1, cf. V 126]. Elsewhere, he can speak as if the soul, under its covering of light, were actually smiling. In the heaven of the sun, one of the lights is said to issue from the smile (*riso*) of Gratian (X 103–4); and when, in the next canto, Dante sees the light of Aquinas grow more intense, he realises that the saint is smiling:

> E io sent' dentro a quella lumera
> che pria m'avea parlato, sorridendo
> incominciar, faccendosi più mera.
>
> ['And within that light which first had spoken to me I heard it begin to speak, while it smiled and grew brighter', *Par.* XI 16–18].

Again, in the heaven of Mars, Cacciaguida's first response to his descendant's anxious questioning takes the form of a fresh coruscation in 'la luce in che rideva il mio tesoro' ['the light wherein was smiling my treasure', XVII 121]. On these occasions, Dante is able to perceive bodily *cenni* even in those blessed souls who appear to him in displays of light.

These examples have shown how, throughout the *Commedia*, Dante displays his interest in the part played by a variety of physical signs in human communication. This interest finds its most curious expression in his representations, in *Purgatorio* x, of what he there calls *visibile parlare* or 'visible speech'. As Dante and Virgil climb the mount of purgatory, they come upon the circle of the proud, and there they see, cut into the white marble side of the mountain, three sculpted scenes. These intaglii present examples of humility to the sinners of the circle: the Virgin Mary at the Annunciation, King David dancing before the ark of God, and the Emperor Trajan encountering the suppliant widow (*Purg.* x 28–99). God himself has carved these images, and his marvellous expressive art surpasses, not only the best human sculptors, but even nature itself (lines 32–3). It is enough for a spectator to see the sculpted figures to have a complete knowledge of what they are feeling, and even of the very words they speak. Postures, gestures and looks here, miraculously, 'speak' out of silence. Thus, the angel of the Annunciation

> dinanzi a noi pareva sì verace
> quivi intagliato in un atto soave,
> che non sembiava imagine che tace.
> Giurato si saria ch'el dicesse '*Ave!*'

> ['before us there appeared so vividly graven in gentle mien that it seemed not a silent image: one would have sworn that he was saying "*Ave*"', x 37–40.]

The answering words of Mary, too, can be read directly from her *atto*:

> e avea in atto impressa esta favella
> '*Ecce ancilla Dei*', propriamente
> come figura in cera si suggella.

> ['and these words were imprinted in her attitude: "*Ecce ancilla Dei*", as expressly as a figure is stamped on wax', x 43–5.]

There are no written words: sight here receives a verbal message otherwise reserved for the hearing.[38] In the Trajan scene, similarly, the emperor and the widow 'seem to say' words which Dante can divine and report (x 82–93). He concludes by observing that it was God who 'produsse esto visibile parlare, / novello a noi perché qui non si trova' ['wrought this visible speech, new to us because here it is not found',

---

[38] In the Old Testament scene, the sight of people singing before the ark 'made two of my senses say, the one, "No", the other, "Yes, they are singing"' (x 59–60).

x 95–6].³⁹ The phrase 'visibile parlare' may recall the 'verba visibilia' of St Augustine; but whereas Augustine spoke metaphorically (*'quasi quaedam verba visibilia'*), Dante speaks, as it were, literally.

The poet may be thought of as imagining here an impossible target for the representation of looks and gestures by a human artist. It is impossible mainly because Dante is not God, but also, perhaps, because he is a writer, not a sculptor. Unlike visual artists, writers cannot directly represent the physical form of expressive *atti* – not even a writer as skilled as Dante in registering bodily movements and positions. Significantly enough, it is in the same circle of pride that he introduces a painter, Oderisi da Gubbio, who speaks of how Dante's near contemporary Giotto now holds the field in that art (XI 95); for Giotto was admired at the time for the illusion of reality created by his pictures, and modern scholars have noticed his mastery of the speaking gesture in scenes such as the Annunciation.⁴⁰ Giotto, unlike Dante, could represent a gesture directly, albeit in a frozen still; but he shared with Dante (but not God) the other problem, the problem of meaning. It was and is not easy for human artists in any medium, when they describe or portray some act of NVC, to fix the precise message required by the context – on those not infrequent occasions, that is, when they cannot be content to rely on the general significance assigned by convention to a bow or a smile, or when the action in question is too singular to have any commonly understood meaning.

The simplest expedient available to the writer was for signers to support their gesture or look by speaking words which articulate its meaning, as Virgil does when he turns and looks at Dante, and then says 'Pay attention': it is that kind of look (p. 160 above). Alternatively, the poet himself may supply the verbal gloss, as in the case of that other look of

---

[39] Benvenuto da Imola observes: 'Here on earth we comprehend the speech of men not by sight but by hearing' (Dartmouth Dante Project).

[40] Boccaccio praises Giotto's realism in *Decameron* VI 5: 'One very often finds, in his works, that people's visual sense is deceived, mistaking what was depicted for the real thing': cited by M. Baxandall, *Giotto and the Orators* (Oxford, 1971), p. 74. See Barasch, *Giotto and the Language of Gesture*, with examples from Giotto's Annunciation, Figures 10 and 38. Barasch observes (p. 12) that 'in Italian culture of the thirteenth and fourteenth centuries – the literary sources strongly suggest – a high degree of awareness of the shape and meaning of gestures prevailed. Giotto's work offers ample witness that the master shared this awareness.'

Virgil's which 'silently said "be silent"' (p. 161 above). Glosses may be introduced, less elegantly, with expressions like 'as if he said', 'as who says', or, in Middle English, 'ascaunces'.[41] Dante employs such a formula in that scene in *Purgatorio* where a spirit looks to the east 'as if he said to God...' (p. 174 above). What most distinguishes Dante from the other writers under discussion here, however, is his use of similes for this purpose – evidence, no doubt, of the influence upon him of Latin poetry. Sometimes these similes serve to define what a person physically did (though not without other implications), particularly with unusual actions such as the Paduan usurer sticking his tongue right out or the sightless Sapia raising her face. More often, however, the main purpose of such similes is to focus on the meaning of a look or gesture. That far-fetched comparison with Malohaut's cough indicates what Beatrice meant by her smile. When Virgil smiles 'as one does to a child that is won with an apple', the comparison leaves no room for uncertainty about what he feels and what he does: it characterises the smile and its tone exactly. Other similes are even more specific and circumstantial. After hearing St Peter's attack on his unworthy papal successors in the *Paradiso*, Beatrice changes countenance:

> E come donna onesta che permane
> di sé sicura, e per l'altrui fallanza,
> per ascoltando, timida si fane,
> così Beatrice trasmutò sembianza.
>
> ['And as a chaste lady who is sure of herself, and at another's fault, only hearing of it, becomes timid, so did Beatrice change her semblance', *Par.* XXVII 31–4.]

One cannot tell from this simile exactly what Beatrice did (blushed?), for it focusses entirely on what her 'sembianza' expressed: a precisely defined species of vicarious shame. Beatrice is abashed by what she hears of others' faults.

It is in part by such devices that Dante achieves, if not *visibile parlare*, at least an extraordinary richness of specification in his rendering of expression, look and gesture, both the physical form of what people do, and also 'what the dumb would say'.

---

[41] For 'ascaunces', see pp. 126 and 129 above, rendering Boccaccio's 'quasi dicesse' at *Troilus* I 292.

6

Afterword

Present knowledge about the forms and functions of non-verbal signs in the past is very patchy and imperfect. The subject has, for one thing, never received the kind of systematic, incremental study that scholars have long devoted to past languages. It has no established discipline corresponding to that of historical philology. Hence, when the book of essays entitled *A Cultural History of Gesture* was published in England in 1991, it could be hailed as 'an excitingly original project which wholly succeeds in its novel aims'.[1] The subject has certainly been neglected (though less by German than by English writers), and much remains to be done – in the first place, by establishing facts and dispelling fancies. Yet historical knowledge about looks and gestures can never hope to match what is known about past languages, for the evidence itself is so much more sparse and limited. Nor can it even begin to approach the knowledge available to experts on contemporary NVC. As Keith Thomas remarks in his introduction to the *Cultural History*, 'it is much harder to study the history of gesture and bodily comportment than to observe their present-day manifestations' (p. 4). Accounts of present-day usage, indeed, make one painfully aware of how much historians are bound to miss in the usage of the past, and not least in the Middle Ages. Sociologists can observe such things as the whole gestural repertoire of a single community at a particular time, tracing in it variations according to class, occupation, gender, or age; and they can also map the differences in usage between one region and another.

---

[1] Bremmer and Roodenburg, eds., *A Cultural History of Gesture*. I cite from the cover of the paperback.

Afterword

Two well-known modern studies of this kind will illustrate such fineness of detail at a level quite beyond historians of the subject. One is an investigation into the gestural behaviour of Eastern Jews and Southern Italians living in New York before the Second World War. The author, Daniel Efron, looked at the gestural repertoires of groups of 'traditional' Jewish and Italian immigrants in that city, and compared them with 'assimilated' groups of the same, showing that the two unassimilated groups behaved in ways very different from each other and from native New Yorkers, whereas the other two groups had largely adapted to American norms.[2] A remarkable instance of purely regional variation appears in the work of Desmond Morris and his collaborators. This concerns two ways of signifying negation with the head: the lateral headshake and the 'headtoss' (a rapid backward jerk). The investigators found that in modern Italy the familiar headshake is regularly employed throughout northern and central parts of the country, but that in the south people will negate with the headtoss. One can identify a gestural boundary, indeed, north of which headtossing hardly occurs. This boundary runs across Italy some fifty kilometres north of Naples, and it may be represented by a line on the map – an 'isokine', as it is called by analogy with the isoglosses with which linguistic geographers map dialect features.[3] Morris observes a further remarkable fact: the headtoss area, to the south of the isokine, corresponds to that part of Italy which was colonised in antiquity from Greece – a country whose inhabitants still to this day employ the headtoss as their sign of negation.[4]

This last finding suggests that here is a gesture boundary which has existed with little change continuously since antiquity. Yet I doubt whether one could find sufficient evidence for it in the intervening centuries. Textual and pictorial sources from the past are simply too deficient. On very rare occasions only, an author has set out to give some general

---

[2] D. Efron, *Gesture, Race and Culture* (The Hague, 1972), originally published as *Gesture and Environment* (New York, 1941). Efron's polemical purpose was to counter theories, then being put about by Nazis and others, that gestural behaviour was a racial characteristic.

[3] Morris *et al.*, *Gestures*, pp. 164–8, 247–59, with maps on pp. 254–5. Kendon has a valuable review article prompted by this book, 'Geography of Gesture'.

[4] On 'nodding up' (negative) and 'nodding down' (positive) in Greek antiquity and in modern Greece, see A. L. Boegehold, *When a Gesture was Expected: A Selection of Examples from Archaic and Classical Greek Literature* (Princeton, N.J., 1999), especially pp. 20–21 and 59–63.

Gestures and looks in medieval narrative

account of the gestures with which he is familiar. The fullest and most remarkable of these is the report on Neapolitan gesture in the early nineteenth century, published by Andrea de Jorio in 1832. This book, *La mimica degli antichi investigata nel gestire napoletano*, is now available in a translation with extensive introduction and notes by Adam Kendon.[5] Kendon describes de Jorio as 'the first ethnographer of gesture'; and his book does provide a unique opportunity to observe in great detail the gestural repertoire employed in one place at one past time. But no such rich source of information is available for the period with which this book has been concerned.[6]

The present study has confined itself to textual sources, with only passing reference to the visual arts. The texts in question quite frequently make reference to gestures and looks, but they do not often describe them in any detail. Chaucer is exceptional when he pauses to specify the form and also the meaning of Criseyde's haughty gaze in *Troilus* – both its direction (a little aside) and its message ('What, may I not stand here?'). English and French writers very rarely devote much space to the matter, contenting themselves with occasionally noting the strength of a handshake or the sweetness of a look.[7] One scholar has made the interesting suggestion that writers under medieval conditions had less need than their modern successors to enter into such details because their texts were intended to be read aloud. So it was left for the performer to realise the appropriate actions, just as an actor will realise the script of a play.[8] There is certainly something in this idea. All the writers under consideration here lived at a time when reading aloud to listeners was common practice; and they were also, to a greater or lesser degree, heirs to a narrative language that had been developed in earlier periods

---

[5] De Jorio, *Gesture in Naples and Gesture in Classical Antiquity*, ed. and transl. Kendon. De Jorio believed that modern Neapolitan behaviour could throw light on gestures represented in the artifacts and texts of antiquity.

[6] I have, however, occasionally drawn upon the seventeenth-century study by Bulwer, *Chirologia: or The Natural Language of the Hand*.

[7] Cf. Ménard, *Le rire et le sourire*: 'La plupart du temps les romanciers courtois se contentent de dire qu'un personnage rit, sans apporter d'autres précisions' (p. 439); and see generally pp. 439–47, 'Qualificatifs et Nuances'.

[8] F. Poyatos, 'Nonverbal Communication in the Novel', in Poyatos, ed., *New Perspectives in Nonverbal Communication* (Oxford, 1983), pp. 277–314. Thus: 'the minstrel would enact Sir Orfeo's gestures and tone of voice, as described in the poem, when he faces the demented queen' (p. 298).

Afterword

when such 'aurality' was commoner still.[9] Geoffrey of Vinsauf, as we have noticed, speaks as if even learned Latin verses are to be read aloud, recommending that the performer should act with *vultus* and *gestus* as well as speech.[10]

Yet it is by no means only medieval narratives that underrepresent the part played by non-verbal as against verbal signs in the dealings between their characters. There are deep-seated difficulties in doing justice to them. Unlike characters' words, which are most often recorded in direct speech, non-verbal signs can be recorded only in their equivalent of indirect speech: since they cannot be transcribed, they must be described. Nor is it easy to describe gestures or looks with any precision, since such actions vary continuously within their physical limits, and even slight variations – in the depth of a bow or the length of a gaze – commonly affect what they mean. Geoffrey of Vinsauf, again, recognised the problem when he included *descriptio gesticulantium* among the examples he gives of 'more difficult and less common' kinds of poetic description (as against easy subjects such as a female beauty).[11] It is as if, one modern commentator remarks, 'gestures do not like being written about'. Novelists in modern times do, of course, benefit from later developments in narrative technique, as well as from the enriched vocabularies of post-medieval vernaculars; yet even they still find it difficult to produce a really satisfactory *descriptio gesticulantium*. It is rare to come across anything in their work as good as the description by Marcel Proust of a wink – the wink by which the snob Legrandin manages to acknowledge his acquaintance with Marcel's family without betraying it to the great lady whom he is escorting to her carriage:

---

[9] See Joyce Coleman on 'aurality': *Public Reading and the Reading Public in Late Medieval England and France* (Cambridge, 1996).

[10] Above, p. 69. In the lines that follow, Geoffrey illustrates his point: a reciter may manifest anger by 'fiery face' and 'agitated gesture' (ll. 2044–5), or imitate a rustic by the appropriate signs (*notulas*) in voice, face, and gesture (ll. 2051–4). Boegehold, *When a Gesture was Expected*, stresses the importance of gesture in the writings of ancient Greeks and in the performance of their writings by reciters, actors, etc.

[11] *Documentum de Arte Versificandi*, II 2, 3–7, ed. Faral, *Les Arts Poétiques*, pp. 271–2. Vinsauf refers to an example of gesticular description which I cannot identify: 'Singula mireris, etc.'. The author of *Ad Herennium* remarked that writers on rhetoric neglect the subject of *pronuntiatio* or delivery, because 'all have thought it scarcely possible for voice, mien, and gesture [*voce et vultu et gestu*] to be lucidly described, as appertaining to our sense-experience': ed. and transl. Caplan, III xi 19.

> He subtilised the refinements of good-fellowship into a wink of connivance, a hint, a hidden meaning, a secret understanding, all the mysteries of complicity in a plot, and finally exalted his assurances of friendship to the level of protestations of affection, even of a declaration of love, lighting up for us, and for us alone, with a secret and languid flame invisible by the great lady upon his other side, an enamoured pupil in a countenance of ice.[12]

No doubt it is partly the absence of anything approaching such virtuosity that accounts for the little attention paid by readers to the multitude of non-verbal signs to be found in medieval narratives. A simple statement such as 'he winked' is easier to overlook than Proust's 'enamoured pupil in a countenance of ice'. Nor have scholars done much to remedy the neglect, in their commentaries or in their explanatory notes. The notes in editions of *Sir Gawain and the Green Knight*, for instance, regularly explain what words meant, but I know of none that explains what kisses meant – despite the fact that the kisses of the lady there can only be properly understood if one takes account, not only of their undoubted sexual provocation, but also of their conformity to social customs of the time.

Like *Sir Gawain*, most of the texts I have considered concern themselves mainly or exclusively with polite behaviour. So I am far from claiming to have given a balanced picture of what, in some countries of medieval Europe, actually went on. My texts give only occasional glimpses of social or regional varieties in behaviour – the kinds of differences observed in modern times by Efron or Morris. Jean-Claude Schmitt, writing of the twelfth and thirteenth centuries, is no doubt right in his observation: 'les distinctions d' "ordres", d' "états" et d' "âges" sont plus marquées que jamais. A chaque groupe il convient d'avoir et d'apprendre d'autres gestes.'[13] Yet with rather few exceptions – Vanni Fucci's *fica*, Wat Tyler's handshake – it is only the behaviour of polite or courtly circles that my texts represent. Nor have I had much occasion to notice regional differences. Writers concerned with knights, ladies, and

---

[12] *Swann's Way: Part One*, transl. C. K. Scott Moncrieff (London, 1955), pp. 170–1.
[13] *Raison des gestes*, p. 224. See pp. 224–9 generally there. In the Middle Ages, according to Norbert Elias, 'the behavioural differences between different classes in the same region are often greater than those between regionally separate representatives of the same social class': *The Civilizing Process*, p. 117.

other such 'gentils' generally show them behaving according to standards of courtesy which were, in all essentials, international. Local variations, such as they were in the upper reaches of society, tend to be suppressed.

On the other hand, it is precisely medieval texts of the sort privileged here which pay the most attention to non-verbal signs. As one scholar remarks, 'court life . . . produces an intense refinement of sentiment and emotion, the ability to detect subtle shades of meaning and expressions of intention and sentiment in the most minute gestures'.[14] Writers with any claim to courtliness or gentility accordingly are alert to the meanings of gestures and glances, and they expect their readers also to have an eye for such things. I guess that the author of the Prose *Lancelot* would not have been surprised – as I certainly was – to find the little cough of his Dame de Malohaut recalled by Dante in the *Paradiso*. Dante noticed it, and so, in the story, did Lancelot. In the world of romance, characters notice such small behaviours, as when Alexander, in *Cligés*, asks Guinevere to explain her little enigmatic smile; but it is the same in the *Commedia*, where Dante's quick 'flash of a smile' prompts Statius to ask what he meant by it. Little actions like that, as well as bigger ones like bowing or kneeling, carry significances which modern readers readily underestimate, or, on occasion, misunderstand. There is a need to pay attention to the non-verbal signs in these texts, as well as to the words; for theirs was indeed, as Le Goff put it, 'une civilisation du geste'.

---

[14] C. S. Jaeger, *The Origins of Courtliness: Civilizing Trends and the Formation of Courtly Ideals, 939–1210* (Philadelphia, Pa., 1985), p. 13. Cf. p. 258: 'Words, gestures, intonation, and facial expression all bear meaning, express policy – no act or gesture is random'.

Bibliography

TEXTS

Aelred of Rievaulx, *De Spirituali Amicitia, Patrologia Latina*, Vol. CXCV, Cols 659–702.
An Alphabet of Tales, ed. M. M. Banks, EETS, 126, 127 (1904–5).
Amis and Amiloun, ed. M. Leach, EETS, 203 (1937).
Ancrene Wisse, ed. J. R. R. Tolkien, EETS, 249 (1962).
The Anonimalle Chronicle, 1333 to 1381, ed. V. H. Galbraith (Manchester, 1927).
Anonymous Short Metrical Chronicle, ed. M. C. Carroll and R. Tuve, *PMLA*, 46 (1931), 115–54.
Anonymous Short Metrical Chronicle, ed. E. Zettl, EETS, 196 (1935).
Of Arthour and of Merlin, ed. O. D. Macrae-Gibson, EETS, 268, 279 (1973, 1979).
Augustine, *De Doctrina Christiana*, ed. and transl. R. P. H. Green (Oxford, 1995).
  De Mendacio, in *Corpus Scriptorum Ecclesiasticorum Latinorum*, Vol. XLI (1900), pp. 413–66.
The Babees Book: Early English Meals and Manners, ed. F. J. Furnivall, EETS, 32 (1868).
Bacon, Sir F., *Francis Bacon: A Critical Edition of the Major Works*, ed. B. Vickers (Oxford, 1996).
Barbour, J., *Barbour's Bruce*, ed. M. P. McDiarmid and J. A. C. Stevenson, 3 vols., STS, 4th Series, 12, 13, 15 (1980–85).
Bernard of Clairvaux, *De Gradibus Humilitatis et Superbiae*, in *Opera*, ed. J. Leclercq and H. M. Rochais, Vol. III (Rome, 1963), pp. 13–59.
Boccaccio, G., *Il Filostrato*, ed. V. Branca, in Branca, ed., *Tutte le opere di Giovanni Boccaccio*, Vol. II (Milan, 1964).
Bokenham, O., *Legendys of Hooly Wummen*, ed. M. S. Serjeantson, EETS, 206 (1938).
Boncampagno da Signa, *Rhetorica Novissima*, ed. A. Gaudentius [Gaudenzi], Biblioteca Iuridica Medii Aevi, Vol. II (Bologna, 1892), pp. 249–97.
Capgrave, J., *The Life of St. Katherine of Alexandria*, ed. C. Horstmann, EETS, 100 (1893).
Carpenter, A., *Destructorium Viciorum* (Paris, 1516).
Catholicon Anglicum: An English–Latin Workbook, ed. S. J. H. Herrtage and H. B. Wheatley, EETS, 75 (1881).

Bibliography

Charles d'Orléans, *Fortunes Stabilnes: Charles of Orleans's English Book of Love*, ed. M.-J. Arn (Binghamton, N.Y., 1994).
   Poésies, ed. P. Champion, 2 vols (Paris, 1982–3).
Chaucer, G., *The Riverside Chaucer*, 3rd edn, ed. L. D. Benson (Boston, 1987).
   Troilus and Criseyde, ed. B. Windeatt (Harlow, 1984).
Chrétien de Troyes, *Le Chevalier de la Charrete*, ed. M. Roques (Paris, 1978).
   Cligés, ed. A. Micha (Paris, 1982).
   Erec et Enide, ed. M. Roques (Paris, 1968).
   Le Roman de Perceval, ou Le Conte du Graal, ed. W. Roach (Geneva, 1959).
   Yvain (Le Chevalier au Lion), ed. T. B. W. Reid (Manchester, 1942).
Cicero, *Orator*, ed. and transl. H. M. Hubbell, Loeb Classical Library (Cambridge, Mass., 1942).
Clariodus, ed. D. Irving, Maitland Club, 9 (Edinburgh, 1830).
The Cloud of Unknowing and The Book of Privy Counselling, ed. P. Hodgson, EETS, 218 (1944).
Commentarius Brevis et Jucundus Itineris atque Peregrinationis, ed. K. Hrdina (Prague, 1951).
Dante, *The Divine Comedy*, ed. and transl. C. S. Singleton, 6 vols. (Princeton, N.J., 1970–75).
   Le opere, ed. M. Barbi *et al.*, 2nd edn (Florence, 1960).
Dives and Pauper, ed. P. H. Barnum, EETS, 275, 280 (1976, 1980).
Douglas, G., *Virgil's Aeneid*, ed. D. F. C. Coldwell, 4 vols., STS, 3rd Series, 25, 27, 28, 30 (1957–64).
Erasmus, D., *The Correspondence, Letters 1 to 141*, transl. R. A. B. Mynors and D. F. S. Thomson (Toronto, 1974).
Froissart, J., *Chroniques de J. Froissart*, ed. S. Luce *et al.*, 15 vols., in progress (Paris, 1869–).
   Les Chroniques de Sire Jean Froissart, ed. J. A. C. Buchon, 3 vols. (Paris, 1852–3).
Geoffrey of Vinsauf, *Poetria Nova* and *Documentum de Arte Versificandi*, in E. Faral, ed., *Les arts poétiques du XIIe et du XIIIe siècle* (Paris, 1924).
The Gest Hystoriale of the Destruction of Troy, ed. G. A. Panton and D. Donaldson, EETS, 39, 56 (1869, 1874).
Gower, J., *Confessio Amantis*, ed. G. C. Macaulay, in *John Gower's English Works*, EETS, E.S. 81, 82 (1900, 1901).
Guy of Warwick, ed. J. Zupitza, EETS, E.S. 42, 49, 59, (1883–91).
Henryson, R., *The Poems of Robert Henryson*, ed. D. Fox (Oxford, 1981).
Ad Herennium, ed. and transl. H. Caplan, Loeb Classical Library (Cambridge, Mass., 1954).
Hugh of St. Victor, *De Institutione Novitiorum, Patrologia Latina*, Vol. CLXXVI, Cols. 925–52.
Ipomadon, ed. R. Purdie, EETS, 316 (2001).
Ipomedon: Poème de Hue de Rotelande, ed. A. J. Holden (Paris, 1979).
The Isle of Ladies, or The Ile of Pleasaunce, ed. A. Jenkins (New York, 1980).
Kempe, M., *The Book of Margery Kempe*, ed. S. B. Meech, EETS, 212 (1940).

Bibliography

Kyng Alisaunder, ed. G. V. Smithers, EETS, 227, 237 (1952, 1957).
Laȝamon, *Brut*, ed. G. L. Brook and R. F. Leslie, EETS, 250, 277 (1963, 1978).
Lancelot do Lac: The Non-Cyclic Old French Prose Romance, ed. E. Kennedy, 2 vols. (Oxford, 1980).
Langland, W., *Piers Plowman: The B Version*, ed. G. Kane and E. T. Donaldson (London, 1975).
Piers Plowman: The C Version, ed. G. Russell and G. Kane (London, 1997).
Piers Plowman: An Edition of the C-Text, ed. D. Pearsall (London, 1978).
The Latin Text of the Ancrene Riwle, ed. C. D'Evelyn, EETS, 216 (1944).
Life of the Black Prince by the Herald of Sir John Chandos, ed. M. K. Pope and E. C. Lodge (Oxford, 1910).
Lybeaus Desconus, ed. M. Mills, EETS, 261 (1969).
Lydgate, J., *Lydgate's Siege of Thebes*, ed. A. Erdmann, EETS, E.S. 108 (1911).
Machaut, G. de, *Le Jugement du Roy de Behaigne and Remede de Fortune*, ed. and transl. J. I. Wimsatt and W. W. Kibler (Athens, Georgia, 1988).
Malory, Sir T., *The Works of Sir Thomas Malory*, ed. E. Vinaver, 3 vols. (Oxford, 1947).
Manning, R., *Robert of Brunne's Handlyng Synne*, ed. F. J. Furnivall, EETS, 119, 123 (1901, 1903).
Martin of Dacia, *De Modis Significandi*, in *Martini de Dacia Opera*, ed. H. Roos, Corpus Philosophorum Danicorum Medii Aevi, II (Copenhagen, 1961), pp. 3–118.
Metham, J., *Amoryus and Cleopes*, in *The Works of John Metham*, ed. H. Craig, EETS, 132 (1906).
Middle English Metrical Romances, ed. W. H. French and C. B. Hale (reissue, New York, 1964).
Le Moniage Guillaume, ed. W. Cloetta, 2 vols., Société des Anciens Textes Français (Paris, 1906, 1911).
Montaigne, M. de, *The Complete Essays*, transl. M. A. Screech (London, 1991).
Le Morte Arthur, ed. J. D. Bruce, EETS, E.S. 88 (1903) (stanzaic *Morte Arthur*).
La Mort le Roi Artu, ed. J. Frappier (Geneva, 1954).
The Northern Passion, ed. F. A. Foster, EETS, 145 (1913).
Nouveau Recueil Complet des Fabliaux, ed. W. Noomen, Vol. VI (Assen/Maastricht, 1991).
Octovian Imperator, ed. F. McSparran (Heidelburg, 1979).
The Oxford Book of Medieval English Verse, ed. C. and K. Sisam (Oxford, 1970).
Partonope of Blois, ed. A. T. Bödtker, EETS, E.S. 109 (1912).
Pearl, ed. E. V. Gordon (Oxford, 1953).
Petrarch, F., *De Insigni Obedientia et Fide Uxoris* (*Epistolae Seniles* XVII iii), in W. F. Bryan and G. Dempster, eds., *Sources and Analogues of Chaucer's Canterbury Tales* (London, 1958).
The Pilgrimage of the Lyfe of the Manhode, ed. A. Henry, EETS, 288, 292 (1985, 1988).
The Poems of the Pearl Manuscript: 'Pearl', 'Cleanness', 'Patience', and 'Sir Gawain and the Green Knight', ed. M. Andrew and R. Waldron (London, 1978).
Promptorium Parvulorum, ed. A. Way, 3 vols., Camden Society, 25, 55, 89 (1843, 1853, 1865).

Bibliography

The Promptorium Parvulorum, ed. A. L. Mayhew, EETS, E.S. 102 (1908).
Proust, M., *Swann's Way, Part One*, transl. C. K. Scott Moncrieff (London, 1955).
La Queste del Saint Graal, ed. A. Pauphilet (Paris, 1949).
Quintilian, *Institutio Oratoria*, ed. and transl. H. E. Butler, Loeb Classical Library, 4 vols. (Cambridge, Mass., 1920–2).
Rabelais, F., *Gargantua and Pantagruel*, transl. J. M. Cohen (Harmondsworth, 1955).
   Pantagruel, ed. G. Defaux (Paris, 1994).
   Le Quart Livre, ed. R. Marichal (Geneva, 1947).
Le Roman de la Rose, ed. F. Lecoy, 3 vols. (Paris, 1965–70).
Ruiz, J., *Libro de Buen Amor*, ed. and transl. R. S. Willis (Princeton, N. J., 1972).
Rymes of Robyn Hood: An Introduction to the English Outlaw, ed. R. B. Dobson and J. Taylor (London, 1976).
Secular Lyrics of the XIVth and XVth Centuries, ed. R. H. Robbins (Oxford, 1952).
Seinte Katerine, ed. S. R. T. O. d'Ardenne and E. J. Dobson, EETS, S.S. 7 (1981).
The Seven Sages of Rome, ed. K. Brunner, EETS, 191 (1933).
Sidrak and Bokkus, ed. T. L. Burton, EETS, 311, 312 (1998–9).
Sir Ferumbras, ed. S. J. H. Herrtage, EETS, E.S. 34 (1879).
Sir Gawain and the Green Knight, ed. J. R. R. Tolkien and E. V. Gordon, 2nd edn revised by N. Davis (Oxford, 1967).
   ed. T. Silverstein (Chicago, 1984).
Sir Orfeo, ed. A. J. Bliss, 2nd edn (Oxford, 1966).
Skelton, J., *John Skelton, The Complete English Poems*, ed. J. Scattergood (Harmondsworth, 1983).
The Tale of Beryn, ed. F. J. Furnivall and W. G. Stone, Chaucer Society Publications, 2nd Series, 17, 24 (1876, 1887).
The Tale of Gamelyn, ed. W. W. Skeat, in *The Complete Works of Geoffrey Chaucer*, 6 vols. (Oxford, 1894–7), Vol. IV, pp. 645–67.
A Talking of the Love of God, ed. C. Horstman, in *Yorkshire Writers*, Vol. II (London, 1896), pp. 345–66.
Thomas, *Tristan*, ed. F. Lecoy (Paris, 1991).
Trevisa, J., *On the Properties of Things: John Trevisa's Translation of Bartholomaeus Anglicus De Proprietatibus Rerum*, ed. M. C. Seymour *et al.*, 3 vols. (Oxford, 1975, 1988).
Tugwell, S., ed., 'The Nine Ways of Prayer of St. Dominic: A Textual Study and Critical Edition', *Mediaeval Studies*, 47 (1985), 1–124.
Twelve Fabliaux, ed. T. B. W. Reid (Manchester, 1958).
Two Wycliffite Texts, ed. A. Hudson, EETS, 301 (1993).
Usk, T., *The Testament of Love*, ed. W. W. Skeat, in *Chaucerian and Other Pieces* (Oxford, 1897), pp. 1–145.
Valentine and Orson, ed. A. Dickson, EETS, 204 (1937).
The Vulgate Version of the Arthurian Romances, ed. H. O. Sommer, 7 vols. (Washington, 1909–13).
The Wars of Alexander, ed. H. N. Duggan and T. Turville-Petre, EETS, S.S. 10 (1989).
William of Palerne, ed. G. H. V. Bunt (Groningen, 1985).

Bibliography

Wycliffite Bible: *MS. Bodley 959 ... The Earlier Version of the Wycliffite Bible*, ed. C. Lindberg, Vol. IV (Stockholm, 1965).
Wynnere and Wastoure, ed. S. Trigg, EETS, 297 (1990).
Ywain and Gawain, ed. A. B. Friedman and N. T. Harrington, EETS, 254 (1964).

DICTIONARIES

Anglo-Norman Dictionary, ed. W. Rothwell, L. W. Stone, and T. B. W. Reid (London, 1977–92).
An Anglo-Saxon Dictionary, ed. J. Bosworth and T. N. Toller (Oxford, 1898); *Supplement*, ed. T. N. Toller (Oxford, 1921); *Addenda and Corrigenda*, ed. A. Campbell (Oxford, 1972).
Dictionary of Medieval Latin from British Sources, ed. R. E. Latham and D. R. Howlett, in progress (Oxford, 1975–).
A Dictionary of the Older Scottish Tongue, ed. W. A. Craigie *et al.*, in progress (Chicago, Aberdeen, 1931–).
Grande dizionario della lingua italiana, ed. S. Battaglia, in progress (Turin, 1961–).
Middle English Dictionary, ed. H. Kurath *et al.*, in progress (Ann Arbor, Mich., 1954–).
Novum Glossarium Mediae Latinitatis, ed. F. Blatt *et al.*, in progress (Copenhagen, 1957–).
The Oxford English Dictionary, ed. J. A. H. Murray *et al.*, 1st edn (Oxford, 1933).
Thesaurus Linguae Latinae, in progress (Leipzig, 1900–).
Tobler–Lommatzsch, *Altfranzösisches Wörterbuch*, in progress (Berlin, 1925–).

STUDIES

Argyle, M., *Bodily Communication*, 2nd edn (London, 1988).
Argyle, M., and M. Cook, *Gaze and Mutual Gaze* (Cambridge, 1976).
Barański, Z. G., 'Dante's Signs: An Introduction to Medieval Semiotics and Dante', in J. Barnes and C. Ó. Cuilleanáin, eds., *Dante and the Middle Ages* (Dublin, 1995), pp. 139–80.
Barasch, M., *Gestures of Despair in Medieval and Early Renaissance Art* (New York, 1976).
  Giotto and the Language of Gesture (Cambridge, 1987).
Bäuml, B. J., and F. H. Bäuml, *Dictionary of Worldwide Gestures*, 2nd edn (Lanham, Md., 1997).
Baxandall, M., *Giotto and the Orators* (Oxford, 1971).
Benson, R. G., *Medieval Body Language: A Study of the Use of Gesture in Chaucer's Poetry*, Anglistica 21 (Copenhagen, 1980).
Birdwhistell, R. L., *Kinesics and Context: Essays on Body-Motion Communication* (London, 1971).
Boegehold, A. L., *When a Gesture was Expected: A Selection of Examples from Archaic and Classical Greek Literature* (Princeton, N.J., 1999).

Bibliography

Botticelli, S., *The Drawings for Dante's Divine Comedy*, ed. H.-T. Schulze Altcappenberg (London, 2000).

Bremmer, J., and H. Roodenburg, eds., *A Cultural History of Gesture: From Antiquity to the Present Day* (Oxford, 1991, paperback, 1993).

Brieger, P., M. Meiss, and C. S. Singleton, *Illuminated Manuscripts of the Divine Comedy*, 2 vols. (London, 1969).

Bulwer, J., *Chirologia: or The Natural Language of the Hand, and Chironomia or the Art of Manual Rhetoric* (1664), ed. J. W. Cleary (Carbondale and Edwardsville, 1974).

Burrow, J. A., *A Reading of 'Sir Gawain and the Green Knight'* (London, 1965).

——— 'Gestures and Looks in *Piers Plowman*', *Yearbook of Langland Studies*, 14 (2000), 75–83.

Callan, H., *Ethology and Society: Towards an Anthropological View* (Oxford, 1970).

Camille, M., *Image on the Edge: The Margins of Medieval Art* (London, 1992).

Chénon, E., 'Le rôle juridique de l'*osculum* dans l'ancien droit français', *Mémoires de la Société des Antiquaires de France*, 6 (1919–23), 124–55.

Coleman, J., *Public Reading and the Reading Public in Late Medieval England and France* (Cambridge, 1996).

Corti, M., 'La teoria del segno nei logici modisti e in Dante', in P. Lendinara and M. C. Ruta, eds., *Per una storia della semiotica* (Palermo, 1981), pp. 69–86.

Craun, E. D., *Lies, Slander, and Obscenity in Medieval English Literature* (Cambridge, 1997).

Darwin, C., *The Expression of the Emotions in Man and Animals* (1872, paperback, Chicago, 1965).

Dinshaw, C., 'A Kiss is Just a Kiss: Heterosexuality and its Consolations in *Sir Gawain and the Green Knight*', *diacritics*, 24.2–3 (1994), 205–26.

Douglas, M., *Implicit Meanings: Essays in Anthropology* (London, 1975).

Eco, U., and C. Marmo, eds., *On the Medieval Theory of Signs* (Amsterdam, 1989).

Eco, U., R. Lambertini, C. Marmo, and A. Tabarroni, 'On Animal Language in the Medieval Classification of Signs', in Eco and Marmo, eds, *On the Medieval Theory of Signs*, pp. 3–41.

Efron, D., *Gesture, Race and Culture* (The Hague, 1972).

Eibl-Eibesfeldt, I., 'Similarities and Differences between Cultures in Expressive Movements', in Hinde, ed., *Non-Verbal Communication*, pp. 297–312.

Ekman, P., 'Cross-Cultural Studies of Facial Expression', in Ekman, ed., *Darwin and Facial Expression*, pp. 169–222.

Ekman, P., and W. V. Friesen, 'The Repertoire of Nonverbal Behavior: Categories, Origins, Usage, and Coding', *Semiotica*, 1 (1969), 49–98.

Ekman, P., W. V. Friesen, and P. Ellsworth, *Emotion in the Human Face* (New York, 1972).

Ekman, P., ed., *Darwin and Facial Expression: A Century of Research in Review* (New York, 1973).

Elias, N., *The Civilizing Process: The History of Manners*, transl. E. Jephcott (Oxford, 1978).

Bibliography

Enciclopedia Dantesca, ed. U. Bosco *et al.* (Rome, 1970–78).
Firth, R., 'Verbal and Bodily Rituals of Greeting and Parting', in La Fontaine, ed., *The Interpretation of Ritual*, pp. 1–38.
Franz, A., 'Seelische und körperliche Bewegung in Dantes Divina Commedia', in *Estudios eruditos in memoriam Adolfo Bonilla y San Martín* (Madrid, 1927), Vol. 1, pp. 415–30.
Frijhoff, W., 'The Kiss Sacred and Profane: Reflections on a Cross-Cultural Confrontation', in Bremmer and Roodenburg, eds., *A Cultural History of Gesture*, pp. 210–36.
Garnier, F., *Le langage de l'image au moyen âge: signification et symbolique* (Paris, 1982).
Genette, G., *Narrative Discourse: An Essay in Method*, transl. J. E. Lewin (Ithaca, N.Y., 1980).
Goffman, E., *Relations in Public* (London, 1971).
Goody, E., '"Greeting", "Begging", and the Presentation of Respect', in La Fontaine, ed., *The Interpretation of Ritual*, pp. 39–71.
Green, R. F., *A Crisis of Truth: Literature and Law in Ricardian England* (Philadelphia, Pa., 1999).
Habicht, W., *Die Gebärde in englischen Dichtungen des Mittelalters* (Munich, 1959).
'Zur Bedeutungsgeschichte des englischen Wortes *Countenance*', *Archiv für das Studium der Neueren Sprachen und Literaturen*, 203 (1966), 32–51.
Havely, N., *Chaucer's Boccaccio: Sources for 'Troilus' and the 'Knight's' and 'Franklin's Tale'* (Cambridge, 1980).
Hinde, R. A., ed., *Non-Verbal Communication* (Cambridge, 1972).
Hooff, J. A. R. A. M. van, 'A Comparative Approach to the Phylogeny of Laughter and Smiling', in Hinde, ed., *Non-Verbal Communication*, pp. 209–38.
Jaeger, C. S., *The Origins of Courtliness: Civilizing Trends and the Formation of Courtly Ideals, 939–1210* (Philadelphia, Pa., 1985).
Jakobson, R., 'Motor Signs for "Yes" and "No"', *Language in Society*, 1 (1972), 91–6.
Jorio, A. de, *La mimica degli antichi investigata nel gestire napoletano* (Naples, 1832); transl. and ed. A. Kendon as *Gesture in Naples and Gesture in Classical Antiquity* (Bloomington, Ind., 2000).
Keen, M. H., *The Laws of War in the Later Middle Ages* (London, 1965).
Kendon, A., 'Geography of Gesture', *Semiotica*, 37 (1981), 129–63.
'The Study of Gesture: Some Observations on its History', *Recherches Semiotiques / Semiotic Enquiry*, 2 (1982), 45–62.
'The Organization of Behavior in Face-to-Face Interaction', in K. R. Scherer and P. Ekman, eds., *Handbook of Methods in Nonverbal Behavior Research* (Cambridge, 1982), pp. 440–505.
'Did Gesture Have the Happiness to Escape the Curse at the Confusion of Babel?', in Wolfgang, ed., *Nonverbal Behavior: Perspectives, Applications, Intercultural Insights*, pp. 75–114.
'Do Gestures Communicate? A Review', *Research in Language and Social Interaction*, 27 (1994), 175–200.
Kirkpatrick, R., 'Dante and the Body', in S. Kay and M. Rubin, eds., *Framing Medieval Bodies* (Manchester, 1994).

Bibliography

Knox, D., 'Ideas on Gesture and Universal Languages, c. 1550–1650', in J. Henry and S. Hutton, eds., *New Perspectives on Renaissance Thought* (London, 1990), pp. 101–36.

Kolve, V. A., *Chaucer and the Language of Narrative: The First Five Canterbury Tales* (London, 1984).

Koziol, G., *Begging Pardon and Favor: Ritual and Political Order in Early Medieval France* (Ithaca, N.Y., 1992).

La Fontaine, J. S., ed., *The Interpretation of Ritual* (London, 1972).

Lateiner, D., *Sardonic Smile: Nonverbal Behavior in Homeric Epic* (Ann Arbor, Mich., 1995).

Leach, E., 'The Influence of Cultural Context on Non-Verbal Communication in Man', in Hinde, ed., *Non-Verbal Communication*, pp. 315–44.

Le Goff, J., *La civilisation de l'occident médiéval* (Paris, 1964).

'Le rituel symbolique de la vassalité', in Le Goff, *Pour un autre moyen âge* (Paris, 1977), pp. 349–420.

Lewis, C. S., 'Dante's Similes', in Lewis, *Studies in Medieval and Renaissance Literature* (Cambridge, 1966), pp. 64–77.

Leyser, K., 'Ritual, Ceremony and Gesture', in Leyser, *Communications and Power in Medieval Europe: The Carolingian and Ottonian Centuries* (London, 1994), pp. 189–213.

Lucke, H. K., 'Striking a Bargain', *Adelaide Law Review*, 1 (1962), 293–311.

MacKay, D. M., 'Formal Analysis of Communication Processes', in Hinde, ed., *Non-Verbal Communication*, pp. 3–25.

McNeill, D., *Hand and Mind: What Gestures Tell us about Thought* (Chicago, 1992).

McNeill, D., ed., *Language and Gesture* (Cambridge, 2000).

Major, J. Russell, '"Bastard Feudalism" and the Kiss: Changing Social Mores in Late Medieval and Early Modern France', *Journal of Interdisciplinary History*, 17 (1987), 509–35.

Mann, J., 'Price and Value in *Sir Gawain and the Green Knight*', *Essays in Criticism*, 36 (1986), 294–318.

Meech, S. B., *Design in Chaucer's 'Troilus'* (Syracuse, N.Y., 1959).

Ménard, P., *Le rire et le sourire dans le roman courtois au moyen âge (1150–1250)* (Geneva, 1969).

Morris, D., P. Collett, P. Marsh, and M. O'Shaughnessy, *Gestures: Their Origins and Distribution* (London, 1979).

Morsbach, H., 'Nonverbal Communication and Hierarchical Relationships: The Case of Bowing in Japan', in Poyatos, ed., *Cross-Cultural Perspectives in Nonverbal Communication* (Toronto, 1988), pp. 189–99.

Mostert, M., ed., *New Approaches to Medieval Communication* (Turnhout, 1999).

Needham, R., ed., *Right and Left: Essays on Dual Symbolic Classification* (Chicago, 1973).

Nicholls, J., *The Matter of Courtesy: Medieval Courtesy Books and the Gawain-Poet* (Woodbridge, 1985).

Nolan, B., *Chaucer and the Tradition of the 'Roman Antique'* (Cambridge, 1992).

Peil, D., *Die Gebärde bei Chrétien, Hartmann und Wolfram: Erec–Iwein–Parzival* (Munich, 1975).

Bibliography

Phillips, K. M., 'Bodily Walls, Windows, and Doors: The Politics of Gesture in Late Fifteenth-Century Books for Women', in J. Wogan-Browne *et al.*, eds., *Medieval Women: Texts and Contexts in Late Medieval Britain. Essays for Felicity Riddy* (Turnhout, 2000), pp. 185–98.

Portch, S. R., *Literature's Silent Language: Nonverbal Communication* (New York, 1985).

Poyatos, F., 'Nonverbal Communication in the Novel', in Poyatos, ed., *New Perspectives in Nonverbal Communication* (Oxford, 1983), pp. 277–314.

Poyatos, F., ed., *Cross-Cultural Perspectives in Nonverbal Communication* (Toronto, 1988).

Putter, A., *'Sir Gawain and the Green Knight' and French Arthurian Romance* (Oxford, 1995).

Réau, L., *Iconographie de l'art chrétien*, 3 vols. (Paris, 1955–9).

Robertson, D. W., *A Preface to Chaucer: Studies in Medieval Perspectives* (Princeton, N. J., 1963).

Roodenburg, H., 'The "Hand of Friendship": Shaking Hands and other Gestures in the Dutch Republic', in Bremmer and Roodenburg, eds., *A Cultural History of Gesture*, pp. 152–89.

Ryle, G., *Collected Papers*, Vol. II (London, 1971).

Schmitt, J.-C., 'Between Text and Image: The Prayer Gestures of Saint Dominic', *History and Anthropology*, Vol. 1, Part 1 (1984), 127–62.

La raison des gestes dans l'occident médiéval (Paris, 1990).

Screech, M. A., *Rabelais* (London, 1979).

Laughter at the Foot of the Cross (London, 1997).

Shapiro, M., *Dante and the Knot of Body and Soul* (Basingstoke, 1998).

Simmel, G., *Simmel on Culture: Selected Writings*, ed. D. Frisby and M. Featherstone (London, 1997).

Simon, G., *Le regard, l'être et l'apparence dans l'optique de l'antiquité* (Paris, 1988).

Spicer, J., 'The Renaissance Elbow', in Bremmer and Roodenburg, eds., *A Cultural History of Gesture*, pp. 84–128.

Stanbury, S., *Seeing the 'Gawain'-Poet: Description and the Act of Perception* (Philadelphia, Pa., 1991).

Stokes, M., 'The Contract of Love-Service: *Lancelot* and *Troilus*', *Litteraria Pragensia*, 9 (1999), 62–83.

Thorpe, L., 'Merlin's Sardonic Laughter', in W. Rothwell *et al.*, eds., *Studies in Medieval Literature and Languages in Memory of Frederick Whitehead* (Manchester, 1973), pp. 323–39.

Toynbee, P., *A Dictionary of Proper Names and Notable Matters in the Works of Dante*, revised by C. S. Singleton (Oxford, 1968).

Trexler, R. C., 'Legitimating Prayer Gestures in the Twelfth Century. The *Penitentia* of Peter the Chanter', *History and Anthropology*, Vol. 1, Part 1 (1984), 97–126.

Weitz, S., 'Facial Expression and Visual Interaction', in Weitz, ed., *Nonverbal Communication: Readings with Commentary*, 2nd edn (New York, 1979), pp. 17–36.

Bibliography

Weldon, J. F. G., 'The Gesture of Perception: The Pattern of Kneeling in *Piers Plowman* B. 18–19', *Yearbook of Langland Studies*, 3 (1989), 49–66.
West, C. B., *Courtoisie in Anglo-Norman Literature*, (Oxford, 1938).
White, R. B., 'A Note on the Green Knight's Red Eyes', *English Language Notes*, 2 (1962), 250–52.
Wildeblood, J., *The Polite World: A Guide to English Manners and Deportment from the Thirteenth to the Nineteenth Century* (London, 1965).
Windeatt, B., 'Gesture in Chaucer', *Medievalia et Humanistica*, n.s. 9 (1979), 143–61.
Wolfgang, A., ed., *Nonverbal Behavior: Perspectives, Applications, Intercultural Insights* (Lewiston, N.Y., 1984).

Index of names and titles

Accursius *Commentary on the Pandects*, 68
Ad Herennium, 183
Aelred of Rievaulx *De Spirituali Amicitia*, 50, 52
Alphabet of Tales, 25 n, 39 n
Amis and Amiloun, 14 n
Ancrene Wisse, 43 n, 46–8
Anonimalle Chronicle, 37–8
Anonymous Short Metrical Chronicle, 112–13
Argyle, Michael, 1 n, 9, 46 n, 57, 60, 69 n, 73 n, 100
Aristotle *Politics*, 66, 67 n
Arthour and Merlin, 43, 80–1
Augustine, St, of Hippo *De Civitate Dei*, 81 n; *De Doctrina Christiana*, 1–3, 4, 25, 88, 141, 157, 172, 175; *De Magistro*, 2 n; *De Mendacio*, 88 n
Austen, Jane, 36 n

Bacon, Francis *The Advancement of Learning*, 67
Barasch, M., 5, 123 n, 178 n
Barbour, John *Bruce*, 78–9, 154
Bäuml, B. J. and F. H., 35, 36 n
Benson, R. G., 5
Benvenuto da Imola *Commentary on the Commedia*, 166–7, 171 n, 178 n
Bernard, St *De Gradibus Humilitatis et Superbiae*, 110 n
Bible: Second Book of Kings, 32; Psalms, 43, 53 n, 59 n, 109; Proverbs, 88 n, 110, 168; Ecclesiasticus, 109; Isaiah, 47 n, 59, 92 n, 170 n; Matthew, 43, 44; Mark, 43; Luke, 106–7; Acts, 59; Romans, 173
Birdwhistell, Ray, 8–9, 35 n, 70 n, 73–4
Boccaccio, Giovanni *Decameron*, 178 n; *Il Filostrato*, 115–16, 117, 118, 121, 122–3, 124, 125, 126, 128–9, 130, 131, 133, 134–5, 159
Boegehold, A. L., 181 n, 183 n
Bokenham, Osbern *Legendys of Hooly Wummen*, 89 n

Boke of Curtasye, 19, 60
Boncampagno da Signa *Rhetorica Antiqua*, 31; *Rhetorica Novissima*, 64, 65, 95, 166
Bone Florence of Rome, 109
Boke of Margery Kempe, The, 66 n
Botticelli, Sandro, 170 n, 171 n
Bulwer, John *Chirologia*, 14 n, 36, 45 n, 182 n

Callan, H., 17 n
Capgrave, John *Life of St Katherine of Alexandria*, 30 n
Carpenter, Alexander *Destructorium Viciorum*, 88
Catholicon Anglicum, 58 n, 108 n
Charles d'Orléans, 50–1, 54, 55, 92–3, 104 n, 151
Chaucer, Geoffrey *Boece*, 91; *Book of the Duchess*, 30, 84 n, 99; *Canterbury Tales*, 13, 14, 15, 17, 22, 31, 40, 44, 53, 54, 55, 58, 62, 63, 64, 71, 72, 74 n, 75, 79–80, 85, 86–8, 95, 106, 124, 125 n, 137; *Complaint of Mars*, 92; *House of Fame*, 14 n, 39 n; *Legend of Good Women*, 40, 54, 65, 90–1, 96; *Romaunt of the Rose*, 41 n, 72, 99, 132 n; *Troilus and Criseyde*, 5, 79, 80, **114–36**, 140, 145, 182
Chénon, Emile, 51
Chrétien de Troyes *Chevalier de la Charrete*, 12–13, 16 n, 23, 45–6, 49, 54, 77, 85 n, 94, 102, 120; *Cligés*, 23 n, 29, 39 n, 40, 54, 77–8, 83, 85–6, 93, 185; *Erec et Enide*, 20 n, 23–4, 40, 42, 48–9, 50, 52, 55–6, 85 n, 92; *Perceval*, 16, 22, 26–7, 33 n, 39 n, 40, 43, 45 n, 50, 79, 81, 82–3; *Yvain*, 14 n, 16, 25–6, 41, 42, 52, 83–4
Cicero *Orator*, 91
Clanchy, M. T., 11 n
Clariodus, 96 n
Cleland, James, 36
Cloud of Unknowing, The, 60
Corti, M., 157 n
Cursor Mundi, 62 n

Index of names and titles

Dante Alighieri *Commedia*, 40n, 126n, 140n, **154–79**, 185; *Convivio*, 157–8; *Vita Nuova*, 94
Darwin, Charles *Expression of the Emotions*, 7–8, 9, 42, 61, 70
Defensoris Liber Scintillarum, 104
De Modo Orandi Corporaliter, 23
Dickens, Charles, 107
Dinshaw, Carolyn, 151n
Dives and Pauper, 17, 19, 22n, 40, 53n
Douglas, Gavin *Aeneid*, 23n, 34, 36, 39
Douglas, Mary, 81n
Dunbar, William, 62n
Du prestre qui ot mere mal gré sien, 106n

Efron, D., 181, 184
Eibl-Eibesfeldt, I., 8, 61n
Ekman, P., 7n, 10n, 70–1, 88–9
Elias, Norbert, 51–2, 184n
Erasmus, Desiderius, 32–3, 52, 117

Fierabras, 104n
Firth, Raymond, 27, 55, 146
Le foteor, 46
Franz, A., 156n, 161n
Frijhoff, W., 52
Froissart, Jean *Chroniques*, 12, 13, 15–16, 18–19, 24, 29–30, 34, 43, 44, 46, 49–50, 52, 53, 65–6, 75–6, 99–100

Gamelyn, 105–6
Garnier, J., 46, 171n
Geertz, Clifford, 111n
Genette, Gérard, 115n
Geoffrey of Monmouth *Vita Merlini*, 81
Geoffrey of Vinsauf *Documentum de Arte Versificandi*, 183; *Poetria Nova*, 69, 183
Gest Hystoriale of the Destruction of Troy, 31, 59
Giotto, 5, 178
Goffman, Erving, 49, 83
Goody, E., 28n
Gower, John *Confessio Amantis*, 15, 17, 22, 23, 25n, 33–4, 39n, 40, 53, 64–5, 66, 72, 74–5, 81, 82, 83, 84, 85, 89–90, 95–6, 98n, 101, 133
Green, Richard, 14, 122, 141n, 147
Guy of Warwick, 89, 100n

Habicht, Werner, 5, 28n, 39n, 82, 89n, 92n, 136, 138, 145
Havely, Nicholas, 116n, 128–9
Henryson, Robert *Fables*, 59, 62; *Testament of Cresseid*, 31
Herodotus *History*, 66, 67n
Hue de Rotelande *Ipomedon*, 49, 55, 60, 97–8

Hugh of St Victor *De Institutione Novitiorum*, 1n, 47n, 110–11

Ipomadon, 49n, 55n, 97–8
Isle of Ladies, The, 93

Jaeger, C. S., 185
Jakobson, Roman, 61
James, Henry, 115
Jolly Jankin, 109
Jorio, Andrea de *Gesture in Naples*, 31, 45n, 159n, 166n, 170n, 182
Joyce, James, 38, 115

Kendon, Adam, 3, 4n, 9n, 10n, 57, 139n, 181n, 182
King Edward and the Shepherd, 32
Koziol, G., 53n
Kyng Alisaunder, 46n, 50, 65

Laȝamon *Brut*, 89
Langland, William *Piers Plowman*, 18, 20, 21–2, 29, 39n, 43, 53n, 53–4, 72, 73, 80, 92, 101–2, 103, 104–5, 124
Leach, Edmund, 8
Le Goff, Jacques, 11, 185
Leo of Rozmital *Commentarius Brevis et Jucundus*, 32, 34
Lewis, C. S., 162n, 169
Leyser, Karl, 16n
Life of the Black Prince, 17n
Livy *History*, 66, 67n
Lucke, H. K., 147n
Lybeaus Desconus, 14n, 39, 141n
Lydgate, John, 62; *Siege of Thebes*, 95n

Machaut, Guillaume de *Jugement du Roy de Behaigne*, 92n; *Remede de Fortune*, 94
MacKay, D. M., 3
Major, J. Russell, 19n, 51
Malory, Sir Thomas *Morte Darthur*, 15, 18n, 20, 21, 22, 23, 24, 30, 33n, 34, 39, 42, 44, 52, 54, 56–7, 63–4, 74, 75, 79, 80, 82, 84, 85, 94–5, 100, 120
Manning, Robert, of Brunne *Handlyng Synne*, 54n, 59, 63
Martin of Dacia *De Modis Significandi*, 157
Ménard, P., 5, 74n, 76, 77, 78, 80, 81, 182n
Metham, John *Amoryus and Cleopes*, 102n
Midsummer Day's Dance, A, 109
Le Moniage Guillaume, 102
Montaigne, 26n, 28n, 67
Morris, Desmond, 7, 170n, 181, 184
Le Morte Arthur, 21n, 39n, 52n, 77, 78, 98
La Mort le Roi Artu, 21n, 40, 75

Index of names and titles

Newton, Humfrey, 96
Nicholls, Jonathan, 136n, 144, 145–6, 150n
Northern Passion, The, 106–7

Octovian Imperator, 39
Ovid *Fasti*, 66, 67n; *Heroides*, 166n; *Metamorphoses*, 65n

Partonope of Blois, 62n
Patience, 88n
Pearl, 30
Pecock, Reginald, 58n
Peil, D., 5, 33n, 39n
Petrarch *De Insigni Obedientia et Fide Uxoris*, 71, 86–8, 130
Pilgrimage of the Lyfe of the Manhode, The, 46n
Poyatos, F., 182n
Promptorium Parvulorum, 58n, 59n, 108
Prose *Lancelot*, 12, 14n, 16, 20, 22n, 24, 25n, 29, 30, 33, 40n, 41, 42, 53, 54, 56, 75, 80, 85n, 93, 98, 99, 102, 145n, 165–8, 185
Proust, Marcel, 115, 183–4
Putter, Ad, 136n, 137n, 144, 167n

La Queste del Saint Graal, 54n
Quintilian *Institutio Oratoria*, 7, 126n, 170n

Rabelais, François *Gargantua and Pantagruel*, 67–8
Rhodes, Hugh *Boke of Nurture*, 138
Robertson, D. W., 127
Robin Hood, 21, 32n, 49n
Roman de la Rose, 22n, 41, 42, 43n, 49n, 53n, 64n, 90, 92, 99n
Roman d'Eneas, 106
Roodenburg, H., 7, 36–7, 38
Ruiz, Juan *Libro de Buen Amor*, 68
Russell, John *Boke of Nurture*, 109
Ryle, Gilbert, 111, 113

Schmitt, Jean-Claude, 1n, 11, 16, 19n, 23n, 59n, 64, 65, 110n, 158, 162, 168, 171, 184
Screech, M. A., 67, 68, 80n
Seinte Katerine, 150n
Seven Sages of Rome, The, 63
Shakespeare, William *Henry V*, 106n

Sidrak and Bokkus, 92
Silverstein, T., 141n
Simmel, Georg, 130
Simon, G., 92n
Singleton, Charles S., 159n, 161n, 170n, 171n, 173
Sir Ferumbras, 104, 105
Sir Gawain and the Green Knight, 5, 21n, 74n, 77, 79, 97, 115, **136–55**, 184
Sir Orfeo, 20–1, 41, 182n
Sir Penny, 30
Skelton, John *Bowge of Courte*, 44–5, 60, 100–1, 106; *Magnificence*, 20n, 31, 60
Spenser, Edmund *Faerie Queene*, 65n
Spicer, Joaneath, 45
Stanbury, Sarah, 138n, 148n
Stans Puer ad Mensam, 42n, 49, 60
Sterne, Laurence, 38
Stokes, Myra, 167n

Tale of Beryn, The, 45, 124n
Talking of the Love of God, A, 44
Ten Commandments of Love, The, 95
Thomas *Tristan*, 49
Thomas, Keith, 180
Thorpe, Lewis, 80–1
Thorpe, William, 17
Trevisa, John *On the Properties of Things*, 40, 65; *Polychronicon*, 58n

Urbanitatis, 19, 30
Usk, Thomas *Testament of Love*, 92

Valentine and Orson, 65
Vulgate *Merlin*, 80

Wars of Alexander, 44, 60, 63, 140
Weitz, S., 91
Wildeblood, J., 29n, 32n, 34–5
William of Palerne, 24, 65
Windeatt, Barry, 117–18, 120n, 124, 126, 129, 132n, 135
Wynnere and Wastoure, 59–60

Young Children's Book, 60
Ywain and Gawain, 16, 24–5, 26, 39n, 41, 42, 52, 84–5

Index of signs

amorous looks, 47, 59, **92–8**, 106, 131–3, 148–9
arm akimbo, 45
arm in arm, 121

beckoning, 38, **57–9**, 160, 164, 172–3
bowed head, 41–2, 94, 98, 158, 165–6
bowing, 4, 6, **17–19**, 20, 21–2, 23, 26, 27, **28–30**, 33–4, 36n, 53, 59, 61, 99, 100, 102, 119, 132, 139, 141, 146–7, 152, 159, 163, 169, 178, 185
breast-beating, 19, 40, 169, 174
bum-baring, 44, 170n

clapping, 39
commanding looks, 102–3, 160–1
coughs, 3, 4, 124, 140, 165–8, 179, 185
curtsey, 20, 36n, 94

doffing headgear, 28, **30–2**, 59, 99, 143–4, 153–4
downward gaze, 93, 123–4, 126, 129, 131, 133, 135, 182

embraces, 27, 28, 29, **32–4**, 35, 52, 53, 54, 55, 56, 117, 125, 135, 144, 146, 154, 160, 162

facial expressions: affectionate, 174, 176; angry, 2, 4, 8, 82–3, 153, 175; humble, 86, 131, 134; impassive, 86–7, 142; joyous, 82, 84, 87, 117, 160, 174, 175; proud, 85, 168; sad, 2, 4, 82, 84, 86; sober, 86, 133; stern, 86
farting, 3, 44, 171
fica, 170, 184
frowns, 4, **71–3**, 96, 139, 153, 171

handclasp, 4, **14–16**, 28, 30, **34–5**, 37, 38, 52, 116, 121–2, 123
hand in hand, 48, **49–50**, 121

handshake, 7, **35–8**, 182, 184
headnod, 18–19, 43, 57, 58, **60–2**, 63, 108, 132
headshake, 6, 43–4, 61, **62–4**, 159, 181
headtoss, 126–7, 135, 168, 181
hiding the face, 125
hm . . . , 124
holding up hands, **13–14**, 16, 19, 20, 23, 117, 118, 141, 174

immixtio manuum, **11–13**

kissing, 4, 5, 12–13, 16, 17, 27, 28, **32–4**, 35, **50–7**, 117, 118, 123, 125, 135, 143, 146, 147, **150–2**, 154, 160, 166–7, 173, 184
kneeling, 6, 12, 13n, 16, 17–18, **19–26**, **28–30**, 32, 34, 37, 52, 53, 93, **117–20**, 135, 141, 144, 158, 172, 185

laughter, 3, 5, 8, 39, 73, 76, 77, **78–81**, 96, 101, 102, 126n, 135, 140, 142, 145, 147, 149–50, 153, 154–5
leading by the hand, 48–9, 145–6
legs crossed, 46–7
looking askance, 43n, 47, **98–9**

pointing, 4, 38, 57, **59–60**, 102, 160, 169, 172
poking, 125
prostration, 18
pursing the lips, 47, 153

raised eyebrows, 126–7, 168

scornful gaze, 47, 99–100, 101, 137–8
self-injury, 40–1, 122–3
slap in the face, 100
smiles, 4, 5, 8, 9, 70, 71, **73–8**, 93, 96, 126, 135, 142, 148, 149–50, 159–60, 161–2, 164–5, 165–7, 172, 174, 176, 178, 179, 185

spitting, 44
staring, 4, 73, **100–1**, 112, 133–5
sticking the tongue out, 44, 170, 171, 179
striking a bargain, 147
swearing on sacred things, 12, **16–17**

tearing clothes, 40, 41
tearing hair, 39–40, 41, 122–3

winks, 4, 6, **103–13**, 161 n, 182–3
wringing hands, 39, 40, 41, 123

CAMBRIDGE STUDIES IN MEDIEVAL LITERATURE

1. Robin Kirkpatrick *Dante's Inferno: Difficulty and Dead Poetry*
2. Jeremy Tambling *Dante and Difference: Writing in the "Commedia"*
3. Simon Gaunt *Troubadours and Irony*
4. Wendy Scase *"Piers Plowman" and the New Anticlericalism*
5. Joseph Duggan *The "Cantar De Mio Cid": Poetic Creation in its Economic and Social Contexts*
6. Roderick Beaton *The Medieval Greek Romance*
7. Kathryn Kerby-Fulton *Reformist Apocalypticism and "Piers Plowman"*
8. Alison Morgan *Dante & the Medieval Other World*
9. Eckehard Simon (ed.) *The Theatre of Medieval Europe: New Research in Early Drama*
10. Mary Carruthers *The Book of Memory: a Study of Memory in Medieval Culture*
11. Rita Copeland *Rhetoric, Hermeneutics and Translation in the Middle Ages: Academic Traditions and Vernacular Texts*
12. Donald Maddox *The Arthurian Romances of Chrétien de Troyes: Once and Future Fictions*
13. Nicholas Watson *Richard Rolle and the Invention of Authority*
14. Steven F. Kruger *Dreaming in the Middle Ages*
15. Barbara Nolan *Chaucer and the Tradition of the "Roman Antique"*
16. Sylvia Huot *The "Romance of the Rose" and its Medieval Readers: Interpretations, Reception, Manuscript Transmission*
17. Carol M. Meale (ed.) *Women and Literature in Britain, 1150–1500*
18. Henry Ansgar Kelly *Ideas and Forms of Tragedy from Aristotle to the Middle Ages*
19. Martin Irvine *The Making of Textual Culture: Grammatica and Literary Theory, 350–1100*
20. Larry Scanlon *Narrative, Authority and Power: the Medieval Exemplum and the Chaucerian Tradition*
21. Erik Kooper *Medieval Dutch Literature in its European Context*
22. Steven Botterill *Dante and the Mystical Tradition: Bernard of Clairvaux in the "Commedia"*
23. Peter Biller and Anne Hudson (eds.) *Heresy and Literacy, 1000–1530*
24. Christopher Baswell *Virgil in Medieval England: Figuring the "Aeneid" from the Twelfth Century to Chaucer*
25. James Simpson *Sciences and Self in Medieval Poetry: Alan of Lille's "Anticlaudianus" and John Gower's "Confessio Amantis"*
26. Joyce Coleman *Public Reading and the Reading Public in Late Medieval England and France*
27. Suzanne Reynolds *Medieval Reading: Grammar, Rhetoric and the Classical Text*
28. Charlotte Brewer *Editing "Piers Plowman": the Evolution of the Text*

29 Walter Haug *Vernacular Literary Theory in the Middle Ages: the German Tradition in its European Context*
30 Sarah Spence *Texts and the Self in the Twelfth Century*
31 Edwin Craun *Lies, Slander and Obscenity in Medieval English Literature: Pastoral Rhetoric and the Deviant Speaker*
32 Patricia E. Grieve *"Floire and Blancheflor" and the European Romance*
33 Huw Pryce (ed.) *Literacy in Medieval Celtic Societies*
34 Mary Carruthers *The Craft of Thought: Meditation, Rhetoric, and the Making of Images, 400–1200*
35 Beate Schmolke-Hasselman *The Evolution of Arthurian Romance: the Verse Tradition from Chrétien to Froissart*
36 Siân Echard *Arthurian Narrative in the Latin Tradition*
37 Fiona Somerset *Clerical Discourse and Lay Audience in Late Medieval England*
38 Florence Percival *Chaucer's Legendary Good Women*
39 Christopher Cannon *The Making of Chaucer's English: a Study of Words*
40 Rosalind Brown-Grant *Christine de Pizan and the Moral Defence of Women: Reading Beyond Gender*
41 Richard Newhauser *The Early History of Greed: the Sin of Avarice in Early Medieval Thought and Literature*
42 Margaret Clunies Ross *Old Icelandic Literature and Society*
43 Donald Maddox *Fictions of Identity in Medieval France*
44 Rita Copeland *Pedagogy, Intellectuals, and Dissent in the Later Middle Ages: Lollardy and Ideas of Learning*
45 Kantik Ghosh *The Wycliffite Heresy: Authority and the Interpretation of Texts*
46 Mary C. Erler *Women, Reading, and Piety in Late Medieval England*
47 D. H. Green *The Beginnings of Medieval Romance: Fact and Fiction, 1150–1220*
48 J. A. Burrow *Gestures and Looks in Medieval Narrative*